# THE BOOK OF BURWELL STUDENTS

## Lives of Educated Women in the Antebellum South

*Margaret Anna Burwell*

Compiled by Mary Claire Engstrom
Hillsborough, North Carolina
April 1979

Historic Hillsborough Commission, Hillsborough, NC 27278
© 2007 by the Historic Hillsborough Commission
All rights reserved. Published 2007
First edition
Printed in the United States of America


12 11 10 09 08 07 06 05 04 03    1 2 3 4 5
ISBN: 978-0-6151-6433-5
Library of Congress Cataloging-in-Publication Data


Cover & book design: Ernest Dollar
Index: Judith Martin

*Cover: Sarah Rebecca Jones Collins (1833–72). Oil on canvas, c. 1858. Artist unknown. (Photograph courtesy of Rebecca D. Warren, Chapel Hill, N.C.)*


*Frontispiece:* carte de visite *of Margaret Anna Burwell (date unknown). She wore the brooch given to her as a Christmas gift in 1855 by her sister, Mary Jane Robertson. After the death of Mrs. Burwell's daughter Fanny, some of Fanny's hair was placed in the brooch.*

*Historian and author Mary Claire Engstrom.*

# Preface

*The Book of Burwell Students* is primarily the work of Mary Claire Randolph Engstrom, who researched and compiled its contents over many years. The book includes all the information Mrs. Engstrom was able to discover about the Burwell School, which existed from 1837 until 1857 in Hillsborough, North Carolina, its students, and its proprietors, the Rev. Robert and Mrs. Margaret Anna Robertson Burwell.

Mrs. Engstrom was a meticulous and tireless historian of Orange County and its county seat, Hillsborough, but she published little of her extensive work. A perfectionist, she was never satisfied that what she had done was complete or completely correct. She nevertheless left an impressive record. She brought to light and publicized in newsletters and newspaper articles almost single-handedly the important history of Hillsborough from its settlement until the end of the 19th century, leaving no person of note, place of memory, or worthy structure unresearched.

The Burwell School and Mrs. Burwell were particularly close to her heart. While her role in helping to make the Historic Hillsborough Commission a reality is undocumented, the importance of her guiding hand was always acknowledged. The commission's purpose was stipulated at its founding as the restoration and preservation of Hillsborough, but it very soon became intensely focused on the purchase, restoration, and maintenance as a historic site of the former Burwell School buildings and grounds.

The Historic Hillsborough Commission became Mrs. Engstrom's special concern and delight. Through the years she wrote dozens of letters in her idiosyncratic and beautiful handwriting (she never learned to type) on behalf of fund-raising and to enlist help from descendants of Burwell students with both the restoration of the buildings and the collection of information and memorabilia relevant to the students. She welcomed anything remotely connected with them, from their jewelry and personal possessions to embroideries and poetry. Her gleanings of facts, letters, drawings, and photographs, together with her own research, make up the substance of this book.

Letters in particular were a primary source for Mrs. Engstrom's research. She was given a handful of originals (now in the commission's collections), which she included in her manuscript. Because of their condition, we have been unable to include reproductions of some of the originals, but we have made and included transcriptions of them all.

In publishing this work, the Historic Hillsborough Commission has adhered as closely as possible to Mrs. Engstrom's format and writing. We have, however, adapted the whole work to current editorial standards and made a few corrections of fact, which we know she would have approved. We have also appended in brackets new information about individual students as well as new sketches of students she was unable to identify. For the convenience of readers, we have also transcribed anything in Mrs. Engstrom's handwriting and have added a short glossary and index.

This entire effort was made possible by a generous grant from the Institute of Museum and Library Services, for which we express our deepest thanks. The grant has made possible the publication of Mrs. Engstrom's manuscript, as well as the additional research and its results.

We want to thank especially Commissioner Elizabeth Woodman, who has served voluntarily as principal editor, for her careful attention and supervision of the project. Thanks are also due to her volunteer assistant editors: Katherine Malone-France, former executive director of the Burwell School site, who has also written the introduction, and Commissioner Jean Bradley Anderson. The new material about the students is for the most part the work of Vanessa Hansen, a genealogist.

Finally, the commission wishes to thank the current executive director of the Burwell School site, Elvan Cobb, for coordinating the work of the editors and for countless other tasks in bringing this effort to fruition.

—JBA
*Hillsborough, North Carolina, 2007*

# Table of Contents

# Introduction

*The Book of Burwell Students* is a testament to the efforts of two women—Margaret Anna Burwell and Mary Claire Engstrom—whose homes in Hillsborough, North Carolina, were two blocks apart but whose tenures in the town were separated by a century. This volume offers proof of their perseverance, their diligence, and their intellect. Had they lived in Hillsborough at the same time, I don't know whether they would have been friends or rivals; perhaps they would have been both. But they are bound together in this work, which cannot be fully understood without having some sense of who they were.

In 1810, Margaret Anna Robertson was born into a life of dwindling privilege. She was the daughter of Scottish merchant William Bruce Robertson and his wife, Margaret Ann Spotswood. On her mother's side, Anna was the great-great-granddaughter of Virginia's colonial governor, Alexander Spotswood; but by the time Anna was a young child, her mother was running a boarding house in Petersburg, Virginia. Whether Anna and her six siblings were orphaned or abandoned is unclear; but they were reared and educated in the home of their maternal aunt and her husband, who placed great emphasis on education and religious practice. Anna began earning a living as a teacher when she was eighteen, after the death of her uncle.

When Anna Robertson married Robert Burwell in 1831, she married into another family that once had wielded political power in colonial Virginia but had lost most of its wealth. Robert Burwell was a graduate of Hampden-Sydney College in Farmville, Virginia, where his father had served as the college's steward, a job that included operating the dining hall and making sure students had firewood. In 1824, Robert was a member of the first class of students at the Union Theological Seminary in Richmond. When he married Anna, he was the pastor of Wood's Church in Chesterfield County, near Petersburg. In 1835, Robert and Anna moved to Hillsborough when Robert accepted a job as minister of Hillsborough Presbyterian Church. Accompanying them were their two small children, John and Mary, and a young enslaved woman named Elizabeth Hobbs. Two years after their arrival, the Burwells opened a school for young women in a small brick building constructed behind the Presbyterian parsonage where they lived.

Though Anna Burwell's name never appears in a deed book as the legal owner of lots 152 and 153, she was firmly in charge of life on the two acres where the Burwells made their home and operated their school. This property, which the Burwells eventually purchased from the Presbyterian church, was located on a rise, three blocks north of Hillsborough's central intersection. The Burwell household, like many others in antebellum Hillsborough, constituted a small, nearly self-sustaining community with gardens, livestock, family residence, a scattering of outbuildings, and population that sometimes numbered more than thirty people. On a daily basis, Anna Burwell directed the activities of her children, a fluctuating group of slaves, and the school's boarding and day students.

The two spheres of Anna's activity—the Burwells' household and their school—were bound even more closely than the ten feet separating the family residence and the brick school building would suggest. She parented both her children and the students living in her home, maintaining some sense of order with the discipline she felt her husband was unwilling to supply. She attended to financial accounts—whether the pocket money account of boarding student Mary Bailey Easley, who favored sweets from Mrs. Vasseur's "downstreet" shop, the wages to the school's drawing and music teachers, or the purchase of a guitar for daughter Fanny who was studying in New York. She educated her own twelve children and was the administrative and entrepreneurial force behind the Burwells' school. In addition to teaching classes in a variety of subjects, Anna Burwell wrote monthly progress reports to each girl's parents and probably wrote the school's catalogue and advertisements. She did all of this while bearing another ten children in the first seventeen years she lived in Hillsborough.

Much of what is known about Anna Burwell's Hillsborough years comes from her all too few diaries and letters, preserved by the Burwell family and the Historic Hillsborough Commission. Written at three different times during her years in Hillsborough, these documents bring Anna and her world to life. The letter she wrote in February 1855 to her daughter Fanny depicts the extent of her responsibilities to her household and her school:

> *We are going on at the same old gait—the same round every day. . . . Yesterday I was out all day about Pork, rather late in the season you will say, but a fine lot was offered to us and we bought it as we had not been able to get a full supply. It was cut out day before yesterday and I'll tell you my day's employment that day and you will say there was variety at least. I attended to my housekeeping as usual, went in school at eleven and taught the*

*writing, then I heard the reading classes, by that time the Pork
came, I changed my dress, went out and with my own hands
trimmed sixty-six pieces of meat, then came in, washed and dressed
up in my best and with Nannie . . . went to Mrs. Heart's, to Dr.
Long's, and thence home. I presided at supper and finished the day
with a long letter to sister Mary.*

Further evidence of Anna Burwell's role in the household
is supplied by her eldest son, John Bott Burwell, in his unpublished
autobiography. He recalled a trip to Virginia with his father, during
which they camped one night with a peddler who traveled often through
North Carolina, selling his goods. Upon learning they were from
Hillsborough, the peddler asked if they knew the "Widow Burwell"
with whom he traded. The description he gave of her home was
unmistakably the Burwells' property. When Robert Burwell asked
why he thought Mrs. Burwell was a widow, the peddler explained
that he assumed she was a widow because she seemed to be responsible
for everything about the household.

Perhaps the most revealing aspect about Anna Burwell's
personal writings is that she was not a 19th century superwoman, as
she sometimes has been portrayed. The most unguarded passages of
her diaries express her exhaustion and frustration. "Indeed my days are
spent in a hurry and I never felt so worn out in my life both in body and
in mind," she wrote one evening. And, yet, there is always the next day's
diary entry: Anna got up the next morning and did it all again. She
summed up her own perseverance in the closing of another letter to
Fanny in early 1856. "Try," she wrote, "there is a sovereign potency
in that little word."

Anna Burwell's letters to her daughter Fanny constitute an
important narrative thread throughout *The Book of Burwell Students*,
shedding light on why she expended so much effort in running a
school. Certainly there were financial motives (and her papers reveal
the school's financial uncertainty, alleviated occasionally, but never
for long, by the arrival of new students). However, it was the idea of
usefulness that supplied a deeper purpose for her efforts. The only
edition of the school's catalogue known to exist was published in 1848
and most likely was written by Anna Burwell. It asserts that the mission
of the school was to produce young women who were "thorough
scholars and useful members of society." Perhaps she was thinking
of her own uncertain childhood or the difficult situations she had

seen neighbors and former students face when she wrote to Fanny on January 19, 1856, ". . . it seems to me so all important that girls should have educations to qualify themselves to help themselves."

*The Book of Burwell Students* offers an important counterpoint to Anna Burwell's own writings because it reveals how Anna Burwell was viewed by the young women she educated and by their parents. In an 1851 letter, Robert Primrose instructed his daughter Mary Anne, a boarding student, to be tolerant of and responsive to Anna Burwell's discipline: "Even if she does scold you . . . you must make allowance for they are doing everything for your advancement in knowledge which is to be hoped will be for your good."

Lavinia Cole, who studied with the Burwells for two years, remembered Anna Burwell as "a wonderful woman. She neglected no duty, kept the house beautifully, had the personal supervision of the thirty boarders, attended to their manners and morals . . . made her own bread, washed the dishes, with our assistance—taught six hours a day— was the mother of twelve beautifully clean, healthy attractive children, dressed well always and entertained as much company as any other lady in the village."

The Burwells' school operated until 1857. During its twenty years, the institution educated more than two hundred young women within a curriculum that seems broad and rigorous by today's standards. Burwell students learned to read and write, but they also studied a range of subjects including Latin, philosophy, literature, astronomy, history, and algebra. Music, drawing, and French lessons were offered for an additional charge.

Historical perspective places the Burwells' school near the beginning of the institutionalization of women's education in North Carolina and the country. In Hillsborough, the Episcopal minister, William M. Green, had established a female seminary in 1825, which remained open until the Civil War, antedating the Burwells. Outside of town, the Anderson Female Academy, founded in 1830, had closed the year before the Burwell School opened. Also in North Carolina, Salem Academy, founded in Winston-Salem by Moravians in 1772 as one of the first two female academies in the United States, and the Louisburg Female Academy, established in 1814, were important examples of the phenomenon. During the 1830s, the Burwell School was one of a number of significant female academies and seminaries throughout the country that opened. They included the LaGrange Female Academy, founded in LaGrange, Georgia, in 1831; the Columbia Female Academy, established in Columbia, Missouri, in 1833; and the Wheaton Female

Seminary, established in Wheaton, Massachusetts, in 1834. In 1837, the same year the Burwells began their school, Mary Lyon opened Mount Holyoke Female Seminary, today Mount Holyoke College, in South Hadley, Massachusetts.

In 1857, the Burwells moved to Charlotte to lead the Charlotte Female Institute, which would become Queens College and later Queens University. Anna Burwell's impact there was also significant. She again took on multiple roles—from formulating the curriculum to teaching to determining plantings around campus. In 1920, Queens' main administration building was named "The Burwell Building" in *her* honor.

Even a cursory reading of her life reveals that Anna Burwell would certainly have merited a mention in North Carolina history or women's education; but the diligent research of this book's author, Mary Claire Engstrom, reveals a complex and multifaceted figure, a fuller portrait of a woman both of her times and ahead of them. It is easy to speculate about what drew Mary Claire Engstrom to Anna Burwell. They were both, in their own way, outsiders in a Hillsborough society that was as interconnected and insular when Anna Burwell arrived by wagon in 1837 as it was in 1959, when Mary Claire Engstrom and her husband purchased the Nash-Hooper House. Yet, they both found their place in town through their intellect—Anna Burwell starting a highly regarded school and Mary Claire Engstrom dedicating herself to documenting and preserving the town's history. Mary Claire Engstrom's references to Anna Burwell as a "superwoman" indicate that she drew inspiration from Anna as she sought to explore every topic she deemed important, lead every group she could organize, and meet every challenge she could anticipate.

Mary Claire Engstrom's impact on Hillsborough is significant. The town we know today—a place whose civic identity is deeply rooted in an appreciation of its history—would not exist without her efforts. In July 1978, a feature article in the *Durham Morning Herald* called her "Hillsborough's Guardian Angel"; and she did, indeed, act as the guardian of Hillsborough's historic resources during a critical period in the 1960s and '70s. Women involved in the historic preservation movement in that era were thought of as "little old ladies in tennis shoes." But I think "smart woman in a smart suit" more accurately describes Mary Claire Engstrom, because there was nothing casual about either her clothes or her actions, which were both always well tailored, to her or to the situation. She did not just research historic buildings; she lobbied for legislative appropriations and wrote numerous successful grant applications to fund their restoration. If the Historic Hillsborough Commission was not her inspiration (many think it was), she wrote its bylaws, filed its articles of incorporation, and secured its legal status as a nonprofit organization.

Interestingly, Mary Claire Engstrom had no long-standing connection to Hillsborough, or even North Carolina, although she dedicated much of her time and energy to preserving their history. Born in Kansas City, Missouri, Mary Claire Randolph studied English and Political Science at St. Teresa's Junior College and the University of Missouri, where she received an MA in English, specializing in 18th century English literature. She then earned a doctorate in English at UNC–Chapel Hill, where she taught during World War II. There, she met and married Alfred G. Engstrom, a professor of romance languages. After the war, when female substitutes were dropped from the faculty, Mary Claire Engstrom found herself without a connection to her original field of study. She began to develop an interest in history. In 1959, when she and her husband moved the Nash-Hooper House in Hillsborough, a home originally built by one of North Carolina's signers of the Declaration of Independence, her focus turned to 18th and early 19th century northern Orange County.

In 1962, Mary Claire Engstrom was one of Gov. Terry Sanford's original appointees to the newly created Historic Hillsborough Commission. In a pattern of quick and carefully outlined actions that would characterize her service, Engstrom's nomination as chair was approved on November 2, she presided over a meeting on November 11 to determine the commission's initial organizational actions; and, sixteen days later, on November 27, she issued a nine-point report to the commission on the accomplishment of those tasks. During her first term as chair, she took on two enormous projects simultaneously: She spearheaded the campaign to restore the original 18th century spelling of Hillsborough (the last three letters having been dropped for more than a century), and, at the same time, persuaded the commission to purchase and restore the Burwell School property. In a letter to Gov. Sanford in 1966, she outlined why it was important that the commission purchase the Burwell School property:

> *New and exciting things have been happening in Hillsborough because the town is at last waking up to a sense of its remarkable potential. . . . But the Commission, after a year, has been completely unable to begin a restoration program of any kind.*

*The one or two historic properties available have been sky high in price and out of all reason. Now, the historically significant old Burwell School, the only remaining one of Hillsborough's many famous schools, has come on the market at $35,000. The price is so low as this partly because the owners want the Commission to have the property and to preserve it. The spacious 7-room frame house is on a strategic corner lot of approximately 2 acres and could provide suitable headquarters for both the Commission and the Historical Society. . . . To put it plainly . . . we must accomplish something tangible at this point. . . . And an opportunity like the Burwell School does not often present itself in Hillsborough. . . . Our Commission pledges to you our continuing effort and interest in historic matters that benefit the state and we assure you of our earnest wish to accomplish good things for the town of Hillsborough.*

In 1965, thirteen members of the Historic Hillsborough Commission, including Mary Claire Engstrom, signed $1,000 notes to guarantee the loan that allowed the organization to buy the Burwell School property. Eleven years later, they burned a copy of the mortgage on the front lawn and owned the property outright. Purchasing the Burwell School is particularly striking in the context of the entire preservation movement, because it happened in 1965, one year *before* the first federal preservation legislation was enacted. Under Mary Claire Engstrom's leadership, the commission provided a local example of historic preservation and its most fundamental principles, just as the movement was receiving its first national and governmental recognition.

But buying the property was only the beginning of Mary Claire Engstrom's work at the Burwell School. Over the next two decades, she campaigned tirelessly for funds for its restoration and spent countless hours consulting about the project with the North Carolina Department of Archives and History. As the restoration began, she drafted and submitted the Burwell School's nomination to the National Register of Historic Places. Again, she ran at the front of the pack. Today, more than 2,400 properties in North Carolina are on the National Register. The Burwell School is number 43, placed on the Register in the very first class of properties in 1970.

During this time, Mary Claire Engstrom also exhaustively researched the Burwell and Spotswood families and the young women who attended the Burwells' school. This research led to what I believe are her two greatest accomplishments. First, she received from the

Burwell family Anna Burwell's diaries and letters, which she then painstakingly transcribed from Anna's spidery script to her own precise handwriting. Written in 1846, 1855, 1856, and 1871, these are remarkable documents. Few historic sites are fortunate enough to have the depth of documentation of daily life that these diaries provide. Anna Burwell's papers undergird the site's interpretive framework, allowing its guided tours, school programs, and special events to portray the Burwell family, the African-Americans enslaved in their household, and students who attended their school in personal and compelling detail.

Mary Claire Engstrom's second great work was this volume, *The Book of Burwell Students*. From the diaries and other sources, she eventually identified 201 young women who attended the school from 1837–57, writing 135 of the 159 biographical sketches included here. *The Book of Burwell Students* is stunning in both its detail and breadth. We will never know how many hours she spent poring over 19th century records and newspapers, or the dead ends or false leads she encountered. Unlike Anna Burwell, she left little documentation of her anxieties or disappointments—all we have is her remarkable final manuscript.

Indeed, *The Book of Burwell Students* could function as a primer on historical research in a pre-Internet world. While she had no personal connection to the Burwells or their school, Mary Claire Engstrom located and received help from dozens of the students' descendents, most notably Alice Noble. In addition to being the granddaughter and great-niece of Burwell School students, Noble had ties to other families with deep North Carolina roots, yielding significant information and artifacts about Burwell students.

Mrs. Engstrom's was a campaign of small victories, waged in dusty courthouse basements and solitary library research rooms as she examined thousands of documents for a small clue, like a receipt for tuition or a line or two about the school in a letter. She consulted church records, county marriage bonds, deed registers, cemetery records, university alumni records, newspapers, family Bibles, and town and county histories. In the historical collections of the UNC–Chapel Hill and Duke University, she pored over business records and personal correspondence. One document often led to another. Before search engines and digitized documents made research quicker and remote from its sources, this was how it was done, and there is something magnificent about the process and its results.

She began with the names of the students, which came from a variety of sources, including the lists of students and patrons in the school's catalogue, given to the Historic Hillsborough Commission by the granddaughter of Burwell student Lavinia Cole. The transcriptions of Anna Burwell's diaries and letters yielded more names, as did an autograph album that Burwell student Mary Bailey Easley brought with her to school in 1852. Other students were identified by their own families. For each name, Mary Claire Engstrom utilized all the documents available to her to methodically recreate the lives of women who had died, in many cases, a century or more before. Often, she eventually located descendents who provided oral histories and gave or loaned artifacts—letters, artwork, photographs, clothes, jewelry, furniture—to the Historic Hillsborough Commission for display at the Burwell School Historic Site.

To examine the research *behind* this book is also to note its perfect timing, and to imagine the consequences of what may be lost when such efforts are delayed. When Mary Claire Engstrom was conducting research in the 1960s and 1970s, she was still able to make contact with Burwell students' granddaughters, nieces, and great-nieces. Some of the women she and Alice Noble spoke or corresponded with had known Burwell students personally. Attending the school was a source of great pride for many women, and they had talked about it to their families. Miss Mattie E. Blackwood wrote to Mary Claire Engstrom in 1965, "My father's mother, Mrs. Martha Jane Craig Blackwood, attended the Burwell School and spoke of that fine school as long as she lived."

But even as this book was being compiled, information about the students was slipping away. Alice Noble died in 1972, while Mary Claire Engstrom was still in the early stages of writing *The Book of Burwell Students*. Mrs. William Bason wrote of her aunt, Burwell student Ann Eliza Nash, "I have collected all I could find about Aunt Eliza. She died before my father was married even and I had to search through his many family notes to find anything at all. . . ." In many cases, though, the descendents of Burwell students had something to share. But had Mary Claire Engstrom begun her search even ten years later, she would not have had access to many of the personal remembrances and artifacts presented here.

Though she devoted a great deal of time to this volume and the work of the Historic Hillsborough Commission at the Burwell School Historic Site, it must be noted that Mary Claire Engstrom's efforts were not focused only on the Burwell School. She was also a charter member and first president of the Hillsborough Historical Society. She compiled research files on most of Hillsborough's historic buildings, families, architects, trees, maps, and cemeteries, and wrote a number of entries in the *Dictionary of North Carolina Biography*. She produced additional unpublished works, wrote numerous newspaper articles, and developed several temporary and traveling exhibits. Her work has been used by countless researchers. Perhaps most significantly, her research on the town's architectural history constitutes the core of the National Register nomination for the downtown historic district that was ultimately written by Catherine Bishir.

When the Historic Hillsborough Commission nominated Mary Claire Engstrom for an award in 1986, the supporting narrative said, "The difference she made in Hillsborough shows today"; and it is still evident two decades later. Without a National Register district in downtown Hillsborough, there would be no Historic District Commission and no status as a Certified Local Government, both important tools that help preserve the area's historic fabric and character. And there certainly might not be a Burwell School Historic Site. To be sure, the preservation of the Burwell School and the historic character of Hillsborough is not the work of Mary Claire Engstrom alone; but her research and advocacy were instrumental in helping the town develop the civic identity and pride that inspired its preservation and sustain that effort to this day.

In 1970, the Engstroms sold the Nash-Hooper House and moved to Chapel Hill, but Mary Claire Engstrom's connection to the Burwell School continued. She devoted much of the next decade to her work on *The Book of Burwell Students*. In 1983, she resigned from the Historic Hillsborough Commission, because of health problems. She died in 1997. The Engstrom Research Room at the Burwell School and the Hillsborough Historical Society's annual Engstrom Award are fitting tributes to her, as is the publication of this book.

Of course, *The Book of Burwell Students* is significant not only because of the women whose work it reflects, but also because of the women whose stories it tells. This volume is a rarity among primary sources and contemporary scholarship about women and women's education in the early 19$^{th}$ century because it examines a number of students from one institution. Most research has focused on the people who founded and taught at schools like the Burwells', but there are fewer sources and scholarship on the women who were educated in those female academies. When such students are studied, it is rare to find so many pupils from a single school profiled in one work.

Thanks to the diligence of Mary Claire Engstrom, the Burwell students emerge from this book as unique and vibrant individuals. The spirited Annabelle Norwood runs up and down the hill in front of the

Burwell residence to warm herself on cold mornings. The impulsive Rebecca Jane Parker elopes with her beloved "Mr. Harris" so quickly that she leaves behind all her dresses and bonnets. The tragic Elizabeth Coit begs her family to pick her up from the Burwells when the term ends, but dies in an epidemic that sweeps through Hillsborough before they can retrieve her. These women and their stories could easily have been lost, but instead are preserved in these pages.

As a group, the students in this book constitute a statistically significant sample from a representative institution. They represent nearly two-thirds of the estimated 250 who attended the Burwells' school from 1837–57. Furthermore, the school they attended is typical of many others founded in the first half of the 19th century, as the education of women in the United States moved out of the home and into private schools. The students' biographical sketches provide a broad sense of who was being educated, how they reacted to that process, how others viewed their education, and what became of them. In doing so, *The Book of Burwell Students* greatly enhances our understanding of the impact education had on women and the larger society at a pivotal moment.

*The Book of Burwell Students* reveals both the diversity and interconnectedness of the students. The student population was not drawn entirely from the top level of the socioeconomic stratum. While the fathers of the boarding students were often wealthy planters, judges, attorneys, congressmen, or prominent ministers, the day students included the children of a local builder, a dry goods merchant, a black-smith, a shoemaker, and a saddler. Bettie S. Morris, daughter of a Hillsborough tavern owner, is listed in this book next to Virginia Moseley, daughter of the first governor of Florida. Despite such class divisions, the lives of the students were often linked, both during and after their school years. Sisters, cousins, and neighbors attended the school together or recommended it to one another. Students brokered romances between their relatives and fellow students. Sarah C. Ray, writing of her friend and fellow student, Kate Murchison, in a letter to her cousin John H. Tillinghast, advised him, "She says that she is gratified that you desire to visit H—and if you will come to Mrs. Burwell's she will contrive to open the parlor door for you." Frederick Nash Strudwick married not one, but two Burwell students—his neighbor Mary Burwell and, after her death, her cousin, Rosaline Brooke Spotswood.

Some of the greatest treasures in *The Book of Burwell Students* are the students' letters, which both illustrate the educational process and capture the young women's unvarnished reactions to it. The students' writings show that the Burwells had a clearly defined and rigorous curriculum. Mary Huske Pearce wrote to her cousin William Tillinghast in 1851 that they were forbidden from reading "novels or tales," so she had turned her attention to history, "Marie Antoinette, for example." Pearce and other students confirm the curriculum's emphasis on writing, including periods of the day set aside for letter-writing and regular composition assignments. Mary Pearce complained to her cousin, "We now have to write compositions every week . . . you would feel sorry for me, if you knew how difficult it is for me, especially as we have to write something Imaginative, and I am nearly exhausted of subject, substance, and everything else."

For some boarding students, the combination of academic work and crowded living conditions in the Burwells' household—probably quite different than those they were accustomed to in their more affluent homes—provoked homesickness and misery. Susan Murphy wrote to her parents, "Sometimes I feel like my heart would break. It appears like I have been here 5 months allredy I never wanted to see home so bad in my life. . . ." However, other young women thrived in the classroom and carried their academic successes with them for the rest of their lives. When eighty-year-old Margaret Isabella Walker wrote her "Reminiscences," she recounted being praised by Robert Burwell in a math class as "the proudest day of my life."

A selection of letters written to the students underscores the attention families paid to their education from afar and their expectations of how the young women would put their studies to use. On March 11, 1838, William Person Mangum, who represented North Carolina in the U.S. Senate, wrote to his daughter Sallie, "I am much pleased to perceive evidence of great improvement in your writing; & trust, My dear, that not only in that, but in all respects you will make all reasonable efforts to improve your time."

Marcus Cicero Stephens's letter to his granddaughter, Mary Anne Primrose, amplified Anna Burwell's own ideas about the need for women to be educated so they could "help themselves." Stephens urged Mary Anne to expand her studies beyond the "usual subjects" of music, drawing, and French.

*Generally speaking, the women have not been treated with Justice by the male sex. It is true the rougher walks of life have very properly been destined to men, and the knowledge necessary for such purposes is also the peculiar study of man. But if the woman be inferior to the man in bodily strength, her mind is equally vigorous as his. The records of ancient and modern History set this matter beyond doubt and I have known several instances in private life where women have exhibited full as much courage, prudence, and strong sense as any men in like circumstances.*

*The Book of Burwell Students* provides compelling evidence that the hopes of Anna Burwell and Marcus Cicero Stephens were realized as many of the students put their educations to good use. As Mary Claire Engstrom wrote in her Prefatory Note, ". . . much solid accomplishment is recorded in these pages." Burwell students continued their educations at other female academies in North Carolina, as well as in New York and Philadelphia. Some pursued more specialized studies, as in the case of Josephine Berry, who attended design school in New York after studying music and art with the Burwells. Many students went back to their homes and became teachers, educating not only their children, but nieces, nephews, cousins, and neighbors. And, in what is likely the most substantive impact of the school, Burwell students organized their own educational institutions, accelerating the spread of women's education in 19th century North Carolina. They played a role in the founding or administration of eight other schools—the Nash-Kollock School, Mrs. Huske's School, Mrs. V.A. Blackwood's School, the Reidsville Female Seminary, the Simonton Female College, Sunnyside, Poplar Hill, and the Almeda School. Two of these schools have connections to educational institutions that exist today—the Simonton Female College became the Mitchell Community College in Statesville, North Carolina, and Nash-Kollock graduates served as the president of Greensboro Female College (now Greensboro College), and on the faculty of the State Normal and Industrial School (now UNC–Greensboro).

Mary Claire Engstrom took particular note of connections between the Burwells' school and contemporary educational institutions. Her correspondence reflects that she was excited to learn that a school operating in southern California—the Webb Schools in Claremont—was in the "direct lineage" of the Burwell School because it was founded by U.S. Senator Sawney Webb, brother of Burwell School student Suny Webb. Senator Webb credited his affinity for education to his sister, who taught him in her Almeda School.

In addition to chronicling an important period in educational history, *The Book of Burwell Students* illuminates the world in which the Burwells and their pupils lived, as both the Civil War and slavery emerge as important themes. Both are seen primarily from the perspective of white Southern women, as only one student—Henrietta Holdich from New York—came from a state north of Virginia or west of Alabama.

Almost every Burwell student had a brother or husband who served in the army of the Confederate States of America. Some were casualties of the war, and one was among those who surrendered at Appomattox. Those who survived the war often returned home to the devastation of their property and financial ruin. On the home front, former Burwell students offered their own responses to the conflict—they managed large planta-tions while their husbands were away, wrote stories supporting the Southern cause that were printed in magazines, and in the case of Emma Newkirk McKoy, saved the hams from the smokehouse of her Cumberland County plantation by hanging them under the very bridge the Union soldiers would use as they approached her property. Emma's husband, Erskine McKoy, eventually returned from the Civil War but died a short time later. Emma then put her Burwell education to use teaching music in the Fayetteville area, driving to and from her students' homes in a horse and buggy.

The institution of slavery also plays a role in *The Book of Burwell Students*, as it did in the lives of those who operated and attended the Burwells' school. The most direct reference to slavery comes in a letter written by fifteen-year-old Sarah Kollock to her grandfather in 1841. She asked that he allow her "to draw on the hire of my negroes to the amount of $20," so that she might buy a calico frock. "Understand, dear Grandpa," she wrote, "tis to be taken from the hire of negroes belonging to me. . . ." Affirming the young woman's view of this transaction as wholly a matter of commerce, she concludes the letter, "You see this is a real business note."

In both antebellum documents—like Sarah Kollock's letter—and this book's 20th century interpretation of them, enslaved African-Americans are seen primarily as an economic commodity. In *The Book of Burwell Students*, Mary Claire Engstrom mentions slaves only when large numbers of them were owned by a student's family or when they were inherited by the students. The years since this manuscript was written have yielded evidence that enslaved people learned even when they were not actively being taught. It is quite probable this was true at the Burwells. Therefore, a discussion of Burwell students should include the people enslaved in the Burwell household.

Anna Burwell's papers and other primary sources show that people were enslaved in the Burwell household throughout the time of the school's operation. Since the household and school shared much of the same physical space, the slaves certainly interacted with the students and worked in areas where classes took place. In an 1856 diary entry, Anna Burwell mentions both Eliza Chavis and Ann as slaves whose duties included building fires in the "girls' rooms," waiting in the dining room during meals, and washing, ironing, and sewing for the students. Enslaved people would also have been charged with cleaning the school building and tending to the fires in its two fireplaces. *The Book of Burwell Students* records that one young woman—Emma Newkirk—brought a slave with her to school; other students may have done so as well.

Although the presence of slaves at the Burwell School and in the household is undeniable, their learning was most likely limited to what they could glean from lessons they overheard while performing other tasks. Anna Burwell's diaries and letters never make even an oblique reference to teaching slaves or to their literacy. However, she did not, at least in the early years of the school, prohibit one of the people enslaved in her household from writing letters. In April 1839, two years after the Burwells' school opened, Elizabeth Hobbs (Keckly), a slave who had been loaned to the Burwells by Robert's family, wrote to her mother, Agnes Hobbs, who was enslaved at the Burwell family home in Virginia. Published years later in Elizabeth Hobbs Keckly's memoir, the letter makes clear that its seventeen-year-old author was highly literate and that Anna Burwell sanctioned its writing:

> *I want to hear of the family at home very much, indeed. I really believe you and the family have forgotten me . . . nevertheless, I love you all dearly and shall, although I may never see you again, nor do I ever expect to . . . however, it is said that a bad beginning makes a good ending, but I hardly expect to see that happy day at this place. . . . I must close now, although I could fill ten pages with griefs and misfortunes; no tongue could express them as I feel; don't forget me though, and answer my letters soon. I will write you again soon, and would write more now, but Miss Anna says it is time I finished. . . . I wish you would send me a pretty frock this summer.*

Could Elizabeth Hobbs Keckly have been permitted to write this letter at the same time of evening that the boarding students were writing letters to their parents? Does her daily exposure to academic lessons as she performed tasks in the schoolroom explain how a seventeen-year-old, born into slavery and without formal access to education, could write a letter that so eloquently evoked her pain? In a striking example of the comparisons *The Book of Burwell Students* prompts, Elizabeth Hobbs Keckly's letter to her mother reveals she wanted the same thing that Burwell student Sarah Kollock did when she wrote to her grandfather about hiring out her slaves. Both young women wanted a new dress.

If Elizabeth Hobbs Keckly were ever included among "Burwell students," she would easily be the school's most famous pupil. She would be the only one to spend considerable time in the White House, as she did while she was dressmaker and confidante of First Lady Mary Todd Lincoln. She would be the only one to have a memoir published by a national press, as *Behind the Scenes: Thirty Years a Slave and Four Years in the White House* was by Carlton and Company in 1868. And she would be the only one whose writings are studied in classrooms today, as *Behind the Scenes* is, and the only one whose handiwork—a dress designed for Mrs. Lincoln—can be found in the Smithsonian Institution.

Despite its omission of a substantive discussion of slavery and the dated tone of some of Mary Claire Engstrom's more subjective assessments, *The Book of Burwell Students* should be viewed as ambitious research for the time in which it was written. It was daring and boundary-breaking simply because it assigned historical significance to the lives of relatively ordinary young women, and such a topic would not have been considered mainstream at the time. When Mary Claire Engstrom was working on the book in the 1970s, the field of women's studies was in its infancy. The first academic program in women's studies began in 1970 at San Diego State University, and many important books on women's education in the United States were not written until the 1980s.

The fact that the study of women's history and women's education is still relatively new, and that important works in these disciplines are still being written, makes the publication of *The Book of Burwell Students* all the more exciting and important. There would certainly be no more fitting legacy for the work of Margaret Anna Burwell and Mary Claire Engstrom than for *The Book of Burwell Students* to provide the basis and inspiration for further scholarship. There is much more of value to be studied and written about the Burwells, the young women they educated, and their representation of times in which they lived. As Mary Claire Engstrom's Prefatory Note proclaims, *"The Book of Burwell Students* should be regarded as the tentative beginning of a larger project."

—*Katherine Malone-France*
*Washington, DC*

# Prefatory Note

The present *Book of Burwell Students* should be regarded as the tentative beginning of a larger project. The one existing *Burwell School Catalogue of 1848–51* lists only 107 students; but there were clearly many more during the school's successful twenty years of existence from 1837 to 1857. Now, in April 1979, 81 additional student names have been authenticated and added to the roster, bringing the known list to a total of 188 girls. Many names have been gleaned from Mrs. M.A. Burwell's letters, from student letters, and from the living descendants of Burwell girls.

The following brief sketches are not intended to be full-scale biographies. They undertake to give as much essential information as possible about each girl: her parents' names; something of her background culturally and geographically; her brothers' and sisters' names, especially if they attended the Caldwell Institute or the Burwell School; her years of attendance at the school, the specific sessions if possible; her church affiliation; her special talents and interests; the date of her marriage and name of her groom; where she lived as an adult; the number and names of her children; and the year and place of her death. A photograph is included if one is available. Most important, the sketches try to note what use the girl made of her Burwell School education.

Most Burwell School girls married in the years just before or at the beginning of the Civil War. Some of their husbands were killed, others injured and maimed, physically or psychologically; and young wives with small children found themselves running plantations, caring for invalids, teaching schools based on the Burwell pattern in their own homes, driving buggies over country roads to give music lessons, and making ends meet in any way they could. *The Book of Burwell Students* is inevitably a sad book.

Medically, the book is a terrifying one. Sudden death overtakes young girls and young brides without warning; ailments are fatal for lack of knowledge and drugs; a lethal summer epidemic in Hillsborough runs on unchecked; nervous ailments have no cure save the asylum. Similarly, although they are rarely mentioned in plain English, 19th century addictions to drink and opium cast a shadow over many marriages and families.

Nevertheless, in spite of such odds, much solid accomplishment is recorded in these pages: New schools and seminaries are begun, some of which still flourish today; careers are attempted as musicians, artists, writers, and horticulturists; and families are educated, scores of whose members are listed in the indexes of North Carolina histories.

Mrs. Burwell's revealing letters of 1855–56 to her daughter Fanny are freely quoted in the following pages, and for these the Historic Hillsborough Commission is indebted to Helen Burwell Styron (Mrs. Charles Styron) of Raleigh who generously placed them in our hands. Our special debt to the late Miss Alice Noble of Chapel Hill is recorded on a separate page as are the commission's grateful thanks to the many friends of the Burwell School who have aided this project by sharing their family records and special information about Burwell girls.

Student names are listed alphabetically in *The Book of Burwell Students*. Two baptismal names and a nickname are sometimes given also (e.g., Eliza [Lizzie] Adam Jones), and the reader should look under each of these. Sketches of a few of the 188 girls are omitted in the present book; the additional sketches, chiefly of Fayetteville girls, will be included as soon as research is completed.

The compiler has written all of the sketches in the book and therefore assumes all responsibility for errors of either fact or judgment.


—*Mary Claire Engstrom*
*Chairman, Historic Hillsborough Commission*
*Hillsborough, North Carolina*
*April 1979*

# Special Acknowledgment to the late Miss Alice Noble of Chapel Hill, North Carolina

Miss Alice Noble, daughter of the late Marcus Cicero Stephens Noble, Professor of Education at the University of North Carolina, and herself the longtime Secretary of UNC's School of Pharmacy, undertook the research on the New Bern students at the Burwell School for this book as a special, affectionate tribute to her grandmother, Mary Anne Primrose (Mrs. Albert Morris Noble), a Burwell student in 1841. Miss Alice was also related to Mary Snead Chapman and had close ties with the Cole sisters.

All told, she worked for many months in 1965 and 1966, wrote scores of letters of inquiry to her old friends, and sent other scores of progress reports to the compiler. Miss Alice meant to purchase the binder to contain *The Book of Burwell Students* as a memorial to her father, Professor Noble, but the compilation of the book was not begun during her lifetime. The commission and the compiler here record their special gratitude and warm thanks to Alice Noble for the store of information she collected to place between these covers. We, too, record here that her work was done in honor of Burwell student Mary Anne Primrose (Sept. 13, 1826–Feb. 1, 1916).

—*MCE*
*Hillsborough, April 1979*

# Acknowledgments

The following persons have generously and graciously contributed information in various forms for the sketches of Burwell students:

Mrs. Carl Anderson (Jean Bradley Anderson), Cabe Ford Rd., Durham, N.C.

Mrs. William Bason (Hannah Willard Ashe Bason), Raleigh, N.C.

Mrs. Ruth H. Bateman, 4908 Starmount Dr., Greensboro, N.C.

Mrs. Bessie D. Beam, 303 Crestwood Dr., Roxboro, N.C.

Mrs. John Berry (Mary Strudwick Berry), 304 Wentworth Dr., Greensboro, N.C.

Miss Isabel Bidgood, Earl Court Apts., 1301 St. Paul St., Baltimore, Md.

Miss Mattie E. Blackwood, Rt. 2, Chapel Hill, N.C.

Mrs. Edward Browne (Catherine Browne), New Bern, N.C.

Mr. James Webb Cheshire, Over-the-River, Hillsborough, N.C.

Mrs. Mary Pride Clark, 500 Forest Lake Rd., Fayetteville, N.C.

Mrs. W.C. Coker (Louise Venable Coker), 609 North St., Chapel Hill, N.C.

Miss Elizabeth H. Collins, Highlands, Hillsborough, N.C.

Mrs. Frederick B. Drane, PO Box 105, Edenton, N.C.

Mrs. James W. Feild (Virginia Epes Feild), 3314 Alabama Ave., Alexandria, Va.

Mrs. W. W. Flowe, 113 Grove Ave., NW, Concord, N.C.

Mr. and Mrs. James E. Gay, Jr., 75 N. Stratford Rd., Winston-Salem, N.C.

Mrs. H.E. Hayes (Ray L. Hayes), 177 Beverly Rd., Danville, Va.

Mr. Clark Slover Hollister, New Bern, N.C.

Mr. Samuel W. Hughes, 123 E. Queen St., Hillsborough, N.C.

Mrs. Elizabeth Hicks Hummel, 415 College St., Oxford, N.C.

Mrs. Irvin Jensen (Sara Irvin Jensen), 634 S. Main St., Reidsville, N.C.

Mr. Kenneth L. Kimmins, 3514 Glenna Ave., Grove City, Oh.

Mrs. Samuel Simpson Kirkland, Ayr Mount, Hillsborough, N.C.

Mr. Edwin M. Lynch, 312 N. Churton St., Hillsborough, N.C.

Mrs. R.Y. McAden (Mary Lacy McAden), 118 E. Peace St., Raleigh, N.C.

Mrs. Colvin McAllister, Fayetteville, N.C.

Mrs. John Malcolm McAllister, 2525 Wake Dr., Raleigh, N.C.

Miss Elizabeth Vann Moore, Edenton, N.C.

Mrs. W.G. Moore, 201 Oakenwald Dr., Marion, S.C.

Mrs. Mattie Burwell Murphy, Davidson, N.C.

Mrs. Frank Nash (Ann Spotswood Strudwick), Colonial Inn, Hillsborough, N.C.

Miss Alice Noble, On Windy Hill, Chapel Hill, N.C.

Mrs. T.O. Pass, Sr. (Nancy C. Pass), Rt. 1, Box 293, Roxboro, N.C.

Prof. William S. Powell, History Dept., 515 Hamilton Hall, UNC, Chapel Hill, N.C.

Mrs. S.R. Prince, High Rock Farm, Rt. 1, Box 465, Reidsville, N.C.

Mrs. Eugenia Richards, 5211 Chesapeake, Houston, Tex.

Mrs. John M. Roberts (Grace Jean Roberts), 143 W. Tryon St., Hillsborough, N.C.

Mrs. J.M. Saunders (Susan Rose Saunders), 326 W. University Dr., Chapel Hill, N.C.

Mrs. Grant Shepherd (Mary Exum Shepherd), 117 W. Union St., Hillsborough, N.C.

Miss Mary Spurgeon, 301 Hillsborough St., Chapel Hill, N.C.

Mrs. Russell Stafford, 1522 31st St., NW, Washington DC

Mr. George Stevenson, Div. of Archives & History, 109 E. Jones St., Raleigh, N.C.

Mrs. Robert Burns Street (Margaret Berry Street), Huntersville, N.C.

Mrs. Charles Styron (Helen Burwell Styron), 373 Williamsborough Ct., Raleigh, N.C.

Mrs. Ivey James Sutton (Annie M. Sutton), 1236A Columbus Cir., Wilmington, N.C.

Mrs. J.A. Warren (Pattie Spurgeon Warren), 301 Hillsborough St., Chapel Hill, N.C.

Mr. A. Earl Weatherly, Greensboro, N.C.

Mrs. John Graham Webb (Mary Leigh Webb), 117 E. Queen St., Hillsborough, N.C.

Miss Louise C. Webb, 101 Ingleside Dr., Concord, N.C.

Mr. Mangum Weeks, 219 N. Royal St., Alexandria, Va.

Mrs. Dorothy H. Wood, Rt. 2, Hillsborough, N.C.

# Burwell School Catalogue of 1848–51

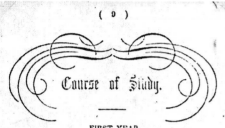

## Course of Study.

### FIRST YEAR.

| | |
|---|---|
| READING AND SPELLING, | COMPOSITION, |
| ENGLISH GRAMMAR, | ELEMENTS OF NAT. PHILOSOPHY, |
| GEOGRAPHY, | HISTORY, |
| PENMANSHIP, | ARITHMETIC, |

### SECOND YEAR.

| | |
|---|---|
| ENGLISH GRAMMAR, (Continued,) | WATTS ON THE MIND, |
| GEOGRAPHY, (Continued,) | LESSONS ON ASTRONOMY, |
| HISTORY, | COMPOSITION, |
| ARITHMETIC, | PENMANSHIP, |
| NATURAL PHILOSOPHY, | READING AND DEFINING, |

### THIRD YEAR.

| | |
|---|---|
| PARSING BLANK VERSE, | GEOMETRY, (Commenced,) |
| COMPOSITION, | ASTRONOMY, |
| PHILOSOPHY OF NATURAL HISTORY, | BOTANY, |
| ALGEBRA, | PENMANSHIP, |

### FOURTH YEAR.

| | |
|---|---|
| GEOMETRY, | CHEMISTRY, |
| RHETORIC, | MORAL PHILOSOPHY, |
| INTELLECTUAL PHILOSOPHY, | EVIDENCES OF CHRISTIANITY, |

ANCIENT HISTORY AND GEOGRAPHY,

## Remarks.

The situation of this School combines the advantages of town and country, and in healthfulness and purity of moral atmosphere, it is thought to be peculiarly eligible.

The primary object of our course of instruction is, to qualify young ladies for the cheerful discharge of the duties of subsequent life. We seek to cultivate in every pupil a sense of her responsibility for time and for eternity.

Our instruction in every branch is thorough. "Not how much, but how well," is our motto.

The character of each recitation is recorded at the time of reciting, and a report sent to the parent or guardian twice in a session.

The Government is as purely parental as possible. An appeal to the reason and affection of the pupil, and to her conscience, as influenced by the precepts of the Bible, is always preferred to the use of sterner means.

On the Sabbath no calls or visits are allowed. When no particular preference is expressed, the pupils will attend the Presbyterian Church. The afternoon of the Sabbath is devoted to the study of the Sacred Scriptures, and the Shorter Catechism.

In the Sleeping Apartments every comfort is provided, and habits of neatness strictly enjoined. Extravagance in dress is discouraged, but every pupil is required to be neatly dressed *at all times.*

## TERMS:

The year is divided into two Sessions, commencing and closing with those of the University of North Carolina.

| | |
|---|---|
| Board and Tuition per Session, | $67 50 |
| Music on Piano or Guitar, | 20 00 |
| Use of Instrument for practice, | 5 00 |
| French, | 10 00 |
| Latin, | 5 00 |
| Drawing, | from 10 to 20 00 |
| Washing, | 5 00 |

It is very desirable that pupils enter at the first of a Session, but they are charged only from the time of entrance. No deduction made for absence except in case of *protracted sickness.* No accounts allowed except by permission of the parents.

# Burwell School Students Revised Roster

## Compiled May 1983

The revised roster of 201 names of authenticated Burwell School students listed alphabetically below includes the 107 names published by the Burwells in their 1848 catalogue, plus 94 additional names discovered in Mrs. M.A. Burwell's letters, her diaries, various student letters, autograph albums, and keepsake books, acquired from the descendants of students. It is certain that the roster given here is by no means complete. The present list records all students authenticated as of May 1983. The roster form used below lists students alphabetically; otherwise the form used in the Burwells' catalogue has been followed:

Alston, Anna—Chatham County, North Carolina
Alston, Eugenia—Chatham County, North Carolina
Alston, Lavinia M.—Chatham County, North Carolina
Alston, Sally—Chatham County, North Carolina
Amis, Fannie J.—Granville County, North Carolina
Amis, Rosa —Granville County, North Carolina
Anders, Ellen—Bladen County, North Carolina
Ashe, Ann Eliza—Wilmington, North Carolina
Ashe, Annie—Waynesborough, Virginia
Ashe, Annie R.—Wadesborough, North Carolina
Ashe, Eliza—Wadesborough, North Carolina
Ashe, Maria—Waynesborough, Virginia
Attmore, Sally—New Bern, North Carolina
Barton, Sally—Caswell County, North Carolina
Bell, Emily Rowena—Plymouth, North Carolina
Bell, Jane Williamette—Plymouth, North Carolina
Benners, Julia—Waynesville, North Carolina
Berry, Elizabeth Ann—Hillsborough, North Carolina
Berry, Josephine—Hillsborough, North Carolina
Berry, Rosanna—Hillsborough, North Carolina
Bridges, Sally—Richmond, Virginia
Bridges, Virginia (Jenny)—Richmond, Virginia
Brook(e)s, Harriet—Halifax, Virginia
Brookes, Sallie—Halifax, Virginia
Brown, Bettie C.—Salisbury, North Carolina
Brown, Charlotte Ann—Hillsborough, North Carolina
Brown, Laura H.—Hillsborough, North Carolina
Bunting, Mary L.—Sampson County, North Carolina

Bunting, Sally—Sampson County, North Carolina
Burwell, Fanny—Hillsborough, North Carolina
Burwell, Mary—Hillsborough, North Carolina
Burwell, Nannie—Hillsborough, North Carolina
Cameron, Annie Ruffin—Hillsborough, North Carolina
Carrington, Betty—Halifax, Virginia
Chapman, Kate—New Bern, North Carolina
Chapman, Mary Snead—New Bern, North Carolina
Coit, Elizabeth—Cheraw, South Carolina
Coit, Martha—Cheraw, South Carolina
Cole, Harriotte Middleton Gillespie—New Bern, North Carolina
Cole, Lavinia Ellis—New Bern, North Carolina
Cooley, Emily Eliza—Hillsborough, North Carolina
Cooley, Mary Cain—Hillsborough, North Carolina
Cowan, Caroline E.—New Bern, North Carolina
Craig, Martha Jane—Orange County, North Carolina
Davis, Anna—Pittsborough, North Carolina
Davis, __ —New Hanover County, North Carolina
Davis, __ —New Hanover County, North Carolina
Douglas, Margaret—Orange County, North Carolina
Easley, Mary Bailey—Cluster Springs, Virginia
Faison, Amelia—Sampson County, North Carolina
Faison, Sallie E.—Sampson County, North Carolina
Faucette, Eliza Jane—Alamance County, North Carolina
Faucette, Martha—Orange County, North Carolina
Faucette, Sally—Orange County, North Carolina
Freeland, Mary—Hillsborough, North Carolina
Fuller, Virginia Ann—Hillsborough, North Carolina
Garland, Victoria—Caswell County, North Carolina
Garrett, Bettie—Chatham County, North Carolina
Garrett, Mary L.—Chatham County, North Carolina
Gilchrist, Fannie—Fayetteville, North Carolina
Gilchrist, Lucy—Fayetteville, North Carolina
Gilchrist, Susan—Fayetteville, North Carolina
Glass, Lizzie—Graham, North Carolina
Grice, Sarah—Sampson County, North Carolina
Hall, S.—New Bern, North Carolina
Hammond, Ella—Waynesborough, Virginia
Harrison, Cassandra—New Bern, North Carolina
Hawks, (Hannah?)—Washington, North Carolina
Holditch, Henrietta—New York, New York
Hollister, Janet—New Bern, North Carolina
Holmes, Bettie A.—Fayetteville, North Carolina
Holt, Annie—Alamance County, North Carolina
Holt, Frances—Alamance County, North Carolina

Hooker, Margaret Parthenia Evelyn—Hillsborough, North Carolina
Horner, (C.?)—Granville County, North Carolina
Howerton, Emily—Hillsborough, North Carolina
Howerton, Maria Louise—Hillsborough, North Carolina
Jeffreys, Mary E.—Caswell County, North Carolina
Johnson, Margaret—Orange County, North Carolina
Johnston, Harriet—_____
Jones, Eliza Adam (Lizzie A.)—Hillsborough, North Carolina
Jones, Fanny Iredell—Hillsborough, North Carolina
Jones, Frances—Wadesborough, North Carolina
Jones, Mary Albertine—Hillsborough, North Carolina
Jones, Mary Cameron—Hillsborough, North Carolina
Jones, Mary Rebecca—Hillsborough, North Carolina
Jones, Sally Rebecca—Hillsborough, North Carolina
Jordan, Ann (Nan)—Orange County, North Carolina
Jordan, Elizabeth (Bet)—Orange County, North Carolina
Kirkland, Annie Ruffin—Hillsborough, North Carolina
Kirkland, Susan Mary—Hillsborough, North Carolina
Kollock, Sara(h) Jane—Hillsborough, North Carolina
Lindsay, Annette Eliza—Greensboro, North Carolina
Lindsay, Mary Virginia—Greensboro, North Carolina
Long, Helen Caldwell—Hillsborough, North Carolina
Long, Margaret Taylor—Hillsborough, North Carolina
Lunsford, Frances Elizabeth—Roxboro, North Carolina
Lunsford, Virginia—Roxboro, North Carolina
Lynch, Elizabeth Palmer—Hillsborough, North Carolina
Lynch, Mary Jane—Hillsborough, North Carolina
McAuley, Caroline—_____
McDiarmid, Annie—Cumberland County, North Carolina
McDiarmid, Catharine—Cumberland County, North Carolina
McKay, Flora—Memphis, Tennessee
McKay, Isabella—Cumberland County, North Carolina
McKeithan, Margaret—Cumberland County, North Carolina
McLester, Margaret—Hillsborough, North Carolina
Mangum, Sally Alston—Orange County, North Carolina
Mebane, Martha F.—Orange County, North Carolina
Mebane, Mary E.—Orange County, North Carolina
Middleton, Jemima—Duplin County, North Carolina
Mitchell, Eliza N.—Chapel Hill, North Carolina
Montgomery, Barbara Maria—Alamance County, North Carolina
Moore, Ann—Hillsborough, North Carolina
Moore, Julia Rebecca—Chapel Hill, North Carolina
Moore, Mary (Mitty)—Hillsborough, North Carolina
Morris, Bettie S.—Hillsborough, North Carolina
Morrow, Martha—Oaks, Orange County, North Carolina

Moseley, Virginia—Tallahassee, Florida (Centerville, Florida)
Murchison, Kate—Cumberland County, North Carolina
Murchison, Margaret—Cumberland County, North Carolina
Murphy, Julia—Sampson County, North Carolina
Murphy, Mary Bailey—Sampson County, North Carolina
Murphy, Susan Moseley—Sampson County, North Carolina
Nash, Elizabeth Simpson—Hillsborough, North Carolina
Newkirk, Emma—New Hanover County, North Carolina
Norwood, Annabella Giles—Hillsborough, North Carolina
Norwood, Margaret Yonge—Hillsborough, North Carolina
Norwood, Robina—Hillsborough, North Carolina
Nunn, Sally—Orange County, North Carolina
Owen, Mary—____
Owen, Sally Roberta—Mayo, Virginia
Palmer, Eliza—Hillsborough, North Carolina
Parker, Jane Rebecca—Hillsborough, North Carolina
Parks, Maria L.—Hillsborough, North Carolina
Pearce, Annie Blount—Hillsborough, North Carolina
Pearce, Mary Huske—Fayetteville, North Carolina
Perkins, Henrietta (Martin)—Caswell County, North Carolina
Pointer, Margaret—Person County, North Carolina
Primrose, Mary Anne—New Bern, North Carolina
Ray, Sarah C.—Fayetteville, North Carolina
Roberts, Susan—Orange County, North Carolina
Robinson, Mary Elizabeth—Bladen County, North Carolina
Ruffin, Rebecca Edwards (Beck)—Hillsborough, North Carolina
Ruffin, Susan Mary—Orange County, North Carolina
Sanders, Bettie—Johnston County, North Carolina
Sanders, Laura—Johnston County, North Carolina
Scales, Emma Jane—Rockingham County, North Carolina
Sellers, Frances A.—Sampson County, North Carolina
Sellers, Rosa—Sampson County, North Carolina
Shepard, Margaret—New Bern, North Carolina
Shepard, Mary—New Bern, North Carolina
Smith, ___—Caswell County, North Carolina
Smith, ___—Caswell County, North Carolina
Smith, Bettie—Cumberland County, North Carolina
Smith, Fanny—Caswell County, North Carolina
Smith, Isabella—Cumberland County, North Carolina
Smith, Julia—Cumberland County, North Carolina
Smith, Lou—Fayetteville, North Carolina
Smith, Mary—Granville County, North Carolina
Smith, Sarah—Granville County, North Carolina
Smith, Sarah—Smithfield, Virginia
Speed, Jennie—Granville County, North Carolina

Speed, Nannie Taylor—Granville County, North Carolina
Spotswood, Rosaline Brooke—Petersburg, Virginia
Stedman, Eliza—Fayetteville, North Carolina
Stevens, Jane Ellen—Sampson County, North Carolina
Stevenson, Elizabeth—New Bern, North Carolina
Thompson, Ann—Hillsborough, North Carolina
Unthank, Narcissa—Greensboro, North Carolina
Vanderford, Emily—Hillsborough, North Carolina
Venable, Isabella—Hillsborough, North Carolina
Venable, Martha—Hillsborough, North Carolina
Waddell, Bella—Hillsborough, North Carolina
Waddell, Maria E.—Hillsborough, North Carolina
Walker, Margaret Isabella—Hillsborough, North Carolina
Watkins, ___—Farmville, Virginia
Watkins, Elizabeth—Farmville, Virginia
Watters, Caroline J.—Wilmington, North Carolina
Webb, Anne H.—Greensboro, Alabama
Webb, Elizabeth G.—_____
Webb, Fannie—____
Webb, Henrietta—Orange County, North Carolina
Webb, Martha Ann—Granville County, North Carolina
Webb, Mary—Hillsborough, North Carolina
Webb, Mary Caroline—Orange County, North Carolina
Webb, Susan A.—Orange County, North Carolina
Whitted, Elizabeth—Orange County, North Carolina
Williams, Bell—Cumberland County, North Carolina
Williams, Cornelia—Person County, North Carolina
Williams, Kate—Cumberland County, North Carolina
Williams, Martha K.—Cumberland County, North Carolina
Williams, Phi—____
Wilson, Mary—Morganton, North Carolina
Witherspoon, Denah McEwen—Camden, South Carolina
Witherspoon, Mary Nash—Hillsborough, North Carolina
Womack, Fanny—____
Woodrow, Mary—____
Woods, Sarah—____
Wortham, Mary—Granville County, North Carolina
Yonge, Annabella—New Hanover County, North Carolina

# Biographical Sketches of Burwell Students

## ANNA ALSTON
## & SALLY ALSTON
Chatham County, North Carolina

Three Alston girls from Chatham County (Anna, Sally, and Lavinia) attended the Burwell School in 1855. Anna Alston and Sally Alston were of separate families. All of the Alstons were music students and may have attended the Burwell School expressly for that purpose.

Although Nannie Burwell loved to teach music in the Brick House she seems to have been somewhat intimidated by the wealthy Alston girls and confessed that she felt like bursting into tears whenever Anna Alston took a lesson. Mrs. Burwell wrote to her daughter Fanny on November 27, 1855, ". . . all the Alstons have left [for Christmas vacation]. They left last Friday, but they will return." On January 19, 1856, Mrs. Burwell wrote Fanny, "Dr. Davis [of Pittsboro] says the three Alstons are coming back. . . . Sally Alston's father is dead, died the day before Christmas." On February 8 (after heavy snows): "We expect the Alstons . . . as soon as the weather is better & they are all Music scholars."

On March 4, 1856, Mrs. Burwell wrote in a letter to Fanny,

> *This evening just at sunset another shout announced Sally Alston's arrival & sure enough she has come, & paid this $30, which I now enclose you, feeling grateful for that kind providence which has always done us good. . . . Sally Alston, I heard, was going to Richmond to school & feeling tenderly interested for her, I wrote when I heard of her father's death, & urged her if she went to Richmond not to board in a school, but to let me introduce her to Mrs. Fay & go there to board. I mentioned in the letter that the sessions in Richmond commenced in October, which would be the best time for her to go, & suggested that she might spend the session here, the summer vacation at home, & go to Richmond in the Fall, she says her mother was so pleased with the plan, that she sent her right off here, & she may go to Richmond in October.*

There is no mention of the other Alstons in Mrs. Burwell's letters of 1856. It seems likely that the Alston girls, used to plantation life, may perhaps have found the Burwell School routine too confining and its living arrangements uncomfortably spartan.

The *Raleigh Register* of October 12, 1859, carried the notice of Sally Alston's marriage on October 3, 1859, to Rodger Grigory in Chatham County.

William W. Alston and Nathanael Macon Alston from Chatham County, perhaps brothers or cousins of the Alston girls, were students at the nearby Caldwell Institute in 1848–49, according to the *Catalogue of the Caldwell Institute 1848–49.*

Mrs. Burwell's letters and the *Catalogue of the Caldwell Institute 1848–49* (printed by Dennis Heartt), 12 pp., are in the archives of the Burwell School.

## LAVINIA M. ALSTON
### Chatham County, North Carolina

Lavinia M. Alston was the first of the four Chatham County Alstons to attend the Burwell School. The Methodist Alstons were well-to-do landowners in Chatham, and the four Alstons seem to have represented at least three different families. All were music students. Lavinia was a student in 1845. A letter from Mrs. M.A. Burwell dated January 17, 1846, to her friends Miss Mary A. and Miss Susan Kirkland, then visiting in Fayetteville, mentions Lavinia:

> *Neither Sarah Smith nor Lavinia Allston* [sic] *have returned. Mrs. Alston has again employed Miss Clarke as a teacher in her family, so we do not expect Lavinia, but still think Sarah may come. . . .*

Lavinia married a Methodist minister, the Rev. William Barringer. *Alumni History of the University of North Carolina* (1924 edition) states,

*BARRINGER, WILLIAM*    *Minister*
*Concord; b. Feb. 18, 1816; d. Mar. 17, 1873; m. Lavinia M.*
*Alston; s. 1833–34; presiding elder in the N.C. and S.C.*
*conferences 20 yrs.; four times mem. gen. conf. Methodist Episcopal*
*church, South; Methodist.*

Lavinia Alston Barringer died on August 18, 1867, in Greensboro, according to an obituary notice in the *Raleigh Register* of August 27, 1867. The Rev. Barringer served the Hillsborough Methodist Church in 1870. He was then fifty-four years of age. He died on March 17, 1873, and was buried in Greensboro.

[    Lavinia Alston was the daughter of John J. and Adaline Williams Alston of Chatham County. Her maternal grandparents were William and Elizabeth Kearney Williams of Franklin County. Her paternal grandparents were Joseph John ("Chatham Jack") and Martha Kearney Alston. Lavinia and William Barringer had the following children:

1. John Alston, b. 1851.
2. Paul Brandon, b. 1853.
3. Victor Clay, c. 1855.
4. Ella, c. 1859.
5. William, Jr., c. 1861.    ]

## FANNIE (FANNY) J. AMIS
1834–June 15, 1862
Granville County, North Carolina

Fannie (Fanny) Amis of Granville County is listed in the *Burwell School Catalogue of 1848–51*, and a student letter pinpoints her as having attended the school in 1849 at the time Capt. John Berry was enlarging the original house and the girls were crowded into cramped temporary quarters in the Parks-Hasell House (the Lemuel H. Lynch House) diagonally across Union Street from the Burwell School.

Fannie Amis (her name is spelled Fannie on her tombstone) appears to have been a friend of the Murphy twins from Cuwhiffle

Plantation in Sampson County and also to have been their roommate for a period in the makeshift quarters of the Burwell School. Susan Moseley Murphy in an undated letter (from 1849) to her mother wrote,

> *Fannie Amis sends her love to you. Fannie Amis has left us and gone upstairs. The night she went upstairs she cried. I felt right sorry for the gal. Laura has not told me how she liked Fannie Amis. I think she flattered but it is very much like her but that is not like Fannie Burwell for Fannie is prettier than that . . .*

Although the final sentence here is confused, it seems clear that Fannie knew the Murphy family well and had perhaps visited them in Sampson County. James A. Amis, who attended the Caldwell Institute in Hillsborough in 1848–49, may have been Fannie's brother or cousin. There is no indication of whether Fannie was immediately related to Rosa Amis, a later Burwell student from Granville.

On June 5, 1855, Fannie J. Amis married John Henry Webb (b. May 26, 1825), the son of John Webb and Margaret Howard Webb of Granville. Fannie was then twenty-one years old. The John H. Webbs had three children:

1. Joseph Amis, Mar. 26, 1856–1908; m. Susan Wiggins Russell.
2. John, July 14, 1858–1923; m. Anna May Devin.
3. Fannie Amis, Feb. 7, 1861–92; m. Samuel Venable Morton.

Fannie Amis Webb, the Burwell student, died on June 15, 1862, at the age of twenty-eight, and was buried in a Webb family graveyard in Granville. Her tombstone was erected by her three children, apparently many years later. Her husband, John Henry Webb, on December 7, 1864, married his second wife, Miss Lucy T. Daniel.

Materials for the above sketch are from the Patrick Murphy Family Letters, owned by Mrs. J.M. Saunders, Chapel Hill, N.C.; and from W.J. Webb et al., *Our Webb Kin of Dixie* (Oxford, N.C., 1940), pp. 88-89, 99. (*See also* Susan M. & Mary B. Murphy, Mary Wortham.)

# ROSA (ROSE) AMIS
Granville County, North Carolina

Rosa (Rose) Amis appears to have attended the Burwell School somewhat later than Fannie Amis, who was enrolled in 1849. Mrs. Burwell's 1855–56 letters, written to her daughter Fanny in New York, mention Rosa Amis's romance as though she were a recent student.
On February 4, 1856, Mrs. Burwell wrote,

> *There was a rumor that Dr. Ed Scott & Rose Amis <u>were married</u>, but Mr. B. saw Billie Scott this evening & she says 'tis not so. They are positively engaged.*

On March 4, 1856, she reported further to Fanny,

> *'Tis a fact that Rose Amis is engaged to Ed Scott—he has bought a plantation on Flat River, but when they are to be married I don't know. Report had them married last winter.*

The *Sessions Book of the Hillsborough Presbyterian Church* carries these entries relative to the Amis family of Granville:

> Mrs. Mary N. Amis—Dismissed July 2, 1863, to Pres. Church, Shiloh, Granville Co.
> Miss Rosa Amis—Dismissed April 1, 1858, to Shiloh, Granville Co.
> Mrs. Bettie Amis—Dismissed July 7, 1867, to Shiloh, Granville Co.

The *Catalogue of the Caldwell Institute 1848–49,* printed in 1849 by Dennis Heartt, listed James A. Amis as a student. These members of the venerable Amis family of Granville were all undoubtedly related.
The *Raleigh Register* (Nov. 16, 1859) published the announcement of Rosa Amis's marriage on October 31 to Lewis Amis of Granville.
Dr. Edward Scott, killed in the Civil War, is buried in Hillsborough's Old Town Cemetery. His military marker reads, "Capt. Edward M. Scot, d. 1863. Co. D. lst Regt. NC Vols. C.S.A. Aged 34."

[    The *Hillsborough Recorder* (Jan. 13, 1864) announced the marriage of Dr. E. M. Scott to Mrs. Lizzie Dudley, youngest daughter of the late

Henry Dusenberry of Lexington, on December 16, 1863. The same issue carried the notice of Dr. Scott's death twelve days later in Hillsborough. Captain of Co. D, 1ˢᵗ Regiment of N.C. Troops, he had served in the battles of Seven Pines and Gaines Mill.     ]

Information in this sketch is from Mrs. M.A. Burwell's letters, Burwell School; *Sessions Book of the Hillsborough Presbyterian Church*, Hillsborough, N.C.; the *Raleigh Register* (Nov. 16, 1859), N.C. Collection, Wilson Library, UNC, Chapel Hill.

## [   ELLEN ANDERS (ANDREWS)
c. 1840– ?
Bladen County, North Carolina

On the roster of students Mrs. Engstrom compiled, she included Ellen Anders, but this young woman's name may have been Ellen Andrews. In the United States Census of 1850, the Burwell family had a student by the name of Ellen Andrews living with them. It is possible that the enumerator made a mistake.     ]

## ANN(E) ELIZA ASHE
March 10, 1833– ?
Wilmington, North Carolina

Ann Eliza Ashe was the sister of Capt. Samuel A'Court Ashe and Miss Willie Ashe, all of whom lived in their youth on the family rice plantation, Eyries, in the Rocky Point area near Wilmington. The parents of these children were Maj. William Shepperd Ashe (1814–62), who had a distinguished career as a member of the U.S. Congress (1850–55), president of the Wilmington and Weldon Railroad (1854–62), and a major in the C.S.A., and his wife, Sarah Ann Green.

Ann Eliza (Ann is mistakenly spelled with an *e* in the *Burwell School Catalogue*), the eldest daughter of the Ashes, was born on March 10, 1833. She attended the Burwell School between the years 1848–51. However, her attendance there was interrupted for a session when the family wintered in Macon, Georgia. Her father was elected to Congress in 1850, and in 1851 Eliza was sent to a convent in Georgetown where the Ashe family lived, before moving into the heart of Washington. The last school Eliza attended was Madame Chegaray's in New York City, a school for young ladies.

In 1854 Maj. Ashe resigned from Congress to return to Wilmington as president of the Wilmington and Weldon Railroad. Eliza was married on January 6, 1857, to Dr. James Arrington Miller with the ceremony being performed by the Rev. Robert B. Drane. Dr. Miller proved immensely valuable during the 1861 yellow fever epidemic in Wilmington, and in 1862 joined the C.S.A. as a surgeon.

The Millers had four children, Thomas Arrington, Samuel A'Court, Ann Grange, and Mary Ashe Miller. The sons died unmarried, and Ann Grange died very young. Mary Ashe Miller married Charles Boyd Tyler, a cotton merchant in Atlanta, Georgia, on April 8, 1885. The Charles Tylers had two children, Sarah Ashe and Charles Boyd, Jr. Sarah Ashe married Robert R. Dillingham, who lived but a short time and left no issue. Charles Boyd Tyler, Jr., married also but left no issue. Thus, Ann Eliza Ashe, the Burwell student, has left no descendants.

The data above was contributed to researcher Miss Alice Noble of Chapel Hill by Hannah Willard Ashe Bason (Mrs. William Bason of Raleigh), daughter of Capt. Samuel A'Court Ashe and Hannah Emerson Willard Ashe. Mrs. Bason writes Ann Eliza without an e on Ann and always calls her Eliza or "Aunt Eliza." "I have collected all I could find about Aunt Eliza. She died before my father was married even and I had to search through his many family notes to find anything at all. . ."

## SARAH (SALLY) SITGREAVES ATTMORE
### 1833–82
### New Bern, North Carolina

An ancestor of Sarah (Sally) Attmore was the well-known Philadelphia merchant William Attmore, who wrote the *Journal of Two Tours of North Carolina* in 1787. On one of his visits to North Carolina, Attmore met Miss Sallie Sitgreaves, the captivating daughter of Judge John Sitgreaves. They married on March 18, 1790. William Attmore died in Philadelphia in 1800 and was buried there.

The Attmores' son, George Sitgreaves Attmore, married Mary Taylor, daughter of Isaac and Hannah Justice Taylor, and the couple had a number of children, one of whom was Sarah (Sally) Sitgreaves Attmore, born in 1833. Sally lived during her childhood and until her marriage in the lovely Attmore-Oliver House at 511 Broad Street, a block from Tryon Palace in New Bern.

The Attmore-Oliver House with its great twin chimneys is said to have been built circa 1790 by Samuel Chapman, a prominent citizen and mason. In 1954, the New Bern Historical Society purchased and restored it, and it serves now as its headquarters.

It is uncertain when Sally Attmore attended the Burwell School, very likely in the late 1840s, but before or at the time the catalogue was printed. She would have been fifteen years old in 1848. Sally was one of a number of New Bern girls at the school: Mary Anne Primrose, Mary Chapman, Kate Chapman, Cuddie Cowan, Janet (Net) Hollister, Cassandra Harrison, and Hannah(?) Hawks.

At the age of twenty-four, Sally married twenty-nine-year-old Scotsman Robert Stuart Primrose of New Bern on December 17, 1857. Robert (b. Oct. 1828, d. June 26, 1870) was the brother of Burwell student Mary Anne Primrose. His brother, Cicero Stephens Primrose, also married a Burwell School student, Mary Chapman. Robert was an 1849 graduate of Princeton; he later studied medicine and became an MD. Dr. Primrose and Sarah (Sally) Attmore had one son, Robert Stuart, Jr., also a physician, who married and died without issue.

Sally Attmore Primrose died at the age of forty-nine and is buried in the old Cedar Grove Cemetery in New Bern, North Carolina.

Data in the above sketch is from the documented Primrose files of the late Miss Alice Noble, granddaughter of Mary Anne Primrose. (*See also* Mary Anne Primrose.)

## SALLY BARTON
### 1835–August 16, 1852
### Caswell County, North Carolina

Sally Barton almost certainly is the Sarah C. Barton (1835–Aug. 16, 1852) who died in Hillsborough at the age of seventeen and was buried in the Old Town Cemetery. Sarah Barton's gravestone is now in the open space to the north of Strudwick Hall; it seems probable that, with other stones, it was moved during construction of the hall. (The cemetery also contains the grave of a Harriet Barton [d. July 13, 1885], buried in the D.D. Phillips plot near the present west wall.)

The summer of 1852 was the dread summer in which a malignant and highly contagious disease broke out in Hillsborough, apparently some form of dysentery with high fever. A surprising number of tombstones in the Old Town Cemetery bear 1852 death dates. At the Burwell School, Elizabeth Coit of South Carolina died; Mary Burwell fell dangerously ill; and a second student, according to a letter written by Eliza Bingham to William N. Tillinghast on June 7 of that year, contracted the ailment. The second unfortunate student was evidently Sarah C. Barton of Caswell County. A student also died at the Episcopal seminary on E. Tryon Street

Nothing further is known of Sally Barton. The Bartons, however, were planters and farmers in northern Orange, Person, and Caswell counties.

## EMILY ROWENA BELL
### 1846–1913
### Plymouth, North Carolina

Emily Rowena Bell was born in 1843 in Plymouth, the fourth child of Dr. James W. and Mary Eliza Walker Bell. A Bell granddaughter, Mrs. Ruth H. Bateman, describes her as "pretty and amiable and especially talented in music. Her mother gave her piano lessons, but she had her academic lessons with a tutor who lived with the family."

Her sister Mary Marcia Bell died when Emily was eleven and she was inconsolable. It was decided in 1857 to send both Emily and her older sister Jane to the Burwell School for advanced musical instruction. Mrs. Bateman notes that the girls' mother was a close friend of Mrs. Burwell, and that the girls lived in the Burwell home.

In 1861, at the age of fifteen, Emily Rowena married Mr. James F. Norman of Plymouth, who went immediately into the Confederate army. She remained with her family until their home was burned during the Battle of Plymouth in 1864. Her only child had been stillborn in 1863, leaving her heartbroken.

In 1869, she and her husband purchased the land on which her parents' home had stood and built a house. Emily gave singing lessons, organized a "singing school," and also organized the first choir of the Plymouth Methodist Church.

Visiting her sister Jane in Halifax County in 1875, Emily became attached to her two-year-old niece, Hope Hunter. She took the little girl home with her, and Hope remained permanently with the Normans and became the daughter of the house. Emily continued to give music lessons to students even after ill health confined her to a wheelchair and until her death in 1913.

*March 18, 1965*

*Dear Mrs. Engstrom:*

*My grandmother and my great-aunt were students at Burwell Female School in 1857. They were Jane Williamette Bell (my grandmother) and Emily Rowena Bell, daughters of Dr. James W. and Mary Eliza Bell (nee Walker), of Plymouth, North Carolina. Jane (1841–1911) was 16 and Emily (1846–1913) was 11.*

*Mrs. Burwell was a close friend of the girls' mother and, as I recall the story, an accomplished musician. Emily was very talented in music and it was for this reason that she was allowed to accompany her sister, in order that she could receive musical training from Mrs. Burwell. (It is my impression that she lived at the Burwell home instead of the School.)*

*When the School was burned Jane was sent to Salem Academy, Pittsfield, Massachusetts, but Emily remained with*

*the Burwells for a time. Both girls were married in 1861, Jane
to Dr. William F. Hunter, of Halifax County, and Emily to
James F. Norman, of Plymouth.*

*Emily Rowena Bell (print made from original daguerreotype).*

*I have daguerreotypes of both girls which I treasure very
highly. I don't know whether they could be reproduced, or whether
photographs are desired. I would be happy to make them available
to you for exhibit if it would serve any purpose. They are about the
ages of their attendance at Burwell in the pictures.*

*Sincerely yours,
(Mrs.) Ruth H. Bateman*

Data for this sketch and the picture were supplied by Mrs. Ruth H. Bateman, 4908
Starmount Dr., Greensboro, N.C.

# JANE WILLIAMETTE BELL
### 1841–1911
### Plymouth, North Carolina

Jane Williamette Bell was born in 1841 in Plymouth, the second child of Dr. James W. and Mary Eliza Walker Bell. Her granddaughter, Mrs. Ruth H. Bateman, writes,

> *She was a beautiful, often fiery child, strong-willed and self-reliant. Her father believed that females and brains were not biologically incompatible and he recognized in Jane a rare intelligence. He gave her every advantage in academic studies. At sixteen (that is, in 1857) she was sent to the Burwell School.*

Jane accompanied her eleven-year-old sister, Emily Rowena, and the two girls were to take advanced music courses. Mrs. Bateman writes that the girls' studies were curtailed when the Burwell School burned.

*Jane Williamette Bell (print made from original daguerreotype).*

There is no record, however, of a fire at the school, although we do not know precisely what happened to the refectory. The school, of course, closed in 1857 for very different reasons when the Burwells decided to remove to Charlotte Female Institute in Charlotte, North Carolina. Afterward, Jane W. Bell attended Salem Academy in Pittsfield, Massachusetts.

In 1861 she married Dr. William F. Hunter of Halifax County as his second wife. When her husband left to join the medical corps of the Confederate army, Jane took on the enormous job of running their Halifax County plantation. She continued to manage it after the war because of her husband's failing health and his despondency over the loss of two sons (by his former marriage) in defense of Fort Fisher.

Jane Williamette Bell Hunter bore nine children, three of whom died in infancy. Three sons and three daughters survived her. She died at age seventy in 1911.

Photo of Jane Bell made from a daguerreotype, made available by Jane's granddaughter, Mrs. Ruth H. Bateman.

## ELIZABETH (LIZZIE) ANN BERRY
### 1840–1909
### Hillsborough, North Carolina

Elizabeth (Lizzie) Ann Berry, born in Hillsborough in 1840, was the daughter of Hillsborough builder-architect John Berry (1798–1870) and Elizabeth Ann Vincent Berry (1803–88), of the Crossroads Community, who was said to have been of French Huguenot descent. Elizabeth Ann, named for her mother, was evidently the third and last of the six Berry sisters to have attended the Burwell School and the only one of them, so far as is known, who became a teacher.

Elizabeth Ann, later to be known in Hillsborough as "Miss Lizzie" Berry, was willed the beautiful little Berry Brick House in Hillsborough by her father. She did not marry, but lived with her sister Carolina Victoria Berry (May 22, 1845–Aug. 23, 1927), who married Benjamin Hardesty Bell (July 25, 1837–June 5, 1909) and had ten children. Her niece Mrs. Margaret Berry Street wrote to the present compiler,

*Elizabeth Ann was the beloved "Aunt Lizzie" of the Bell children with whom she was a delightful companion and teacher. She inspired them with a love of classical literature which has persisted throughout their lives. One of the children, Mr. Franklin Wilhelm Bell, became a collector of rare books and all the children have a loving recollection of their Aunt.*

It may have been Elizabeth Ann Berry who planted the beautiful boxwood path now grown to maturity at the Berry Brick House, or it may have been her mother, Elizabeth Ann Vincent Berry. Elizabeth Ann Berry died at sixty-nine at the end of a most useful life and was buried in the Berry plot in Hillsborough's Old Town Cemetery.

*Elizabeth Ann Berry.*

The picture accompanying this sketch and part of the data in it are from Capt. John Berry's granddaughter, the late Mrs. Margaret Berry Street, Huntersville, N.C.

## JOSEPHINE BERRY
1833–1912
Hillsborough, North Carolina

Josephine Berry, born in 1833 in Hillsborough, was the third of the eight children of Capt. John Berry (1798–1870), self-taught architect, brick mason, and politician, and Elizabeth Ann Vincent Berry (1803–88), daughter of a thrifty French Huguenot family of the Crossroads Community. Josephine was unusually talented in both music and art, especially the latter. She was apparently the first of three Berry daughters—Josephine, Elizabeth Ann, and Rosanna—to attend the Burwell School. The Berry girls lived in the delightful little Berry Brick House at 208 W. Queen Street, and all would have been day pupils at the Burwell School. It is probable that all three girls took music and art courses.

Josephine's granddaughter, Mrs. Annie Lee Holt Wood, of Monterey, Virginia, recalled to the present compiler in 1966 that Josephine always spoke of "finishing," not "graduating," at the Burwell School, and that at her "finishing" exercises, the principal (the Rev. Robert A. Burwell, probably, after 1848) in introducing Josephine before her musical selection said, "Josephine is proficient in art as well as music." According to Mrs. Wood, Josephine "finished" in both music and art.

Josephine's father, Capt. John Berry, is said to have recognized her marked artistic talent and to have sent her north to a school of design in New York. The pen sketch, "The Vine-Gatherer's Daughter," below, may have been done either at the Burwell School or at art school in New York (Berry family tradition says at the Burwell School). It would appear to be an extremely proficient copy of an Italian original.

Josephine Berry married Dr. Daniel Archibald Montgomery of Alamance County who is listed as a Patron of the Burwell School in the 1848–51 catalogue, which also includes on its student roster the three Berry sisters and Dr. Montgomery's sister, Barbara Maria Montgomery.

*"The Vine-Gatherer's Daughter,"* a pen-and-ink drawing by Josephine Berry.

The Scots-Irish Montgomery family had come to Alamance County before the American Revolution. Dr. William Montgomery (1789–1843) in the third generation had become a U.S. Congressman and a power in area politics for many years. He married as his second wife Sara (or Sarah) Albright, only daughter of "Postmaster Daniel" Albright, and the third of their ten children was Dr. Daniel Archibald Montgomery. It seems certain that Capt. Berry would have known Dr. William Montgomery's family well, even before Josephine Berry met Maria Montgomery at the Burwell School. Daniel and Josephine Berry Montgomery had seven children.

Information is from Sallie W. Stockard's *History of Alamance County* (Raleigh, 1900), pp. 112, 114, 115. (*See also* Barbara Maria Montgomery.)

## ROSANNA BERRY
1836–60
Hillsborough, North Carolina

Rosanna Berry, born 1836 in Hillsborough, was the daughter of Hillsborough's well-known builder-architect, Capt. John Berry (1798–1870) and Elizabeth Ann Vincent Berry (1803–88) of French Huguenot ancestry. Rosanna, named for her paternal great-grandmother, was considered to be the most beautiful and charming of the six Berry daughters. A daguerreotype shows Rosanna to have been a distinctly Spanish type of beauty with dark eyes and dark hair. She apparently attended the Burwell School in the 1850s and may, like her artist-sister Josephine, have been sent north for further study. Her sisters Elizabeth Ann and Josephine both attended the Burwell School.

Rosanna Berry died when she was twenty-four years old—in 1860, just on the eve of the Civil War. She is buried in the Berry plot in Hillsborough's Old Town Cemetery. A lamb surmounts her tombstone, decorated with oak leaves, a grapevine and leaves, which carries this inscription:

*ROSANNA BERRY*
*1836–1860*
*GONE HOME*

*Rosanna Berry.*

*Dearest Mrs. Engstrom:*

*. . . it has only been recently that I have been able to procure pictures of two of Captain Berry's daughters and I have been able to find out very little about them although I tried to get data from both Mary and Gertrude Bell.*

*Rosanna Berry (1836–1860) was the daughter of John Berry (1798) and Elizabeth Ann Vincent (1803) and was considered to be the loveliest and most charming of the Berry sisters. She attended the Burwell School . . . with two of her sisters—Josephine and Elizabeth Ann. She died when she was 24. Elizabeth Ann Berry (1840–1909) was one of the six daughters of John Berry and Elizabeth Ann Vincent. She and two of her sisters, Josephine and Rosanna, attended the Burwell School. She was willed the little Brick House in Hillsborough by her father. She did not marry, but lived with her sister Caroline Victoria Berry (May 22, 1845–August 23, 1929), who married Benjamin Hardesty Bell (on January 16, 1867) and had ten children. . . .*

*Enclosed are the two pictures. Mrs. Wood promised to send*
*you a picture of her grandmother, Josephine, who married Doctor*
*Daniel Montgomery of Alamance County, who became one of the*
*Trustees of the Burrell* [sic] *School.*
*With love and best wishes,*
*Margaret Berry Street*

Information about the Berry daughters is from the late Mrs. Margaret Berry Street, Huntersville, N.C., and Mrs. Annie Lee Holt Wood, Monterey, Va.

## SALLY BRIDGES &
## VIRGINIA (JENNY) BRIDGES
Richmond, Virginia

These two little girls were Mrs. Burwell's own nieces, daughters of her sister, Mary Dandridge Robertson, who had married Mr. James Robertson Bridges of Richmond, Virginia, in 1835 as his second wife. James Bridges's first wife had been a Miss Calloway by whom he had two children, Edward and Nannie.

Little Sally and Jenny Bridges were probably not paying students at the Burwell School. Mrs. Burwell writes frankly of her "Sister Mary's" difficult position, and it is obvious that the Bridges girls spent their vacations at the Burwell School. James Bridges, it seems clear, had neither income, job, nor position. Mrs. Burwell wrote to her daughter Fanny on January 12, 1856,

> *. . . poor sister Mary . . . I do think her situation is a most*
> *pitiable one. Jenny & Sally (& may be 'tis well they have not a*
> *sense of it) don't seem to realize at all their parents' situation—*
> *they seem to think they can get any thing by "writing to Mama"—*
> *Sally is to be ruined by her expectations from Aunt Sally—poor*
> *child! . . . I feel sorry from my heart for the whole family . . . I hope*
> *to do them good. I try by precept and example to show the good of*
> *industry & energy in whatever is undertaken.*

The Bridges children spent Christmas vacation of 1855 at the school, as Mrs. Burwell wrote in the letter cited above: "I felt sorry for Jenny & Sally they are accustomed to so much at Christmas—but their mother has sent them a box. I positively have no money to buy candy. or toys with. . . ."

Jenny and Sally Bridges evidently shared Nannie Burwell's room—since they were cousins. . . . Jenny appears to have shared Nannie's bed; Sally slept on the couch at the foot of the big bed, according to Mrs. Burwell's letter to her daughter Fanny, dated January 19, 1856.

In her correspondence to Fanny on January 5, 1856, Mrs. Burwell particularly regretted Jenny's lack of cheerfulness:

> *I want you to be <u>cheerful</u>—if you could know what a vacation I've spent with Jenny Bridges's long discontented face always before me you would not wonder. She don't mean it. I suppose she is as happy here as she would be anywhere, but she has not a happy cheerful temper which so lightens life's sorrows—& she is to be pitied—I don't know how to correct it.*

On March 4, 1856, Mrs. Burwell wrote to Fanny,

> *Jenny Bridges has been very unwell for two weeks, is not well now. I don't know what is the matter with her unless it is want of exercise & too close study. Sally will never suffer from either of these causes. She is greatly improved—but is <u>forward</u> still & I am afraid always will be*
> *. . . . James Bridges is still out of employment. . . .*

The materials in the above sketch came from the commission's *Burwell-Spotswood Genealogy* and from the letters of Helen Burwell Styron.

[ **SALLIE BROOK(E)S** (1833–April 26, 1865)
&
**HARRIET BROOK(E)S** (1841– ?)
Black Walnut, Halifax, Virginia

Sallie and Harriet Brookes were the daughters of James F. Brookes and Sarah Atkinson. James Brookes, a wealthy Virginia planter, was originally from North Carolina, which may be why he chose to send his daughters to the Burwell School. (Other Brookes daughters were sent to school but do not appear on the Burwell School roll.) Other families from Black Walnut also sent daughters and sons to the Burwell School and Caldwell Institute.

According to the *Hillsborough Recorder* (Aug. 24, 1853), "Sallie Brooks dtr. of James F. Brooks of Black Walnut, Va.," married Charles B. Easley, who had attended the Caldwell Institute from 1848–49, corresponding to the time Sallie attended the Burwell School. Perhaps they met as students in Hillsborough.

By 1860, the Easleys had returned to Black Walnut, Virginia, where Charles was a wealthy planter, and Sallie was raising their three children: Thomas, Elizabeth, and Sallie. They lived close to the Owen and Carrington girls, who also attended the Burwell School. During the Civil War, Charles joined the C.S.A. Sallie died on April 26, 1865, a few weeks before the war officially ended.

(Information on Harriet has not been found to date.)      ]

**CHARLOTTE ANN BROWN** (September 26, 1838– ?)
&
**LAURA H. BROWN** (September 6, 1840– ?)
Hillsborough, North Carolina

These two sisters, Charlotte Ann and Laura H. Brown, separated in age by only two years, were very likely enrolled in the Burwell School at the same time, probably in the late 1840s and early 1850s. They were the fifth and sixth of the twelve children of the Hillsborough shoemaker and tanner, William H. Brown (July 6, 1809–Mar. 26, 1866), and his wife, Mary L. (Lewis?) Vasseur Brown (July 27, 1813–July 6, 1868), daughter of the little French Huguenot lady, Mrs. Charlotte Vasseur, who kept a candy shop in downtown Hillsborough until nearly the time of her death on September 8, 1856. Mrs. Vasseur has been described by various persons as an attractive old lady who wore frilled and fluted white caps in her confectionery shop which Burwell students patronized (see Mary Bailey Easley's pocket money account of July 1852).

The Vasseur-Brown Family Bible contained the following notation: "Moved in Halifax, N.C., September 16, 1830." And Allen A. and Pauline O. Lloyd have this note in their *History of the Churches of Hillsborough, N.C.: CA, 1766–1962*:

> *Mr. W. H. Brown (grandfather of N.H. Brown) came to Hillsborough in the year 1840. He was on his way to Tennessee and was persuaded by a Mr. Kirkland to live in Hillsborough. His home was located near Walker's Funeral Home (i.e., near the NW corner of Churton and E. Tryon Sts.). He owned the land where the Corner Drug Store and Mary's Shop are now located. Mr. Brown owned Dimmock Mill and a Tannery west of Hillsborough and was the leading member in the old Methodist Church. His wife was a French woman.*

The owner of the Vasseur-Brown Bible, Mrs. Ray Hayes, writes,

> *We have an old bible that belonged to an aunt of ours (now deceased) which contains quite a bit of information on the Vasseurs . . . The Vasseurs were French Huguenots. Mary L. Vasseur was my great grandmother on my mother's side. I have a small hand made rolling pin which her family brought to this country from France.*

The names of three Burwell School students (Charlotte Ann Brown, Laura H. Brown, and their sister-in-law Margaret Parthenia · Hooker [Brown], who named a daughter Anne Vasseur) appear in the Vasseur-Brown genealogical table.

Data for this sketch is from the Vasseur-Brown Family Bible, Ray Hayes (Mrs. H.E. Hayes), Danville, Va., and from *History of the Churches of Hillsborough, N.C.: CA, 1766–1962*, Allen A. and Pauline O. Lloyd. (*See also* Margaret Parthenia Hooker.)

# MARY L. BUNTING (c. 1833– ?)
## &
## SALLY BUNTING
Sampson County, North Carolina

These two girls were the daughters of Dr. Thomas Bunting, physician of Sampson County, whom the Burwells listed as a Patron of the School in their catalogue. Mary L. Bunting, evidently the older, attended the school about the time the catalogue was being compiled (1848–51). Sally, the younger, was a student in 1855: "This is really a busy time," Mrs. Burwell wrote on November 27, 1855, to her daughter Fanny in New York, "& since I've commenced this letter I've had to stop . . . to give Sally Bunting who has a cold a seidlidtz powder. . . ."

Dr. Thomas Bunting is listed in the *Alumni History of the University of North Carolina* (1924 edition):

> BUNTING, THOMAS        *Physician*
> *Sampson co.; d. April 19, 1871; s. 1822;*
> *state sen. 1836–38; 1850–52.*

This sketch of Dr. Bunting is given in the first of the *James Sprunt Historical Monographs*:

> *Dr. Thomas Bunting, born August 1, 1801, was a native Sampsonian. He was of English-Irish extraction, his paternal ancestors emigrating from Derbyshire, England, in 1642, and settling near Philadelphia. His parents were Richard and Mary (Clinton) Bunting.* [This information is incorrect.] *He attended the state university in 1822; then studied medicine which he afterward practised to some extent, but later devoted his entire time to farming. Dr. Bunting served in the State Senate in 1836, '38, '50, and '52. He was delegate to the National Democratic Convention in Baltimore in 1852 and was, for a number of years, Clerk and Master in Equity. He believed in secession as one of the reserved rights of the State and that the South had just cause to withdraw from the Union. He died April 19, 1871.*

The above citation is from "Personnel of the [N.C. State] Convention of 1861," by John Gilchrist McCormick, *James Sprunt Historical Monographs*, No. 1 (Chapel Hill, 1900), pp. 22–23.

[      The Bunting girls' parents were Dr. Thomas Bunting and Elizabeth Holmes, daughter of North Carolina Gov. Gabriel Holmes. The girls' grandparents were David Bunting and Elizabeth Clinton, daughter of Penelope Kenan and Richard Clinton, an American Revolutionary War hero and one of the first members of Congress.

Mary Louisa married her cousin, John H. Hill, a druggist and son of Dr. John Hampden Hill of Wilmington, North Carolina. Mary and John had six children: Thomas, John H., Mary, Elizabeth, Louisa, and Minnie.

Information is from *The Heritage of Sampson County, North Carolina*, Oscar M. Bizzell, ed., 1983. ]

## ANN(A) (NANNIE) ROBERTSON BURWELL
### August 31, 1836–August 25, 1895
### Hillsborough, North Carolina

Ann(a) Robertson Burwell, always called Nannie, born on August 31, 1836, was the third child of the Burwells and the first to be born in the Hillsborough house. Like Mary, Nannie received her entire academic schooling in her mother's school and, upon graduation, went to New York to stay with her Uncle Richard and Aunt Mary Jane Robertson for six to eight months while she took advanced music lessons and studied French. Mary Jane Robertson seems to have been the perfect chaperone and guide in New York, helping the girls with their clothes, taking them to concerts, and giving them the assurance and polish they could not have acquired in Hillsborough. Said Mrs. Burwell in a letter to Fanny on December 29, 1855, "Mary Jane will ever have my gratitude & love for all she has done for my children."

When Nannie returned to Hillsborough, she began the arduous routine of teaching that went on until 1866 in Charlotte, with only the six-week summer vacations as any considerable breaks. Again she shared the sunny, pretty southeast room upstairs in the Burwell home with Mary and Fanny until Mary's marriage in 1854. When Fanny, too, went to New York in 1855, Nan shared it with her two Bridges cousins and two other young students. The room today has a trundle bed, muslin curtains, and a little stagecoach trunk very much as it might have had in Nannie's day. Nan probably returned from New York in 1852, just in time to become accustomed to teaching before Mary's marriage and departure.

Nan's morning classroom seems to have been in the Brick House where she met her music students and taught French. Mrs. Burwell wrote to Fanny on November 27, 1855,

> *Nan likes teaching music better than anything else . . . she gets up from breakfast & goes into the Brick room with a nice fire & Rose seated at her work to wait on her & I tell her [she] has a* <u>*nice*</u> *time especially since all the Alstons have left—she said she felt like crying every time Anna took a lesson.*

In March 1856, Nan was taking music lessons from the new music master, Mr. Hunt, "in the back part of Berlini," according to Mrs. Burwell (in correspondence to Fanny on March 10, 1856). A letter a few days later on March 15 to Fanny indicates that she was less enthusiastic about grammar and composition:

> *Nan has the lack of the Burwells vis,* <u>*promptness & decision*</u>*, she teaches very well, but she don't depend on herself enough, says "can't" too often—when I say anything about not teaching, Nan says, "Oh, Mother, I* <u>*can't*</u> *teach Grammar . . . I can't teach writing"—just because she has never done it and has the notion that she can't.*

Nevertheless, Nan taught faithfully and well without salary, with almost no new pieces of clothing (she was still young), and with few vacations or trips. When the Burwell educational team removed to Charlotte in 1857, Nan accompanied them as part of it, although she was never mentioned formally.

On September 27, 1866, when she was thirty, she married William Henry Crow of Raleigh. They had five children:

1. Robert Burwell, May 7, 1868–89.
2. William Henry, Oct. 24, 1870–8-.
3. Anna Robertson, Dec. 7, 1872– ?
4. Edmund Burwell, Aug. 18, 1874– ?
5. Harriet Holcomb, Apr. 27, 1877–Sept. 19, 1887.

Mrs. M.A. Burwell died in Nannie's Raleigh home in 1870 while visiting her, and the Rev. Burwell spent his last years with Nannie and also died in her home, in March 1895. Nannie herself died six months later on August 25, 1895, at the age of fifty-nine and is buried in Raleigh in Oakwood Cemetery, Heck Section, Lot 2. Three of her five children died in her lifetime.

The Historic Hillsborough Commission owns a little volume, *The Pianoforte Primer*, used by both Nannie and Fanny Burwell and autographed by both of them. Their room, which Mary also once shared, is the southeast room near the head of the stairs.

## FRANCES (FANNY) ARMISTEAD BURWELL
May 17, 1838–April 12, 1856
Hillsborough, North Carolina

Frances A. Burwell, always called Fanny or Fan, was born on May 17, 1838, the fourth child of the Burwells. She followed the same pattern of education as her older sisters, Mary and Nannie, that is, training at the Burwell School until she was sixteen, and then staying in New York with Richard and Mary Jane Robertson to take piano and guitar lessons and perhaps other coaching.

The Historic Hillsborough Commission owns Xerox copies of fifteen letters written by Mrs. Burwell—from November 27, 1855, to March 15, 1856—to Fanny during her New York stay. These were evidently preserved by Fanny and returned to Mrs. Burwell by Mary Jane Robertson after Fanny's untimely death on April 12, 1856. The letters reflect a good deal of Fanny's daily life in New York, and make it clear that she is being "educated" like Mary and Nannie, so that she can return home to teach in the school and help her parents educate her brothers.

Like her sisters, she depended heavily on Mary Jane Robertson's common sense, good taste, and sound advice. Wrote Mrs. Burwell to Fanny on March 4, 1856, "Your Aunt Mary's counsel & advice always get—she has most excellent judgment—as I've proved often."

The long, painful debates over whether they could afford to buy a guitar, whether they could afford one quarter's guitar lessons for Fanny, whether Fanny should look about for a new piano in a "plain case," made clear the fact that the Burwells and their twelve children lived near what modern sociologists would call "the poverty line."

Mrs. Burwell's letters are sprinkled with little lectures and advice to Fanny: Get all the "good" you can from New York; be cheerful and actively cultivate daily fullness, especially with Mary Jane; go to musical concerts, even operas, and improve your musical taste; never succumb to "the blues"; learn to be affectionate and show affection—it sweetens life—and so on.

Fanny's last letter was received in mid-March 1856, and Mrs. Burwell's last letter to her was written on March 15, 1856. Both the Rev. and Mrs. Burwell hastened to New York when the Robertsons alerted them to Fanny's serious danger. She had erysipelas, a disease which often proved deadly. They decided to bring her home by way of boat to Norfolk, but she died at dawn on April 12 aboard the little steamer, *Thames*. Her body was brought to Hillsborough and she was buried in the Strudwick plot in the Old Town Cemetery, the only Burwell to be buried in Hillsborough. Years later, her brother John Bott Burwell placed a modest tombstone (now eroded and covered with moss) over her grave.

## MARY (MOLLIE) SUSAN BURWELL
December 17, 1832–July 3, 1859
Hillsborough, North Carolina

Mary (or Mollie) Burwell seems to have been a universally beloved and admired person—and a splendid example of the Burwell method of education. Mary, born December 17, 1832, in Chesterfield County, Virginia, was the eldest of the Burwells' twelve children, and only three years old when the family moved to Hillsborough in December 1835. Mary would certainly have been one of her mother's pupils in the new "Brick House" in August 1837. She apparently continued to be taught at the Burwell School until she "graduated" and went to New York in 1848 or 1849 to spend a few months with her uncle and aunt, Mr. and Mrs. Richard Spotswood Robertson, and acquire a little urban "polish," in addition to taking a course of music lessons on the piano and perhaps on the guitar. Mrs. Burwell remarked to Fanny in a letter of December 29, 1855, that she had heard that when the Burwell School was once being discussed, a lady had commented that she was "'sure Mrs. Mary Strudwick's being educated there was a sufficient recommendation'—quite a compliment to Mollie—but New York did a great deal for Mary."

Mary returned to take her place as a teacher of French in the Burwell School, replacing former student Sara(h) Jane Kollock. Mary H. Pearce wrote in a letter of September 27, 1851, to her cousin, William H. Tillinghast, "I expect you will be glad to hear we have changed our French teacher. Miss Molly Burwell now fills Miss Kollock's place, and is much more gentle." Mary was an example of unselfishness to the entire family, Mrs. Burwell wrote to Fanny, when Mary had loaned her easy chair to the dying Dr. Shepard K. Nash: "I felt proud that I had such a child as Mary . . . I could hardly keep back the tears."

Mary married young Frederick Nash Strudwick, who lived next door, on June 27, 1854, and the young couple went "across the lot" to live with the Dr. Edmund Strudwicks. Mary's first child, Mary Nash, was born on March 25, 1855, and died two and a half months later on June 12. Mary was in a stupor of grief, and she seems to have become partially paralyzed. The Strudwicks took her to Philadelphia to a Dr. Bauer who placed her in an "instrument" which she used for nearly a year. Her second child, Robbie, Robert Cincinnatus, was born on August 24, 1857.

Frederick Strudwick was genuinely interested in farming, and removed his young family to Choctaw County, Alabama, in 1858. The Burwells in Charlotte were cruelly shocked in July 1859 to learn that Mary had died on July 3. There had been no warning of her illness, and it was a severe blow from which they could not recover.

Mary, aged twenty-five years, seven months, was buried in a cemetery (evidently a country cemetery) at Arcola, Alabama. Her grave apparently was never marked.

Frederick Nash Strudwick married as his second wife another Burwell student, Rosaline Brooke Spotswood of Petersburg, Virginia. The Historic Hillsborough Commission owns a daguerreotype of Rosaline holding her little stepson, Robbie.

Robert Cincinnatus Strudwick (Aug. 24, 1857–Jan. 9, 1932) married Sally Patterson Lewis (May 19, 1861–June 6, 1913) of Albemarle County, Virginia. He had a successful career as a lawyer and judge in Seattle, Washington, and died in Greensboro at the home of his daughter Mary Burwell Strudwick, who had married Dr. John Berry. Mary Burwell Strudwick Berry's children are 1) Mary Strudwick and

2) John. Judge Strudwick's second daughter was Roberta Burwell Strudwick, who married 1) Robert Glenn, with issue Robert Glenn, Jr., and 2) Lenoir Chambers, with issue Elizabeth Chambers. Mary Burwell has thus left behind her four great-grandchildren and a number of great-great-grandchildren not listed in this sketch.

Data in the foregoing sketch is from Mrs. Burwell's letters, Burwell School; W.N. Tillinghast Papers, Ms. Collection, Perkins Library, Duke Univ.; Genealogy and Letters of the Strudwick, Ashe, Young and Allied Families, comp. by Betsy Lawson Strudwick et al., 1971. (*See also* Rosaline Brooke Spotswood.)

## ANNIE RUFFIN CAMERON
July 16, 1842–November 15, 1915
Hillsborough, North Carolina

*Annie Ruffin Cameron.*

Annie Ruffin Cameron, born July 16, 1842, was the third daughter of Paul Carrington Cameron (Sept. 25, 1808–Jan. 6, 1891) and Anne Ruffin Cameron (June 3, 1814–May 29, 1897). Her grandparents included Chief Justice Thomas Ruffin and Duncan Cameron. She was named both for her mother Anne Ruffin, daughter of the chief justice, and her grandmother, Anne Kirkland Ruffin, daughter of the Scots merchant William Kirkland of Ayr Mount.

Annie Ruffin Cameron is not listed in the Burwell catalogue and probably attended the school only in its closing years, 1856 or 1857, when she would have been fourteen or fifteen. It was probably due to Annie that Mrs. Burwell's music master, Signor Antonio di Martino, was given a home in the old James Hogg cottage at Burnside, the Cameron home. [He had lived at Fairntosh with the family before they moved to Burnside in 1836.] Signor di Martino was going blind, and when eventually he could not safely walk without the help of the Cameron girls, he shot himself with one of his own Sicilian cavalry pistols.

Annie Ruffin Cameron at the age of eighteen in 1860 married George Pumpelly Collins (Dec. 26, 1835–Aug. 30, 1903) of Somerset Place, Lake Phelps. His tombstone in St. Matthew's Churchyard, Hillsborough, carries this data:

> *Son of Josiah and Mary Riggs Collins of Somerset Place, Lake Scuppernong [Phelps], Washington Co., N.C. b. New York City; d. Hillsborough. Planter; Major C.S.A. QM Pettigrew-Kirkland-McRae's Brigade. NC Vols. ANV. C.S.A.*

Annie's father, Paul C. Cameron, in 1856 purchased the old Norwood-Mickle-McNair House (partly of logs) across from Eno Lodge; and in 1877 he enlarged the house to the east, added a porch and new roof and presented it to the George Pumpelly Collins family as their home. Mr. Cameron in his will left the property, known as Highlands, to Mrs. Collins for her lifetime, then to his grandson and namesake, Paul Cameron Collins.

Five children of Maj. George Pumpelly Collins and Annie Ruffin Cameron Collins are buried in St. Matthew's Churchyard near their parents:

1. Mary Arthur, Nov.14, 1866–Dec. 20, 1871.
2. George William Kent, Apr. 17, 1869–Jan. 29, 1946.
3. Henrietta Page, Sept. 11, 1870–Mar. 19, 1955.
4. Alice Ruffin (m. Frank Carter Mebane),
    June 30, 1874–Dec. 4, 1958.
5. Paul Cameron, May 7, 1877–Jan. 14, 1961.
[Collins children also included another Mary Arthur, who died young; Anne Kirkland; and Rebecca Anderson.]

Miss Elizabeth H. Collins, daughter of Paul Cameron Collins and Mary McNeill, and granddaughter of Annie Ruffin Cameron and Maj. George Pumpelly Collins, lives at Highlands today.

Materials for this sketch came from Annie Ruffin Cameron's granddaughter Miss Elizabeth H. Collins of Highlands and from granddaughter, Mrs. Frederick B. Drane, Edenton, N.C. Mrs. Drane also gave the commission the photograph of Annie Ruffin Cameron. Tombstone data is from M.C. Engstrom's records of St. Matthew's Churchyard.

## BETTIE CARRINGTON
Halifax, Virginia

Bettie Carrington was a student at the Burwell School in 1855–56, according to Mrs. Burwell's letters to her daughter Fanny in New York. Although various Carringtons resided in northern Orange County, it seems probable that Bettie was the daughter of William Carrington of Halifax, Virginia, and that William Carrington and George Carrington of Halifax who attended the Caldwell Institute in 1848–49 were her brothers or cousins.

Mrs. Burwell mentions Bettie Carrington in a letter to Fanny, dated January 12, 1856:

> I recd a nice affectionate letter from Bettie Carrington yesterday—she & Harriet Brooks came back but Lizzie Watkins & her sister have gone to Warrenton to learn her _Music_. If this weather continues no scholars from a distance can come.

On January 25, 1856, she wrote to Fanny, "Lou Smith and the 'Sanders' came on Monday morning & on Wednesday Bettie Carrington & Ella Hammond."

On February 4, 1856, she wrote,

> Lou Smith & Bettie Carrington have just been in to say Goodnight. They stood & talked so long that now I must hurry to a close. I sent them to Nan to look up some Jelly & Cream & expect they will bring me some. Will _you_ have some?

On February 8, 1856, she reported that Bettie Carrington played for dancing in the parlor:

*The girls are "kicking up a dust" literally in the other room. They have been so confined that I told them tonight to dance for exercise. Bettie Carrington is playing, & I went to the door just now & could hardly see across it for the dust.*

These references are the only ones in the commission's files concerning Bettie Carrington. They represent her as thoughtful, affectionate, and fun-loving with an ability to play the piano (although Mrs. Burwell does not mention her as a music student).

Sources include Mrs. Burwell's letters and the *Catalogue of the Caldwell Institute 1848–49* (Hillsborough, 1849), 12 pp, from the Records Room at the Burwell School.

## CATHARINE (KATE) CHAPMAN
### 1834– ?
### New Bern, North Carolina

Catharine (Kate) Chapman and her sister, Mary Snead Chapman, of New Bern were both enrolled in the Burwell School in Hillsborough in the late 1840s, and both of their names appear in the *Burwell School Catalogue of 1848–51*. They were the daughters of Dr. Samuel Edward Chapman (1807–62) and Eliza Snead Chapman of New Bern.

Kate Chapman was the older of the sisters by one year. The New Bern Census of 1850 gives Kate's age as sixteen, which means she was born in 1834, and Mary Snead's age as fifteen, born therefore in 1835. Kate seems to have suffered extremely bad health and never married. The late Miss Alice Noble of Chapel Hill wrote in 1965 to the present compiler,

*During later years her condition was distressing. She was devoted to Mary Snead's children and there are many letters showing her devotion. . . . No information has been found about the dates of*

*death of the sisters. Mary Snead is thought to have died ca. 1877.*
*Older residents of New Bern remember "Kate," and this means she*
*lived to an old age.*

Kate Chapman appears to have lived the life of the dedicated
spinster aunt so often found in the South.

Data in this sketch is from the documented Primrose family files of the late Miss Alice
Noble, Chapel Hill, N.C.

## MARY SNEAD CHAPMAN
### 1835–77
### New Bern, North Carolina

Mary Snead Chapman and her sister, Catharine (Kate), were
direct descendants of Samuel Chapman, Sr., who erected the handsome
house on Lot 102, 511 Broad Street (ca. 1790), in New Bern, now
known as the Attmore-Oliver House and the home of the New Bern
Historical Society.

Samuel Chapman, Sr., first married Christiana Williams of Bertie
County; after her death, he married Kitty Backhouse on November 4,
1804. Kitty and Samuel had two children: Caroline and Samuel Edward.
Upon the death of Samuel, Sr., the Broad Street house descended to the
daughter, Caroline, who sold it since she was living in New York.

The son, Dr. Samuel Edward Chapman, married Eliza Snead,
daughter of John and Mary Chase Snead of New Bern, on December
20, 1832. *Alumni History of the University of North Carolina* (1924 edition)
gives this brief account of him:

*CHAPMAN, SAMUEL EDWARD*     *Physician New*
*Bern; b. 1807; d. 1862; A.B., 1826; M.D., Univ. of N.Y.*

Catharine (Kate) and Mary Snead were the children of Dr.
Samuel Edward Chapman and Eliza Snead Chapman. Kate was born
in 1834, Mary Snead in 1835. Both girls are listed the *Burwell School
Catalogue of 1848–51,* so they may be presumed to have attended the
school together in the late 1840s when they were twelve or thirteen

years old.

Mary Snead Chapman, the healthier of the two sisters and consequently the brighter and livelier, married Cicero Stephens Primrose of New Bern, son of the Kilmarnock Scotsman, Robert Stuart Primrose, on February 11, 1857. Cicero Stephens Primrose was born in New Bern in 1830 or 1831. He was the third child of Robert Stuart and Anne Stephens Primrose. His sister, Mary Anne, was a student at the Burwell School; and his older brother, Robert Stuart Primrose, Jr., married a Burwell girl, Sarah (Sally) Sitgreaves Attmore.

Two children were born to the Cicero Stephens Primroses:

1. Caroline, March 1858, died in childhood.
2. Mary Ellis (Min), birth date unknown; has descendants living in both Carolinas.

Mary Snead Chapman Primrose is known to have died when her daughter, Min, was seventeen, a circumstance which suggests she died about 1877. Her husband, Cicero Stephens Primrose, had died in 1867, and their daughter, Mary Ellis (Min), was taken to rear by her aunt, Mary Anne Primrose Noble (Mrs. Albert Stephens Noble).

Data in this sketch is from the documented Primrose family files of the late Miss Alice Noble, Chapel Hill, N.C.

## ELIZABETH COIT
1837–June 4, 1852
Cheraw, South Carolina

Elizabeth Coit of South Carolina was one of two Burwell School students who died during the terrible summer epidemic of 1852. Fifteen-year-old Elizabeth Coit died at the school on June 4; the other student, Sarah C. Barton, who died on August 16, may have died elsewhere. Both girls are buried in Hillsborough's Old Town Cemetery.

Elizabeth Coit's name does not appear in the 1848–51 catalogue; evidently she had entered the January 1852 session and spent only five months at the school. Her tombstone in the Old Town Cemetery states that she was the daughter of David and Maria Coit of Marlborough District, South Carolina, and various letters indicate that she was an orphan living on the bounty of her "Uncle [John?] Coit" of Rose Hill. Her cousin, Sarah C. Ray, had also been a student at the Burwell School.

On February 16, 1852, Sarah Anne Tillinghast of Fayetteville appended this postscript to her mother's letter to Sarah Anne's brother John, then a student at the Bingham School at Oaks, Orange County:

> *Mrs. Ray said you had written to Sarah. I suppose you heard by her that Mr. Coit's neice [sic] was going to Hillsboro to school. She is not pretty, being very much like the old gentleman.*

Little Elizabeth Coit may have felt solitary and alone at the Burwell School, for the Tillinghast Papers state that her cousin, Sarah C. Ray, was paying an extended visit to Uncle Coit at Rose Hill, and that Mary Huske Pearce, a Fayetteville student at the Burwell School whom she might have known well, had remained in Louisburg for the winter.

On June 7, 1852, three days after Elizabeth Coit's death, Eliza Bingham of Oaks wrote to her cousin William N. Tillinghast in Fayetteville:

> *So much sickness in Hillsborough . . . I never heard of so many sudden deaths. . . . Miss Coit is, I believe, the first one of Mrs. Burwell's boarders who has died there. Isn't she, or rather wasn't she Sarah Ray's cousin? Poor Sarah must be much distressed, more especially as we heard it was partly through her influence that the young lady went to Mrs. Burwell's school. Another of the girls is very ill now, and Mollie [i.e., Mary] Burwell is quite sick too.*

The deadly 1852 epidemic, which began in April and continued until October, appears to have been a compound of dysentery, high fever, and delirium. W. J. Bingham remarked in a June 5, 1852, letter to William Tillinghast, "Uncle Walter [Dr. Walter Norwood] says cherries and plums are perfect poison this year and you know the Hillsboro doctors never have been very particular about such things."

Bodies were interred almost immediately because of the high summer heat. Fifteen-year-old Elizabeth Coit was buried just to the west of the walkway in the Old Town Cemetery in the area that has come to be known as the Students' Walkway. It seems improbable that any of her family could have attended her funeral at which the Rev. Burwell doubtless officiated; but her Uncle Coit may have erected her tombstone which reads,

## ELIZABETH COIT
*Dau. of David and Maria*
*Coit of Marlborough*
*District, S.C. Died*
*while at School in this*
*Town on the 4th day of*
*June, 1852. Aged 15*
*years, 2 mos.*

Copies of two letters written by Elizabeth Coit at the Burwell School, one on April 10, one on May 29, 1852, only six days before her death on June 4, accompany this sketch.

*Hillsboro No. Ca. April 10ᵗʰ '52*

*My Dear Sister,*
    *I received your note and Cathie's letter last Monday, and I now seat myself to answer it. In the first place, I must tell you, that I am not so very negligent in answering Uncle John's letter as you may suppose, for I have answered it three or four weeks ago, I think that it must have miscarried. if so you must tell me in your next letter, and I will write again. Tell him that Mr. Burwell said, that he did not think that it was necessary to answer his letter.*
    *Do you not think that it is time for me to wear my berage [?] delain [de laine=woolen] dress? I have not worn it yet. All of the girls (nearly) have got new white linen bonnets, and I got one too. Mrs. Burwell said that they would be so nice to go to walk in, in summer. Mrs. Burwell has sent to Petersburg for our bonnets. She did not send for more than three or four. Mine is going to be trimed with pink. I told Mrs. Burwell that I had thought some of having it trimed with white, but Mrs. Burwell said that she thought that white looked too old for a school girl, and it is also going to do for a summer and a winter bonnet. When have you heard from Davis?*
    *Oh! I must not forget to tell you that Peter Mr. Eakin, came up to see me last Saturday, from Chapel-Hill. He said that they were all very well at home, and also that Davis was coming up to see him in four or five weeks, and if he does he will be sure to come here to see me, and if he does, I will be so happy that I won't know*

*what to do. You must try and persuade him to come in his
vacation.*

*Sisty you need not think that it was so very bad in me...but
no matter, I won't say any thing about it.*

*Tell Cather Bunting that I intend to answer her letter next
Saturday.*

*Mrs. Burwell bought me a very pretty neck ribbon, the other
day, and I intended sending it to you in this letter, and if it does
not make it too heavy perhaps I will, but I am afraid (almost) that
you will think it is so foolish, and you may not like it very much.
but it is not my taste, for Mrs. Burwell brought it to me, from
downstreet. Tell Georgie that I hope that he has not given up
writing to me. for I am expecting his letter every mail-night. You
know you told me in your note that he was going to write to me.*

*Have the eggs all been eaten up yet? I suppose that you and
Miss Becky have fine times, and after you have finished the eggs,
Miss Becky only taking a little every now and then, and after you
have finished the eggs, drinking some ashes and water. Do you
sleep with her now? And if you do, who sleeps in our room?*

*Do you get up in the morning any earlier than you used used
to? If you sleep with Miss Becky, I do not think that she lets you.
Remember me to all the people at home. Give my love to Aunt
Jane and Ann and tell Ann that I think she ought to write to me
first. Give my love to all Uncle John's and Cousin Hennie's
family.*

*From your affectionate sister
E Coit*

*P.S. Mary Easeley* [sic] *told me to give her love to you, and tell
you that she was not going to make me a bad girl. Yours,
Elizabeth Coit*

Written around three edges of the last page of the letter is the
following text:

*You said that I never said hardly anything in my letters about
Annie Gilchrist. I do not know what to say about her this time.
She said that Miss Gilchrist said in her letter that she almost
knew me and sent her love to me. so you must send yours to her
sometimes, even if I do not say so much in my letter about her as
she does about me maybe. . . . I have not got Don't you remember*

*those pills you gave me, all the girls in our room laugh at me so much about them.*

Elizabeth makes no mention of feeling unwell in the May 29 letter, but she does remark that Mary Bailey Easley had been ill. Her roommates as well as her special friends, the Gilchrists of Fayetteville, are leaving for the long six-weeks summer vacation, but Elizabeth herself is staying on, probably because no one from Cheraw or Rose Hill planned to come for her. The second letter shows marked composition improvement over the first one and provides clear evidence of the success of Mrs. Burwell's methods.

The May 29 letter was probably the last one to her sister:

*Hillsboro', May 29th 1852*

*My Dear Sister,*
*Our sessions will soon be out, the girls have begun to go home already, five of our boarders went off this morning. Two of them were my roommates, Jennie Speed & and Mary Wortham, Mary Wortham is my bedfellow.*

*Most all the others that are going, will go next wednesday. Fannie Gilchrist is going then. I do not know what I shall do without Fannie. She is the sweetest girl that I ever saw. I wish that you could see her, I know that you would love her dearly. She is going to the north this summer, (if nothing happens) that is she is going as far as Carlisle, Pennsylvania. Fannie is a Christian too.*

*. . . Write often to me, remembering that it is in the vacation and nearly all the girls will have gone home. Give my love to all inquiring friends, and believe me affectionate Sister*

*Lizzie Coit*

Materials are from the W.N. Tillinghast Papers, Ms. Collection, Perkins Library, Duke Univ. Elizabeth Coit's letters of Apr. 10 and May 29, 1852, were given to the commission by Mrs. W.G. Moore, Marion, S.C. (*See also* Sarah C. Ray.)

# HARRIOTTE (HATTIE) MIDDLETON GILLESPIE COLE
September 8, 1827– ?
New Bern, North Carolina

Harriotte (Hattie) Middleton Gillespie Cole, born September 8, 1827, was the fourth daughter of James Cole and Mary Catharine Snead Cole of New Bern. According to information from surviving members of her family (the Dr. Isaac Taylor family of Chapel Hill), "Miss Hattie" attended the Burwell School at the same time her youngest sister, Lavinia, was there. Lavinia is listed in the 1848–51 catalogue, and she herself states that she attended the school in 1848–49. Miss Hattie, therefore, may have begun her schooling as early as 1842 or 1843.

After the Civil War, Miss Hattie and her oldest sister, Mary Catharine, Miss Cattie, went to Chapel Hill to live with their sister Sarah Anne Cole (Mrs. Alexander Taylor) in the beautiful house (no longer standing) on W. Franklin Street, later known to Chapel Hillians as the Cole House. Mrs. Taylor had two sons, Dr. Isaac Taylor and James Cole Taylor. When Miss Hattie's sisters died, she continued to live in the house with her nephew, James Cole Taylor, taking care of her.

Artist William Meade Prince in his book, *The Southern Part of Heaven*, described going to tea as a small boy with his mother at Miss Hattie Cole's and hearing her stirring reminiscences of the "War Between the States":

> *She [Miss Hattie Cole] lived in a house set back from Franklin Street, with a big wisteria vine on the pillars of the porch. Mother used to go to see her sometimes, and I went along. We would sit down in the parlor, and Mother and Miss Hattie would have tea, which Miss Hattie poured from a big, fancy china teapot, with bright flowers painted on it. She told me it was an heirloom. She always had some lemonade for me. There was a sturdy Windsor chair she always made me sit in. I think it was Mr. Jim Taylor's chair—her brother-in-law—who ran the bank. They must have been very rich, with all that money, but some of their chairs were very wobbly, and, I thought, unsafe.*

When Miss Hattie became extremely feeble, she and her nephew James moved to Morganton, North Carolina, where Dr. Isaac Taylor, her other nephew, was head of the Broadoaks Sanatorium. She died in the Isaac Taylors' Morganton home "at a ripe old age." She never married and was known always as "Miss Hattie." She was an ardent Methodist and a strong church worker "whose Christian virtues and generous hospitality adorn[ed] her lovely home in Chapel Hill."

*A sketch of "Miss Hattie" at her tea table, from William Meade Prince's book,* The Southern Part of Heaven. *[Notations by Mary Claire Engstrom.]*

Harriotte ("Hattie") Middleton Gillespie Cole
(1829 - 19

Dau. of James Cole, Newbern

—

Never married. Here (ca. 1905), "Miss Hattie" is telling stories of the Civil War to little William Meade Prince and his mother at the old Cone house in Chapel Hill.

Miss Alice Noble collected information concerning the Coles from her own family archives and from the Dr. Isaac Taylor family. Citation from William Meade Prince, *The Southern Part of Heaven* (New York, Rinehart & Co., 1950), pp. 54–55.

# LAVINIA (VENE or VENIE) ELLIS COLE
## March 14, 1833–1923
### New Bern, North Carolina

The Coles of New Bern were descended on the maternal side from a Frenchman, Jean Blanchard, who settled in New Jersey. Jean's grandson, Andrew Blanchard, had three daughters who all lived in North Carolina after their marriages. Elizabeth Blanchard married Isaac Cole and lived in New Bern. One of their two sons, William, died in childhood; the other, James Cole (Feb. 18, 1795–Oct. 14, 1864), married Mary Catharine Snead (Aug. 25, 1818–Jan. 29, 1862). James and Mary Catharine Snead Cole had nine children; two of them, Harriotte Middleton Gillespie Cole, the fourth daughter, and Lavinia Ellis Cole, the sixth daughter, attended the Burwell School in Hillsborough.

Lavinia Ellis Cole, "the gentle Lavinia," was interested in languages, music, and art, and achieved considerable distinction in all three fields, especially with her beautiful flower paintings, one of which (probably painted about 1880) appeared on the cover of *Popular Gardening* in July 1957. The accompanying feature article sketched her life, calling her "a young lady of quality" who had attended Mrs. Burwell's Female School in Hillsborough, North Carolina, where she studied drawing and French with "Cousin Sarah Kollock" for two years, 1848 and 1849. Next, she attended Mme. Gardel's School in Philadelphia to study art, music, Italian , Spanish, and French—and finally M. Picot's, also in Philadelphia, where only French was spoken. Venie's sweet singing voice, it was said, was often compared to that of Jenny Lind, just then nearing the height of her fame.

At the age of twenty-five, Lavinia returned to New Bern, where on January 19, 1858, she married the rising young lawyer Frederick Cox Roberts, son of J. M. Roberts and a Princeton graduate. *Alumni History of the University of North Carolina* (1924 edition) carries this sketch of Frederick Cox Roberts:

> *ROBERTS, FREDERICK COX, New Bern;*
> *b. Jan. 15, 1836; d. Aug. 25, 1911; s. 1851–52; A.B.*
> *Princeton, 1855; A.M., ibid., 1858; lawyer 1858–79; clerk and master in equity, 1858–68; sec.-treas. A. & N.C. Ry. co. 1879–98; bookkeeper ice co. 1900– ; capt. 5th N.C. cav. C.S.A.*

Handwritten notation on image:

Flower-
Painting
(ca. 1880)
by
"Venie" Cole
Roberts

(Used as cover
of
Popular Gardening
July, 1957)

*Flower painting (ca. 1880), by Lavinia Cole, featured on the cover of* Popular Gardening *in 1957. [Notations by Mary Claire Engstrom.]*

When the Civil War shattered Lavinia's placid, elegant New Bern life, leaving her house in ashes and her garden a mud puddle, she fled to Warren County. Eventually, the New Bern house was rebuilt and the garden recreated. She kept extraordinarily careful garden records and plant lists—e.g., on February 28, 1882, she gathered over one thousand jonquils, narcissi, "king's thumbs," etc., with some twenty-two varieties of other flowers. There were five hundred rose bushes of three hundred varieties in her garden.

As she aged, her family brought her flowers indoors for her to sketch and paint. Sometimes she used watercolors; sometimes she used embroidery silks for her delicate, precise "paintings." Her talent and industry in reproducing flowers are reminiscent of Mrs. Burwell's Aunt Bott who fashioned them in wax. Venie also wrote a number of Civil War stories which appeared in Southern magazines. She died in 1923 at the age of ninety, leaving behind a slender portfolio of flower prints which members of her family cannot now locate. *Popular Gardening* also published a dark, not very successful photo of Lavinia Cole Roberts taken on her ninetieth birthday.

Venie Cole Roberts admired Mrs. M. A. Burwell greatly and never ceased to do so. She wrote to her at intervals and visited her after leaving the school. It is Venie's catalogue of the Burwell School which the Historic Hillsborough Commission uses today as well as an 1848 list of students in Venie's handwriting. Venie also left the following sketch of the Burwell School and Mrs. Burwell in her own handwriting, the original of which a descendant preserves and treasures today:

## THE BURWELL SCHOOL
### By Lavinia (Venie) Cole Roberts

*Miss Sarah Kollock taught French and Drawing in Mrs. Burwell's School in Hillsboro. I was her pupil for two years 1848 and 1849. It was a most excellent school. The teachers were all conscientious and faithful. I feel deeply indebted to them for their careful training. Mrs. Burwell was a wonderful woman. She neglected no duty, kept the house beautifully, had the personal supervision of the thirty boarders, attended to their manners and morals, saw that their beds were properly made—was particular about their health—kept house, made her own bread, washed the dishes, with our assistance—taught six hours a day—was the mother of twelve beautifully clean, healthy attractive children, dressed well always and entertained as much company as any other lady in the village.*

*Mr. Burwell told me they had traced out the families of over 3,000 pupils that had been under their care during the many years they taught, and that with few exceptions, the girls they sent out into the world had become useful wives and mothers and had become a power in the land. After such a life of labor, trials came where they looked for joys. Three of their four young daughters died—all grown—one, Mrs. Strudwick married. Five sons were in the Army—two were killed. I think a third one died—one daughter, the only remaining one married W. Snow, of Raleigh— she too is dead. The other sons have been successful men. Many of her favorite sayings come back to me. When she opened the school room door, and found us not doing our duty, her only reproof was to say, "Oh, constancy, thou art a jewel." She said we studied Rhetoric in the school room and she taught us Logic in the dining room and so our definition of Logic was "Washing Dishes."*

Lavinia Cole Roberts's papers came to the Historic Hillsborough Commission through the courtesy of her late granddaughter, Catherine Browne (Mrs. Edward Browne). The *Popular Gardening* issue cited above was from July 1957 [Vol. 8, No. 7].

# EMILY ELIZA COOLEY
April 26, 1837–December 30, 1869
Hillsborough, North Carolina

Emily Cooley's rose-decorated tombstone in the Phillips plot in Hillsborough's Old Town Cemetery reads,

*EMILY ELIZA COOLEY*
*Dau. of Charles L. and*
*E.A. [should be A.E.] Cooley*
*b. April 26, 1837*
*d. December 30, 1869*
*Aged 32 yrs., 8 mos., 4 days*

Emily Cooley's father, the Rev. Charles Loveland Cooley (June 28, 1794–Nov. 7, 1866) was, according to his tombstone, born in Glastonbury, Connecticut, the son of Rhoda and Elihu Cooley. On January 25, 1826, he married Ann Eliza Chapman (1806–83), who lived near Fayetteville. Both Cooley parents are buried in the Old Town Cemetery. The *Hillsborough Recorder* (Nov. 14, 1866) announced his death at age seventy-two. He had come to North Carolina in 1815. He was a minister first in the Methodist Episcopal Church and then in the Methodist Protestant Church.

The Cooleys had a large family of at least four daughters and three sons. They were an impecunious family and lived in a small house in the southeastern quadrant of the town from which they were once evicted for nonpayment of rent. The Rev. Cooley was a Methodist lay minister with no settled income. In 1877–78 he served one term as mayor of Hillsborough; his autographed copy of Town Ordinances is now preserved in the North Carolina Collection, Wilson Library, UNC.

Emily Cooley attended the Burwell School probably about 1850 when she would have been thirteen years old. She would have been a day pupil and, one imagines, somewhat lost and lonely among girls from old Carolina plantations. She died unmarried at the age of thirty-two and is buried with other members of the Cooley family in the D.D. Phillips plot in the Old Town Cemetery. D.D. Phillips on May 31, 1843, had married her sister Tarmesia (Feb. 11, 1827–Oct. 26, 1899), and Phillips shared his purchased burial ground with the Cooleys.

Three Cooley sons, all Confederate soldiers, are buried in the New Town Cemetery (Hillsborough Memorial Cemetery):

1. Charles Sterling, 1839–Apr. 17, 1900; Co. G 27th Regt. N.C. Vols. C.S.A .
2. Joseph G., July 4, 1846–Sept. 11, 1930; Co. H 24th N.C. Inf. C.S.A.
3. Thos. L., June 27, 1878; Co. G 27th Regt. N.C. Vols. C.S.A.

Descendants of the Rev. Charles Loveland Cooley still live in Siler City, North Carolina

## MARY CAIN COOLEY
Hillsborough, North Carolina

Mary Cain Cooley was the daughter of the Rev. Charles Loveland Cooley, originally of Glastonbury, Connecticut, and Ann Eliza Chapman Cooley. The Rev. Cooley, who may have been a Baptist lay minister, had at least four daughters:

1. Tarmesia M., Feb. 11, 1827–Oct. 26, 1899; m. Daniel D. Phillips.
2. Caroline M., Feb. 1831–Aug. 15, 1853; m. John D. Wilbon.
3. Mary C.; m. Wesley J. Newton.
4. Emily Eliza, Apr. 26, 1837–Dec. 30, 1867; d. unmarried.

Besides these children there were three Cooley sons (see Emily Eliza Cooley). Mary C. Cooley is listed in the *Burwell School Catalogue of 1848–51*, as is Emily, and it may be that the sisters were enrolled at the same time or very nearly at the same time. The Rev. Cooley and his wife and two of their daughters are buried along the western brick wall of D.D. Phillips's cemetery plot [Old Town Cemetery]. Tarmesia and Daniel Phillips are buried at an imposing obelisk nearer the center of the plot. Inscriptions on the Phillipses' tombs make it clear that the Phillips family were ardent Baptists. Mary C. Cooley, who married Wesley Newton on January 3, 1855, with L. H. Newton as bondsman, is not buried in the Old Town Cemetery with other members of her family, nor with her brothers in the newer Hillsborough Memorial Cemetery. There are no references to Mary C. Cooley in any Burwell School papers acquired by the Historic Hillsborough Commission.

Information in this sketch is from the Hillsborough Cemetery Records and Orange Co. Marriage Bonds.

## CAROLINE (CUDDY) E. COWAN
### New Bern, North Carolina

Caroline (Cuddy) E. Cowan was the first boarder at the Burwell School and consequently had a special place in Mrs. Burwell's memory. In a letter to her daughter Fanny, dated January 25, 1856, she remarked,

> *I had a long affectionate letter from Vene Cole the other day & one from <u>Cuddy Green</u> (Cowan that was). She was the first boarder I ever had, was a little child when she lived here. She has now three children & they say her husband is killing himself <u>drinking</u>. She sent me a beautiful embroidered white crape scarf— much too youthful for me. Nan will have it. I valued the expression of kind feeling—how such little affectionate attentions sweeten life.*

Cuddy Cowan is not mentioned in the 1849–51 catalogue; it seems likely she may have been a boarder in the early 1840s. A Miss Susan Cowan joined the Presbyterian Church on July 27, 1831, but the *Sessions Book of the Hillsborough Presbyterian Church* records her removal and dismissal in 1837.

It may have been that the young Cuddy Cowan regarded the Burwell School as a second home or the home she did not have. She apparently was an orphan. The announcement of her marriage to James G. Green on April 11, 1848, published in the *Hillsborough Recorder* of April 19, 1848, stated that she was the daughter of John Cowan, deceased. It was unusual to publish notices of student marriages in the *Recorder*; in this case, it may have indicated that Cuddy had a special place in the Burwell family. Eight years later she was still writing affectionate letters to Mrs. Burwell and sending her Christmas gifts—"how such little affectionate attentions sweeten life."

Materials for this sketch are from Mrs. M.A. Burwell's letters to Fanny, Burwell School; *Sessions Book of the Hillsborough Presbyterian Church*, p.4; *Hillsborough Recorder*, April 19, 1848 (microfilm), N.C. Collection, Wilson Library, UNC, Chapel Hill.

## MARTHA JANE CRAIG
September 23, 1838–August 11, 1912
New Hope, Orange County, North Carolina

Martha Jane Craig, born September 23, 1838, was the daughter of David Craig and Nancy Moore Strayhorn Craig of the New Hope community. Her name does not appear in the *Burwell School Catalogue of 1848–51,* a fact that indicates she entered the school about 1852. Her granddaughter, the late Miss Mattie E. Blackwood, local historian of the New Hope community, stated to the present compiler (letter of May 19, 1965),

> *My father's mother, Mrs. Martha Jane Craig Blackwood, attended the Burwell School in Hillsborough and spoke of that fine school as long as she lived.*

Miss Mattie E. Blackwood believed that Martha Jane may have stayed in Hillsborough with her relatives, Robert Phillips Blackwood and Alice Moore Craig Blackwood, and attended the Burwell School as a day pupil. Miss Blackwood owned a picture of Martha Jane Craig in her later years, but the Historic Hillsborough Commission does not possess a copy of it.

On December 12, 1861, at the beginning of the Civil War, Martha Jane Craig married Samuel D. Blackwood (June 6, 1836–

Apr. 26, 1894) of the patriarchal Blackwood family. Samuel D. Blackwood's tombstone in the new New Hope Cemetery states, "Member of Lane's Brigade, Co. F, 33 N.C. Regiment, C.S.A. In active service from July, 1862. Surrendered at Appomattox, 1865." Samuel D. Blackwood was an Elder of New Hope Presbyterian Church in 1871 and lived to the age of fifty-eight years.

Martha Jane Craig Blackwood died on August 11, 1912, aged seventy-four years (eighteen of them spent as a widow) and is buried in the new New Hope Cemetery (west side of new Highway 86) in Row EE, Grave 1. Her husband, Elder Samuel D. Blackwood, who died on April 26, 1894, is buried beside her.

The information in the foregoing sketch was supplied in part by the late Miss Mattie E. Blackwood, local historian of New Hope Presbyterian Church and Community, and from M.C. Engstrom's Orange County Cemetery Survey.

## [ANNA] DAVIS
Pittsborough, North Carolina

This little girl is mentioned as the daughter of Dr. Davis of Pittsborough in Mrs. Burwell's letter of January 19, 1856, to her daughter Fanny:

> *Dr Davis of Pittsboro' brought his daughter quite an intelligent nice looking little girl of about twelve—she looks as if it would be no trouble to teach her—she is to learn Music.*

## ___DAVIS &
## ___DAVIS
### New Hanover County, North Carolina

These two young girls came to Hillsborough with their grandmother, Mrs. Joseph Watters II (Mary Elizabeth Hyrne Watters), and with an older sister, Rebecca Davis, in attendance. Their mother, Mary Elizabeth Watters, who had married Thomas Davis, Jr., on September 5, 1810, had died and left nine children, two of whom were to be sent to the Burwell School. Mrs. Robina Hogg Norwood recounted the circumstances in a July 9, 1846, letter to her daughter Jane Tillinghast in Fayetteville:

> *My worthy old friend Mrs. Watters is now with us. She came up to bring two of her Grand Daughters Mrs. Davis's youngest children to school to Mrs. Burwell. Mrs. D. left nine—2 sons & seven daughters think of that—but the youngest is almost grown. Mrs. W. seems very weak & feeble but . . . Miss Rebecca Davis an older sister is with her to take care of her.*

The Davis girls would have attended the autumn session of 1846 and possibly succeeding sessions, but there is no mention of their names in the 1848–51 catalogue. It is probable that the Dr. Davis of Pittsborough, who brought his daughter to the Burwell School in January 1856, was also a member of the Watters family.

The letter from Robina Norwood to Jane Tillinghast is in the W.N. Tillinghast Papers, Ms. Collection, Perkins Library, Duke Univ.

## [ MARGARET DOUGLAS
### c. 1842– ?
### Orange County, North Carolina

The United States Census of 1850 lists eight-year-old Margaret Douglas of Orange County as the daughter of John and Rachel Douglas. On January 3, 1859, Margaret Douglas married Willie N. Strayhorn of

Orange County. Willie was a successful farmer. They had a daughter named Rachel. Little is known of Margaret and William Strayhorn after 1860. According to Civil War records, a William Strayhorn, who enlisted in the C.S.A. in 1861, worked his way through the ranks, eventually becoming a sergeant. He was fatally wounded in 1865. If this was Margaret's husband, it's possible she remarried, thus vanishing from records as "Margaret Strayhorn."

Sources include Holcomb, Brent H., *Marriages of Orange County, North Carolina, 1779–1868* (Baltimore: Genealogical Publishing, 2001). **]**

## MARY BAILEY EASLEY
November 25, 1834–November 8, 1928
Houston (now Halifax), Virginia

Mary Bailey Easley, born November 25, 1834, was a younger member of Thomas Easley's large family who lived not far over the Virginia–North Carolina line at Houston (now Halifax), Virginia. Her sisters, who may also have attended the Burwell School, were

1. Mittie (Brookes).
2. Harriet (Owen), 1827–1901.
3. Fannie (Craddock), 1827–85.

Her brothers were

1. Capt. William Henry of the Black Walnut, Va. Cavalry Co.
2. Lt. Thomas, Jr., a West Point graduate killed in the Mexican War.

William Henry Easley and a Charles B. Easley were both students in 1848–49 at the Caldwell Institute in Hillsborough, only a few blocks from the Burwell School. It may be that Mary Bailey Easley and her brother William Henry were in their respective schools during the same years.

Mary Bailey Easley's little mother-of-pearl-backed autograph album carries the date 1852 on a front leaf, and Mrs. M. A. Burwell's autograph is dated May 29, 1852 (that is, the end of the spring session). Names and initials (all identifiable) in the book include

| | |
|---|---|
| Mary L. (or S.) B. | Emma Scales |
| Cattie | Lenox Castle |
| Betty S. | Rockingham, N.C. |
| Lou V. Moseley | |
| F. G. | Centerville, Florida |
| R. B. S. | Sallie Brookes |
| Fannie Webb | Jennie S. |
| Kate Williams | |

A copy of Mary Bailey Easley's invaluable pocket-money account for July 1852 is appended to this sketch. The pocket-money accounts, made up monthly by Mrs. Burwell, were the records of the small sums girls spent for postage, candy, fruit, ribbons, and the like on their Saturday trips "down-street." Mary Bailey, it will be noted, had a sweet tooth and visited Mrs. Vasseur's confectionery shop twice in July. The date of her account indicates that she returned for the autumn session of 1852. Parents or guardians deposited suitable sums of pocket-money with Mrs. Burwell, and she prepared accounts at intervals. On November 27, 1855, Mrs. Burwell wrote wearily to her daughter Fanny in New York:

> *You know tis the last of the [fall] session & tonight I've had all those tedious pocket money accs to make out, all the store accs to look over, the sewing work bills to make out, & it has taken me ever since supper.*

Elizabeth Coit's letter of May 29, 1852, possibly her last letter, written to her sister in Cheraw, South Carolina, mentioned Mary Easley:

> *Mary Easley told me to ask you, why you have not sent your love to her. She has been sick too [with the infectious fever of 1852], she says that it would have done her so much good to have you send it. . . .*

Mary Bailey Easley thus appears to have been outgoing and warm-hearted and a friend of the Coit girls of Cheraw.

Mary Bailey Easley married Dr. John W. Craddock, also of Houston, Virginia, and the two lived at Black Walnut, Virginia, now renamed Cluster Springs. Like many another schoolgirl's autograph book, the blank pages of Mary Easley's book were obviously used for children's scribblings.

*Mary Bailey Easley's Pocket Money Account.*

*1852 July — Miss Mary Easley*
*To M A Burwell Dr*

| | |
|---|---|
| *To Cash paid for lining & cloth* | $2.15 |
| *Collection 20, Melons 10, Peaches 10* | .40 |
| *Melon 10, Postage 05* | .15 |
| *Cash* | 2.11 |
| *Peaches 05, Postage 05* | .10 |
| *Paid for needle Book* | 2.50 |
| *Napkin ring* | .25 |
| *Paid Mrs. Kern for fixing bonnet* | .25 |
| *Ground peas 05, Mrs. Vasseur 40* | .45 |
| *Books—bought at Dr Schoolfields* | 1.50 |
| *Stamps 15, Mrs. Vasseur 25* | .40 |
| *Paid Mrs. Waddill making dress* | 1.50 |

*Cr*
*By Cash*    *10.00*
*Do*          *6.00*
             *16.00*
             *11.76*
             *$4.24*

*This balance I paid you when I settled up all the girls' pocket money.*

Mary Bailey Easley's granddaughter, Marye Lawson Hardin (Mrs. Ernest Lauriston Hardin), Salisbury, N.C., contributed information to this sketch. Mrs. Burwell's and Elizabeth Coit's letters are in the Burwell School archives. Mary Bailey Easley's autograph album and pocket-money account were given to the Historic Hillsborough Commission in 1974 by Mrs. Charles O. Willis, Alexandria, Va.

## MARY AMELIA FAISON
### March 5, 1831– ?
### Sampson County, North Carolina

Mary Amelia Faison, always called Amelia, was born March 5, 1831, the ninth child of William (Billie) A. Faison and Susan Moseley Faison, and therefore the younger sister of Eliza Ann Faison, who married Patrick Murphy, Esq., and also the youthful aunt of the twins, Mary Bailey and Susan Moseley Murphy.

William A. Faison was one of the wealthy planters of Sampson County, and Amelia Faison was therefore in no sense a pensioner of the Murphy family. Since she was three years older than her nieces, the Murphy twins, it may be that Eliza Ann Murphy regarded her as a sort of youthful chaperone.

All of the girls from Cuwhiffle Plantation and the surrounding neighborhood—Mary Bailey and Susan Moseley Murphy, Amelia Faison, Julia Murphy, and Sallie Grice—entered the school for the fall term of 1848, which began on July 17, and presumably stayed two years.

Amelia Faison is frequently mentioned in the twins' letters to their mother at Cuwhiffle: "Sally and Amelia send their love to you";

"Sally and Amelia are going down street now"; "Sister sends her love . . . so does Sallie, Amelia, and Julia."

On November 4, 1851, Amelia Faison, then twenty, married John Gillespie McDougald. There seems to be no record of the termination of the marriage. On December 7, 1858, she married a Presbyterian minister, Dr. B. F. Marable. Their children were

1. Sula, d. in early womanhood.
2. Belle, d. Jan. 1909; m. ___Dean; issue: Christine, Marable, Carlton, Dorothy, Gladys, David.

The information in this sketch came chiefly from Robert Murphy Williams, *Williams and Murphy Records* (Raleigh, N.C., 1949), p. 285. (*See also* Mary Bailey Murphy, Susan Moseley Murphy.)

## ELIZA JANE FAUCETTE
March 18, 1834–October 17, 1905
Alamance County, North Carolina

Eliza Jane Faucette of Alamance County is listed as a Burwell School student in the 1848–51 catalogue. Nothing is known of her, save for her marriage announcement in the *Raleigh Register* of January 13, 1857. On January 7 in Alamance County Eliza Jane Faucette was married to the Rev. Edwin W. Beale of the Eastern Virginia Conference (of Methodist ministers).

[   Eliza(beth) Jane, the fourth of thirteen living children, was born into the prominent family of Chesley Farrar Faucette and Margaret (Peggy) Hayes Shutt/Shult. C.F. Faucette was a wealthy, slave-holding merchant who served in the North Carolina State Legislature and ran for the U.S. House of Representatives.

On January 7, 1858, according to the *Hillsborough Recorder,* Eliza married: "Married—Rev. Edwin W. Beale of the Eastern Virginia Christian Conference, to Eliza Jane (Faucett) eldest dtr. of Chesley F. Faucett, Thursday evening 7th inst. by Rev. W.B. Wellons, all of Alamance."

Edwin, the son of John Spratley Beale and Jane Williams, was born on January 1, 1834, in Southampton County, Virginia. Edwin served as lay-delegate from the Eastern Virginia Conference to the Southern Christian Convention at Union Chapel in Alamance County in 1856, when he probably met Eliza Jane. After he married Eliza, he continued to rise in the Eastern Virginia Conference and became both a respected Elder and teacher.

According to the United States Census of 1860, the Beales and their children were living with the Faucettes, perhaps because Edwin, as an itinerant minister, would have been often away from home.

By 1880 the Beales had eight children. They were living in Nansemond County, Virginia, where Edwin had a church. Edwin died in 1881 and was buried in Cedar Hill Cemetery, Suffolk, Virginia. Eliza died in October 1905. Her epitaph there reads, "Blessed Pure In Heart For They Shall See God."

Sources include *Hillsborough Recorder*, Jan. 13, 1858; P.J. Kernodle, *Lives of Christian Ministers* (1909). ]

## MARTHA FAUCETTE &
## SALLY FAUCETTE
Orange County, North Carolina

Martha Faucette was apparently the daughter of the carpenter and woodworker John Faucett(e) and Temperance (Tempy) Palmer Faucette, whose marriage bond was dated March 29, 1821. Martha is listed in the student roster in the *Burwell School Catalogue of 1848–51*. A notation in the Account Book of Josiah Turner, Jr., mentions that he was trustee for Mrs. Tempy Faucett(e) as of 1850, that he hired out Mrs. Faucett(e)'s negroes, and that on September 20, 1856, he paid $16 to Robert Burwell "for tuition," apparently for a ward. Tuition for day students was $16 to $18 in the 1850s. Since Martha is listed as a student in the 1848–51 catalogue, she would have been enrolled considerably earlier than 1856. Martha Faucett(e)'s marriage bond to John A. Paul was recorded on December 20, 1855, with Gaston Farmer as witness.

The student for whom Josiah Turner, Jr., as trustee had paid tuition on behalf of Mrs. Tempy Faucett(e) in September 1856 was evidently Martha's younger sister, Sally. Mrs. Burwell mentioned Sally in a letter to her daughter Fanny written March 15, 1856: "You asked in one of your letters if Sally Faucette was here last session. No—she left the session before."

Information for this sketch is from the Josiah Turner Jr. Papers, Southern Historical Collection, UNC, Marriage Bonds of Orange Co. (p. 106), and Mrs. Burwell's letters to Fanny, Burwell School.

## MARY FREELAND
### 1834–July 31, 1848
### Hillsborough, North Carolina

Mary Freeland, as she is listed in the *Burwell School Catalogue of 1848–51*, may be the "Mary Ann Freeland, aged 14 years, daughter of J. & L. Freeland" who died July 31, 1848, and is buried in the Old Quaker Cemetery at Mars Hill, near Hillsborough on Highway 57.

The Freelands were longtime members of the Eno Meeting of Friends, and their farm still adjoins the cemetery. Freelands now have homes on two sides of the old burial ground. Mary or Mary Ann would have undoubtedly boarded in Hillsborough since the distance from Mars Hill to Hillsborough was too far to walk and the "Great Road" (Highway 57), then but a wagon track, would have been difficult for farm wagons in winter.

[    Mary Ann Freeland was the daughter of Joseph Freeland and Lydia Miller Freeland, whose marriage took place on January 23, 1826, in Orange County.

Mary Ann's death was recorded in the *Hillsborough Recorder*. The August 9, 1848, issue reported the death of "Mary Ann Freeland, 14, dtr. of Mrs. Lydia Freeland in this county Monday 31st of Consumption."

Her grave reads, "Daughter of J. and L. Freeland. Aged 14 Yrs."

Sources include Holcomb, Brent H., *Marriages of Orange County, North Carolina, 1779–1868* (Baltimore: Genealogical Publishing Co., 2001).    ]

# VIRGINIA ANN FULLER
September 27, 1835–August 5, 1905
Hillsborough, North Carolina

Virginia Ann Fuller, born September 27, 1835, was the daughter of the well-known Hillsborough saddler, Solomon W. Fuller (Feb. 1812–Apr. 1, 1851) and his wife, Eliza May Phillips Fuller, who later, on November 18, 1852, married as her second husband, John Y. Adams. Eliza May Phillips, baptized October 6, 1817, was the daughter of the prominent saddler, James Phillips (Mar. 10, 1765–Oct. 30, 1847), and Nancy Lockhart Phillips (1782–June 14, 1847). Virginia Ann, therefore, was born into families of saddlers on both sides of her ancestry.

James Phillips, who was one of the ten organizers of the Hillsborough Presbyterian Church in 1815–16, was later dismissed by the Session of the Church for variances in point of view and became chief sponsor of the little white frame O'Kellyite Christian Chapel on the southeast corner of Lot 103. His son-in-law Solomon W. Fuller was also a member of the chapel. James Phillips had his saddler's shop above Dr. James Webb's medical office on Lot 83, and the Phillips home was nearby, to the east where the Hill-Webb-Matheson House stands today (the Phillips home comprises the east portion of that spreading house).

James and Nancy Phillips appear to have had these children: William Henry, Ann M., Eliza May, Susan A., Sally, Frances B., Thomas, and James. Various members of the family are buried in the little (42' x 42') stone-walled cemetery on E. Tryon Street, known as the Lockhart-Phillips Cemetery.

Eliza May Phillips married the saddler, Solomon Fuller, on October 9, 1833. The Fullers had four children:

1. Virginia Ann, b. Sept. 27, 1835; m. John M. Blackwood, Dec. 17, 1860.
2. Susan Amanda; m. Thomas Adam, Nov. 17, 1852.
3. Mary J., b. Apr. 27, 1845; m. Thomas D. Tinnin, Apr. 27, 1869.
4. James Thomas.

Solomon W. Fuller, however, had a severe chronic ailment of the chest and throat and died on April 1, 1851, at the age of thirty-nine, when Virginia was sixteen.

Virginia Ann Fuller is the only member of the James Phillips family to be listed in the Burwell School catalogue. She almost certainly attended the school as a day student in the 1840s. It is likely that she began to teach to help support herself. The Fullers lived near the Episcopal Academy on E. Tryon Street, and it is possible that Virginia found her first employment there. Ruth Blackwelder's *The Age of Orange* states that Virginia A. Fuller was principal of the academy, apparently near the end of its existence.

On December 17, 1860, Virginia married John M. Blackwood (Sept. 19, 1832–Mar. 22, 1917) of the patriarchal Blackwood family of New Hope. Her young husband left almost immediately to serve in Co. F, 33 NC Regt., C.S.A. Exactly when Virginia opened her own school in the Blackwood home in Hillsborough is problematical. On December 6, 1865, she advertised in the *Hillsborough Recorder* that her school would open on January 25, 1866, for the spring term and continue twenty weeks. She thanked her former patrons and gave the impression that the school was continuing its schedule. Her terms,

| | |
|---|---|
| *Primary English* | —$12.50 |
| *Higher English* | —15.00 |
| *Drawing* | —10.00 |
| *Painting* | —12.50 |
| *Incidental Expression* | —5.00 |

One-half the fees were to be paid in advance, one-half at midterm, but provisions were to be accepted in lieu of payment. It seems unlikely that Mrs. Blackwood's school could have long survived the competition of the Nash & Kollock School on W. Margaret Lane and Mrs. Huske's (Annabella Norwood's) School at Poplar Hill.

The Blackwoods had three children: William, Pearle Hellen (Nov. 28, 1877–Jan. 5, 1909), and Fuller. A picture of the entire family was owned by Miss Eleanor Craig of New Hope. Virginia Ann Fuller Blackwood and John M. Blackwood with their daughter, Pearle Hellen, are buried in the Hillsborough Memorial Cemetery. Virginia's sister, Mary J. Tinnin, and her husband are also buried there in the Tinnin plot.

Biographical materials in the foregoing sketch were compiled from Phillips family letters provided by Mrs. Eugenia Richards, 5211 Chesapeake, Houston, Tex.; from data collected by the late Miss Mattie E. Blackwood of New Hope; *Orange Co. Cemetery Survey*; *Sessions Book of the Hillsborough Presbyterian Church*; the *Hillsborough Recorder* (microfilm), N.C. Collection, Wilson Library, UNC, Chapel Hill; and Ruth Blackwelder, *The Age of Orange* (Charlotte, 1961), p. 140.

## VICTORIA GARLAND
### c. 1836–c. 1911
### Caswell County, North Carolina

Victoria Garland was evidently the daughter of Dr. John T. Garland, Caswell County, listed in the 1848–51 catalogue as a Patron of the Burwell School. Victoria is listed in the catalogue and probably attended the school in 1850 or 1851. No other mention of her has as yet been found.

Glenn Garland of Milton, North Carolina, is listed as a student at the nearby Caldwell Institute in its 1848–49 catalogue, printed by Dennis Heartt in 1849, and it seems probable that he may have been a brother of Victoria, and that the Dr. John T. Garland family lived at Milton. Thomas Garland of Milton (b. 1828, d. 1869) is listed in the 1924 *Alumni History of the University of North Carolina* (p. 214) as having been a UNC student, 1845–47.

[    Christina Victoria Garland was the daughter of John Tabb Garland and Christina Isabella Glenn. According to an article entitled, "The Original Bloomsburg–1797," published in the *Record-Advertiser*,

> *Christina [Glenn Garland] was educated at Salem Academy, was married to John Tabb Garland, M.D., of Fairview, Milton, North Carolina, and later of Longwood, Caswell County. Dr. Garland purchased Fairview, located on North High Street, from a Mr. Saunders, its builder, in 1822, and Mr. Saunders built Longwood as his new home. Only two years later, however, in 1824, the two men exchanged houses so that Mr. Saunders could entertain William H. Crawford of Georgia, a presidential candidate in '24, in the town house. The Garlands made their home permanently at Longwood.*

In October 1855, Victoria married Colin Neblett, son of Dr. Sterling Neblett, Sr., and Ann S. Macfarland. When the Civil War started in May 1861, Colin joined the C.S.A. as a lieutenant. In June 1862, Colin returned home to his family and farm.

By 1870 the family included two girls, Bella S. (most likely Isabella) and Ann M., and two boys, John Tabb and James H. They lived in Loch Leven, Lunenburg County, Virginia.

On March 5, 1906, Colin died. Though Victoria was still alive in 1910 and living with her son and his family, she apparently died before the United States Census of 1920 was taken. ]

Sources include the *Record-Advertiser*, June 15, 1972, by Kenneth H. Cook; U.S. Census, 1870, Lunenburg Co., Va.

## BETTIE (ANNE ELIZABETH) GARRETT
### &
## MARY LEA GARRETT (October 2, 1841–February 3, 1911)
### Chatham County, North Carolina

These girls came from Chatham County, perhaps from Pittsborough. They were students in 1855–56, and both took music courses. On January 19, 1856, Mrs. Burwell wrote to her daughter Fanny in New York: "Dr. Davis [of Pittsborough] says the three Alstons are coming back & so are the Garretts." On February 8, she wrote, "We expect the Alstons & Annie McDiarmid & the Garretts as soon as the weather is better & they are all Music scholars."
On February 20, she reported to Fanny,

> *The Garretts came day before yesterday. Mary has again stopped Music, finally I presume. You never saw anyone grown as she has. She is as tall as Nannie.*

The *Raleigh Register* of December 12, 1860, reported the marriage on November 8, 1860, of Mary L. Garrett of Chatham to R.J. Powell of Powellton.

[      Mary Lea and Anne Elizabeth Garrett were the daughters of Dr. Richard Garrett and Mary Lea Garrett of Chatham County. After their mother's early death, the girls lived with their grandfather, Woodson Lea, the son of Joseph Lea, who had settled in Chatham County in the 18th century.
Mary Lea's husband, Robert James (Jim) Powell, became a captain in the C.S.A. After the war, he returned to farm in Chatham County. He died at the age of fifty-four on January 31, 1893; Mary lived

on until February 3, 1911. Both are buried in the St. Bartholomew's Episcopal Church cemetery in Pittsboro. They had at least one child, Woodson Lea Powell.

Bettie's life remains undocumented.

Sources include *Chatham County, 1771–1971* (Durham N.C.: Moore Publishing Co., 1971), p. 407.    ]

## FANNIE GILCHRIST &
## LUCY GILCHRIST &
## SUSAN GILCHRIST
Fayetteville, North Carolina

The three Gilchrist girls were the daughters of the Rev. Adam Gilchrist (later D.D.), who was in 1849 pastor of the First Presbyterian Church in Fayetteville, North Carolina. The Rev. Gilchrist was listed as a Patron of the Burwell School in the 1848–51 catalogue. All three girls are listed in the catalogue, and various student letters mention them. Their signatures also appear occasionally in remembrance albums.

Elizabeth Coit's letter to her sister, written on May 29, 1852, says that Fannie Gilchrist is leaving on Wednesday for her summer vacation at home. Elizabeth Coit was spending her own vacation at the Burwell School:

> *I do not know what I shall do without Fannie. She is the sweetest girl that I ever saw. I wish that you could see her, I know that you would love her dearly. She is going to the north this summer (if nothing happens) that is, she is going as far as Carlisle, Pennsylvania. Fannie is a Christian too.*

Lucy Gilchrist is mentioned by Mary H. Pearce of Fayetteville as being a student in September 1851 (according to a letter to W. N. Tillinghast), and Elizabeth Coit mentions "Susy" Gilchrist in a postscript to an April 10, 1852, letter to her sister:

> *You said that I never said hardly anything in my letters about Fannie Gilchrist. I do not know what to say about her this time,*

*she says that Susy Gilchrist said in her letter that she almost knew me and sent her love to me so you must send yours to her sometimes even if I do not say so much in my letters about her as she does about me.*

Susan Gilchrist, at home in the spring session of 1852, may have attended the Burwell School earlier. John A. Oates's *The Story of Fayetteville and the Upper Cape Fear* mentions that the Rev. Adam Gilchrist established the first Sunday school for "colored" people in Fayetteville and that "a daughter of Reverend Gilchrist" served as a teacher in it.

Sources include the Elizabeth Coit letters, Records Room, Burwell School; W. N. Tillinghast Papers, Ms. Collection, Perkins Library, Duke Univ.; and John A. Oates's *The Story of Fayetteville and the Upper Cape Fear* (Charlotte, 1950), p. 699. (*See also* Elizabeth Coit.)

## [ SARAH (SALLIE) GRICE
Sampson County, North Carolina
*(See also* Mary Bailey Murphy.) ]

## ELLA HAMMOND

Ella Hammond was a student at the Burwell School in 1855 and 1856, and nothing further is known of her. Mrs. Burwell wrote to her daughter Fanny on December 10, 1855, " . . . next morning all the Halifax girls left—Ella Hammond with them." After the Christmas holidays, Mrs. Burwell reported on January 25, 1856, that the girls were returning ". . . on Wednesday Bettie Carrington and Ella Hammond." Since Ella was mentioned in connection with Halifax, Virginia, girls, she perhaps lived in Halifax County or very near the North Carolina–Virginia line.

Mrs. M.A. Burwell's letters are in the Records Room, Burwell School.

## CASSANDRA HARRISON
New Bern, North Carolina

Cassandra Harrison of New Bern was the daughter of James and Cassandra Harrison. (Her mother's maiden name is unknown.) Their children included Maria (who died in 1847 and left a Will [on file in the Craven County Courthouse]), Daniel S., John Martin Franck, and Cassandra (the Burwell School student).

Cassandra apparently came to Hillsborough in the late 1840s or 1850, for her name appears in the *Burwell School Catalogue of 1848–51*. She married Bryan S. Rhodes in New Bern on April 1, 1859, the ceremony being performed by Presbyterian minister Thomas G. Wall, the husband of another Burwell girl, Janet Hollister. It may be that Cassandra and Janet were schoolmates in Hillsborough.

Cassandra's brother John M.F. Harrison became the Master of St. John's Masonic Lodge in 1860, having successively held offices in the lodge since 1847. It would appear that Cassandra's mother married a second time, Martin Miller (see Stephen Miller's *Recollections of New Bern*).

The facts concerning Cassandra Harrison and her family were collected by Miss Elizabeth Vann Moore of New Bern and the late Miss Alice Noble of Chapel Hill.

## HANNAH HAWKS
1825–1908
Washington, North Carolina

Hannah Hawks was not listed in the 1848 catalogue; but the information that (Hannah) Hawks, daughter of the New Bern and Washington, North Carolina, lawyer John Hawks, was a student at the Burwell School in 1841–42 is contained in a letter dated November 7, 1841, from Marcus Cicero Stephens, formerly of New Bern but then of Quincy, Florida, to his granddaughter, Mary Anne Primrose (see Mary Anne Primrose). This excerpt from the letter states,

*. . . When I was at John's [John Stephens Hawks's] in*
*Washington [N.C.] there was a daughter of his in pantalets*
*that I called Ben to plague her. Ask her if she is the one. I mean*
*John Hawks' daughter now in Hillsboro . . .*

(M.C. Stephens moved from New Bern to Quincy, Florida, in 1836–37
which date helps to confirm Hannah Hawks's movements.)

John Stephens Hawks (b. March 21, 1796, in New Bern; died
1865 in Washington, N.C.) was the second child and eldest son of
Francis Hawks (1769–1831) and Julia Airay Stephens (1773–1813).
Francis Hawks was the son of John Hawks, the architect of Tryon
Palace, who had married Sarah Rice, daughter of Secretary of the
Crown, John Rice. Thus, the little girl Hannah Hawks "in pantalets"
was the great granddaughter of Tryon's architect, John Hawks. Hannah
Hawks had been preceded to Hillsborough by two Hawks relatives: her
aunt Phoebe Rice Hawks (b. 1805), the daughter of Francis, who had
married Walker Anderson in 1822 and moved there; and her uncle, the
brilliant, handsome Francis Lister Hawks, who bought a house (the
Ruffin-Roulhac House) and settled there briefly with his first wife in
1825. Both uncle and aunt, however, had removed from the town by
the time sixteen-year-old Hannah Hawks came to the Burwell School,
[which] in 1841 [was] just beginning to be established.

John Stephens Hawks, Hannah's father, married on January 13,
1820, Mary Halliday, daughter of Gen. Thomas Halliday of Greene
County. Hawks was an attorney of considerable eminence and, although
he and his bride began their married life in New Bern, in June 1820, they
removed to Washington, North Carolina, where they lived the
remainder of their lives.

The John Stephens Hawks had four children:

1. Francis Halliday (1822–66); lawyer, planter; AB, UNC,
   1844; moved to Ala.–ca. 1849.
2. Thomas; moved to St. Louis, Mo.
3. Hannah (1825–1908); attended Burwell School; m.
   Samuel Latham, 1855.
4. Mary Halliday (1842–96); m. John Drake Williams,
   1860.

Hannah died in 1908 at the age of eighty-three years.

The above data came from the archives of the late Miss Alice Noble, Chapel Hill,
direct descendant of M.C. Stephens, the brother of Julia Airay Stephens who married
Francis Hawks.

# HENRIETTA H. HOLDICH
New York

Henrietta H. Holdich (or Holditch, as the Burwell catalogue lists her) belonged to the famous Shepard Kollock, Jr., family of New York and Elizabethtown, New Jersey, who were, in the mid-19th century, the acknowledged reigning princes of the American Presbyterian Church. No fewer than five members of the Shepard Kollock family served as Moderators of the General Assembly of the Presbyterian Church, the highest honor within the gift of the American Church. Two grand-daughters of the Shepard Kollock family, Henrietta Holdich and Sara(h) Jane Kollock, attended the Burwell School as students.

Henrietta Holdich was the daughter of Lydia Kollock, the ninth child and youngest daughter of printer-editor Shepard Kollock, Jr. (1750–1839), and Susannah Arnett Kollock (1755–1846). Lydia married the Rev. Joseph Holdich (pronounced Holditch or Holdish), D.D., Secretary of the American Bible Society, and named her daughter Henrietta after her older sister Henrietta Kollock, who had married the Rev. John McDowell, D.D., of Elizabethtown, New Jersey. (See the chart of the Kollock family attached to this sketch.) Thus, Henrietta Holdich and Sara(h) Jane Kollock were first cousins—in a North Carolina town already teeming with Kollock relatives.

Their aunt, Mary Goddard Kollock, had married the lawyer, Frederick Nash, and lived on Margaret Lane with a collection of their cousins; another aunt, Susan Davis Kollock, had married the Rev. Dr. John Knox Witherspoon, and the Witherspoons returned to their country home, Tusculum, south of Hillsborough, after unhappy pastorates in South Carolina. A revered great aunt, Abigail Arnett Brown (1768–1835), lay buried under a picturesque tombstone in Hillsborough's Old Town Cemetery; another great-aunt, Hannah Arnett, had married Dr. Robert Hett Chapman, an early president of UNC; and the Chapmans alternated between Chapel Hill and Hillsborough. Finally, an uncle, the Rev. Shepard Kosciusko Kollock, D.D., pastor in Norfolk, Virginia, had married first a young lady from Oxford, North Carolina, Miss Sarah Blount Littlejohn, mother of Burwell student Sara(h) Jane Kollock, and second a Miss Sarah Harris of Norfolk. Even without the Nash & Kollock School, which opened in 1859, the Kollock family impact on 19th century Hillsborough was already extraordinary.

Henrietta Holdich almost certainly roomed and boarded with her "Aunt Nash" on Margaret Lane, as did her orphaned Kollock cousin, Sara(h) Jane. It is likely that she attended the Burwell School in the late 1840s or early 1850s since she would have been younger than Sara(h) Jane Kollock. Our sole record of her is a dramatic, highly competent essay, "Hannah Arnett's Faith . . . A Centennial Story . . . " preserved on eight typescript pages in the Francis Nash Papers. The essay was probably not written at the Burwell School, but was preserved in the Nash family papers. The famous Revolutionary heroine Henrietta wrote about was her great-grandmother, Hannah White Arnett (Jan. 15, 1733–Jan. 10, 1823), wife of Isaac Arnett (May 30, 1726–Nov. 19, 1801) of Elizabethtown, New Jersey.

Both cousins, Henrietta and Sara(h) Jane, were representatives of a most remarkable early American family.

## THE KOLLOCK FAMILY

| Isaac Arnett | m. | Hannah White |
|---|---|---|
| b. May 30, 1726 | | (the Rev. heroine) |
| d. Nov. 19, 1801 | | b. Jan. 15, 1733 |
| "an Associate of Elizabethtown" | | d. Jan. 19, 1823 |

| Susannah | m. | Shepard Kollock, Jr. | Hannah | | Abigail |
|---|---|---|---|---|---|
| b. Sept. 30, 1755 | | b. Sept., 1750 | m. Robert Chapman, | | b. 1768 d. 1835 |
| d. Apr. 13, 1846 | | d. Jun. 28, 1889 | Pres. UNC | | m. Wm. Brown, |
| Phila. | | | | | Buried in Hillsborough |

*1) the Rev. Henry Kollock, D.D., Prof. at Princeton
2) Mary Goddard Kollock  m. Frederick Nash
3) Sarah (Sally) Kollock  m. 1) Judge Samuel King, New Bern
                                    2) Judge Edward Harris, New Bern
4) Isaac Kollock
5) Henrietta Kollock  m. *the Rev. John McDowell, D.D. Elizabethtown, N.C.
6) Jane Hall Kollock  m. *the Rev. Wm. A. McDowell, D.D.Pastor, Third Presb. Church, Charleston, S.C.
                              Trustee of Princeton University
7) Susan Davis Kollock  m. *the Rev. John Knox Witherspoon, D.D.

*8) the Rev. Shepard Kosciusko Kollock, D.D. Pastor, Norfolk*
*m. 1) Miss Sarah Blount Littlejohn, Oxford*
*2) Miss Sarah Harris, Norfolk*
*9) Lydia Kollock m. the Rev. Joseph Holdich (Holditch), D.D.,*
*Sec. of the American Bible Society*
*Moderators of the General Assembly of the Presbyterian Church

The Kollock Family chart came from Alice Read [Rouse], "The Reads and their Relatives" (Cincinnati, 1930), pp. 443–44. (*See also* Sara[h] Jane Kollock.)

## JANET (NET) HOLLISTER
January 25, 1833– ?
New Bern, North Carolina

Janet (Net) Hollister of New Bern appears to have been one of the wealthiest and most privileged girls to have attended the Burwell School. The Hollisters (Hollis— "Holly Terra"—Holly Land) had come early from England to Connecticut, and then about 1800 had migrated to New Bern. William Hollister (1777–1844), a prosperous merchant, whose ships sailed from New Bern to the West Indies, was forty years old when he married his first wife, Julia Hollon, who died in 1827 at the age of thirty years. Eighteen months later, on April 7, 1829, William Hollister married Janet Taylor, then aged thirty-four.

Janet Taylor was the daughter of another wealthy New Bern merchant, also a seafaring man, the Scotsman Isaac Taylor, who is said to have sailed his own brig from Scotland to New Bern. He and his wife, Hannah Justice Taylor, had seven children including Janet. It was Isaac Taylor who in 1792 built the beautiful Taylor-Ward House on Lot 50 at 228 Craven Street in New Bern, still standing and recognized as one of New Bern's architectural treasures and show pieces. On Isaac Taylor's death in 1846 he willed one-seventh portion of his slaves to his daughter, Mrs. Janet Taylor Hollister.

William and Janet Taylor Hollister had two children:

1. Janet, b. Jan. 25, 1833; attended the Burwell School in the 1840s and married Rev. Thos. G. Wall (see below).

2. William, Jr., b. Mar. 23, 1834, d. Apr. 2, 1891; attended the Caldwell Institute in Hillsborough in 1848–49 about the time his sister, Janet, attended the Burwell School; married Sarah King Slover.

In 1840 William Hollister decided to build the handsome Hollister-Swan House at 613 Broad Street for his wife, Janet. This was the house where his daughter, Janet Hollister, the Burwell School student, lived. Five generations of the Hollister family have now lived there, and Mr. and Mrs. Hugh Swan (Helen Hollister) now occupy the house. A description of the house, compiled by Mary Bryan Hollister and her son, Charles Slover Hollister, is included with this sketch.

Janet Hollister's name was listed in the 1848–51 catalogue of the Burwell School, and several of Mrs. Burwell's preserved letters mention Net as being exceptionally generous and thoughtful. Janet married a Presbyterian minister, the Rev. Thomas George Wall, a native of Nova Scotia, who had been graduated at Nassau Hall (Princeton) in 1848 and afterward entered Princeton Theological Seminary. The Rev. Wall came to New Bern in 1854 and married twenty-two-year-old Janet Hollister early in 1855.

A letter written by Mrs. M.A. Burwell to her daughter Mary on August 17, 1855, gives disquieting news of the young bride Janet Wall:

> I hope you may meet _Janet Wall_ in your travels, she has gone on North, _where_ I don't know—Miss Hall from New Berne told Nannie that she was very much disfigured by St. Vitus's dance, that all one side of her face was continually moving—poor thing— how I do feel for her. . . .

A second letter written by Mrs. Burwell on December 22, 1855, to her daughter Fanny mentions Net's little boy, George Barry Wall:

> I had a very affectionate letter from Janet Wall today and a present of a beautiful french calico—suitable for spring. . . . Net said she had never heard . . . of Mary's being in New York. . . . Her little boy named "George Barry" is nearly two months old—she said nothing of her health I presume it is much better.

A third letter written to Fanny on January 5, 1856, describes Mrs. Burwell's garb for a wedding. She wears "the piece of three cornered lace that Janet sent me fixed in a head dress by Mrs.Owen. . ."

Janet Wall and her family spent sixteen months on an extended European tour in 1857–58. L.C. Vass's _History of the Presbyterian Church in_

*New Bern, North Carolina* mentions that in April 1857, the Rev. Thomas G. Wall "made a trip with his family to Europe, and was absent until August, 1858." Few Burwell girls could have had such an opportunity just before the Civil War.

## THE HOLLISTER HOUSE
### By Mary Bryan Hollister & Charles Slover Hollister

*In 1840, when he was sixty-three years old, William Hollister built the Hollister House at the corner of Broad and George Streets which is still owned and occupied by his descendants. He had only four years to enjoy it, but those four years must have been filled with a sense of achievement and satisfaction. He must have been very proud of his new home, and he had reason to be. It is a beautiful type of old New England architecture, situated on an elevation reached by brown stone steps, with "Holly Trees" on each side, and surrounded by a high, ivy-covered wall (retaining) of brick. On top of the house, between the two chimneys, is one of the city's several "Captain's walks." These roof porches, or platforms surrounded by banister and reached by trap doors from the attic, were used by ship-owners when they scanned the river for expected vessels, and they were also used for access to the roof, particularly in case of fire.*

*The property originally occupied three-fourths of the block—extending to Metcalf Street on the east and to the present Mohn property on the south. To the east was a very large vegetable garden, with flower gardens on both sides of the house. Originally, there was a picket fence on top of the retaining wall.*

*The interior has elaborate woodwork on doorways and panelled windows similar to that in the First Presbyterian Church, and delicate floral designs in plaster of Paris as a frieze above the cornices and also around massive wrought iron chandeliers.*

*The black marble mantels are features of beauty. The wide hall extending through the house is divided by a beautiful arch, and has an early American stairway with solid mahogany stair rail.*

*The house was used as Pay Master's headquarters during the occupation of New Bern by Federal troops during the Civil War. The family had to leave hurriedly when Federal troops began bombarding the town from the Neuse River—they refugeed to*

*High Point, N.C., and remained there for the duration of the war.
This, of course, was the family of William Hollister, Jr.*

The materials in this sketch were collected in part by the late Miss Alice Noble. Mr. Charles Slover Hollister made available the description of the Hollister House and other family records as well as Rose G. McCullough's "The Hollister Family of New England—and New Bern" (based on court records, old letters, family Bibles, and other material collected by Mary Bryan Hollister and now in the possession of her son, Charles Slover Hollister Jr.). Information also came from L.C. Vass's *History of the Presbyterian Church in New Bern, N.C.* (1886), p. 164; and from records of the Taylor-Attmore-Oliver families; from Rose G. McCullough's *Ghosts on the River: The Sailing Ships of William Hollister of New Bern* (Raleigh, 1972). Mrs. Burwell's letters are in the Records Room, Burwell School.

## BETTIE A. HOLMES
Fayetteville, North Carolina

Records concerning Bettie A. Holmes's stay at the Burwell School are exceedingly scanty. Her name appears in the 1848–51 catalogue, and Bettie herself is known to have attended the school in 1848. Susan Moseley Murphy, one of the Murphy twins from Cuwhiffle Plantation, wrote to her mother, Mrs. Eliza Ann (Faison) Murphy, at Taylor's Bridge, Sampson County, and remarked in a postscript:

> *Bet Holmes came this morning. I think she is a gret deal pirtier than she was when I saw her.*

The *Raleigh Register* of January 14, 1852, reported the marriage of Bettie A. Holmes of Fayetteville to Dr. John London Meares of Wilmington on January 6, 1852, at Wilmington.

The *Alumni History of the University of North Carolina* (1924 edition) carries this entry on Dr. Meares:

> *MEARES, JOHN LONDON     Physician
> From Wilmington.     San Francisco, Cal.;
> A.B. 1843.*

Bettie A. Holmes Meares, it would appear, lived in San Francisco after her marriage.

According to St. James Parish Historical Records at Wilmington, John London Meares, b. July 23, 1823, was the second son of William B(elvidere) and Catherine Meares. John London Meares was thus twenty-nine years of age at the time of his marriage. The St. James records also mention his elder brother, William Gaston Meares, b. March 3, 1821. Their father, William Belvidere Meares, is entered in the *Alumni History of the University of North Carolina* (1924 edition):

> *MEARES, WM. BELVIDERE.*        *Lawyer.*
> *Wilmington; b. 1787; d. 1841; s[tudent] 1802; mem. house of c.*
> *1818; state sen. 1828–30 and 1833.*

Information is from *Alumni History of the University of North Carolina* (1924 ed.), p. 422.

## ANNIE HOLT
? –1918
Alamance County, North Carolina

Annie Holt of Alamance County was Dr. James Webb's granddaughter, the daughter of his fourth child and third daughter, Anne or Annie, born July 22, 1814, who on November 14, 1838, married Dr. Michael William Holt (1811–58) of Alamance, at least the third Michael Holt in that old Dutch family. Annie was their first child.

There is no official record of Annie Holt's student years at the Burwell School save the fact that her name is entered in the catalogue of 1848–51. Tombstones in Hillsborough's Old Town Cemetery record the deaths of her mother, Mrs. Ann(e) [Webb] Holt, on August 28, 1850, and of a ten-month-old baby sister, Mary Jane Holt (born Oct. 25, 1849) on the same day, August 28, 1850. The tragedy may have ended Annie Holt's stay at the Burwell School. Annie, her sister Sallie Holt, and her brother William Michael (Jim) Holt all became wards of Mr. William J.

Long of Randolph County, the husband of their aunt, Mary Webb. A cousin, Mary Alves Long, recorded the event in her book, *High Time to Tell It*, although she does not make it entirely clear whether the young Holts came to live permanently at the Long plantation.

Webb family accounts of Annie Holt's wedding differ as to the first name of her groom. Mary Alves Long gives an eye-witness account of the wedding in *High Time to Tell It*, but she was only "about four" years old at the time:

> *About the first of my memories was Cousin Annie Holt's wedding to her first cousin, Isaac Foust, which took place when I was about four. Still remembered are the cakes on the table, the bridal pair standing up together and Lena Foust in a white dress with a pink sash—and Mother calling me and Mary Shepherd a few days later to give us the last of the wedding cake.*

Annie Holt's father, Dr. Michael W. Holt, died on May 16, 1858, before her marriage, and is buried beside his wife and baby daughter in the Webb-Long plot in Hillsborough's Old Town Cemetery.

A Webb genealogy, *Our Webb Kin of Dixie*, by W. J. Webb, states that Annie Holt, daughter of Dr. Michael W. Holt and Ann Webb, in 1867 married William H. Foust of Randolph County, and that the couple had these children:

1. Isaac H., 1871–1938; m. 1898 Rosa Petty.
2. Mary Margaret, 1872– ?
3. James Holt, 1875–95.
4. Sallie, 1879– ?

Annie Holt Foust's death date is given as 1918 in this account. Accounts agree that the marriage occurred in the late 1860s and that the groom's surname was Foust.

Resources include Mary Alves Long, *High Time to Tell It* (Durham, 1950), pp. 5, 119, and W.J. Webb, et al., *Our Webb Kin of Dixie* (Oxford, N.C., 1940), p. 22. (*See also* Mary Webb.)

# [ FRANCES ANN HOLT
## 1837–1918
### Alamance County, North Carolina

Frances Ann was the oldest daughter in Emily Farish and Edwin Michael Holt's family of ten children. Her paternal grandparents were Michael Holt III (1778–1842) and Rachel Rainey Holt (1774– ?). Frances's father was the pioneer in the cotton manufacturing business that over several generations owned a small empire of mills up and down the Haw River in Alamance County.

Frances Ann was born in a house in Burlington (now the Alamance County Historical Museum) where she lived until her teens. At that time, her father built a new house across the road based on the plans provided by the noted New York architect, Alexander Jackson Davis, but modified to suit Mr. Holt's own needs.

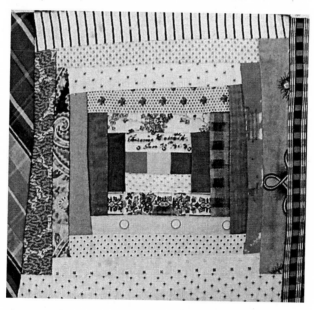

*Friendship quilt made by Frances Holt Williamson and friends for her sister. Central square is signed in ink by "Fannie Holt W. Jan. 30 1868."*

Frances spent one year (1849) at the Burwell School. In 1862, she married a distant cousin, Thomas Slade of Caswell County. He was killed two years later in the Civil War battle of Cold Harbor. She then married Dr. John L. Williamson, who became her father's business partner. They had the following children: Edwin Holt, Emma, Lawrence, Finley, Walter, and Banks.

After her husband's death, Frances inherited his share of the mill business and passed it on to her four surviving sons at her own death. Frances's brother Thomas became governor of North Carolina.

Information courtesy of William M. Vincent, director, Alamance County Historical Museum, Burlington. Above photo courtesy of Commissioner Elizabeth Matheson. The quilt is in the Alamance Co. Historical Museum (Accession #89.81.163). **]**

## MARGARET PARTHENIA HOOKER
March 11, 1839–April 21, 1923
Hillsborough, North Carolina

Margaret Parthenia Hooker of Hillsborough is the last name on the list of students in the Burwell School catalogue; but of all Burwell students, she probably had the longest and most intimate association with the school's grounds and buildings. For nearly all of her long life (eighty-four years) she was scarcely a stone's throw from the school; as a bride she actually lived in the Burwells' former home for five years, and at least two of her children were born there.

Margaret Parthenia Hooker was the second daughter of Nathan Hooker (1793–1848) and Julia A. Hooker (1804–73). A younger sister, Cornelia B. Hooker (June 19, 1836–July 8, 1852), died at sixteen in the terrible summer epidemic of 1852, but Cornelia is not listed in the Burwell catalogue, although it is possible that she may have attended the school. The Hookers lived on the northern edge of Hillsborough only a short distance, north-northwest, from the Burwell School, and indeed a wing of their house, the relic of a fire, survives today at the intersection of N. Wake and W. Corbin streets.

Margaret Hooker would have been a day student, very likely in the late forties and early fifties. One thing points to her special interest in stones and minerals: Her gravestone in the Hooker-Brown plot in Hillsborough's Old Town Cemetery is an enormous rounded piece of scintillating native white quartz which she is said to have selected herself. At the age of sixteen, on July 25, 1855, she married Henry Nicholas (Nate) Brown (Aug. 16, 1831–Jan. 14, 1908).

The young Browns rented the Burwell School property as a residence when the Burwells removed to Charlotte in 1857, and tradition says they remained there for approximately five years. Henry Nicholas Brown planted the great sugar maple tree on the front lawn in 1857 to mark the birth of his first son, LeClair Hooker Brown; and descendants Mr. and Mrs. J.E. Gay of Winston-Salem provided the bronze plaque marking the tree and the event. (In 1979 the 122-year-old tree, no longer the largest sugar maple in North Carolina, is visibly dying, and the plaque, also slightly damaged, is in the Records Room.) Other children of the Browns were,

> Anne Vasseur, Aug. 1, 1859–Dec. 11, 1884;
> d. unmarried.
> Julia Estelle, Oct. 16, 1861–Nov. 8, 1885; d. unmarried.
> Henry Nicholas, Jr., May 13, 1864–Oct. 9, 1922;
> m. Annie E. Wilson (Jan. 9, 1867–Apr. 30, 1893).

Anne Vasseur Brown was evidently also born in the old Burwell dwelling house.

*Margaret Parthenia Hooker Brown.*

*Henry Nicholas Brown.*

In July 1867 Henry N. Brown acquired the controlling interest (Deed Book 37, 479) in Dr. Edmund Strudwick's property (Lot 59) next door to the Burwells on the south, although the Browns may have been living there some years earlier. Lot 59 was on February 10, 1874, formally conveyed to Margaret P. Brown (Deed Book 42, 199). The Brown family continued to own the property until 1955, but in 1960 the "old Strudwick House" was razed. The renovated separate brick kitchen still stands, however, as does an *allée* of trees leading to an iron garden gate opening to the Burwell grounds.

Margaret Parthenia Hooker Brown was a widow for some fifteen years before her own death on April 21, 1923, at the age of eighty-four.

(*See also* Charlotte Brown and Laura Brown.)

## ___HORNER
Granville County, North Carolina

This student from Granville County, whose first name remains unknown, was brought to the Burwell School by her father in a buggy [or wagon] on a freezing January day in 1856. Mrs. Burwell described the incident to Fanny in a letter on January 19, 1856:

> . . . *Her Father asked me to look over her books. I found first Hedge's Logic!!! Botany—Chemistry & Philosophy & as the boys say "sent them sailing." I then prepared to teach her the logic of "a verb must agree with its nominative case"—She plays on the Piano—that is puts her foot on the Pedal and makes a rumbling—I'll report her improvement which I flatter myself will be perceptible in a short time. . . .*

In a January 5 letter to Fanny, Mrs. Burwell had anticipated extravagant dress where the new students from Person and Granville counties were concerned:

*We have heard of three new scholars—two from Person, one named "Williams," the other "Pointer"— & one from Granville named "Horner." They are all from the counties that love dress & the first thing I anticipate is the sight of a gold pencil hanging around the neck & a locket alongside. . . . I'll soon straighten the rest.*

Miss Horner, however, seems to have had no pretensions to gold pencils or lockets. It may be that she spent only one session at the school (the commission has no letters written by Mrs. Burwell after Fanny's death on Apr. 27, 1856).

*See also* Margaret (Mag) Pointer (or Porter).

## EMILY HOWERTON
Hillsborough, North Carolina

Emily Howerton, daughter of Maj. Thomas Howerton and Maria M.M. Howerton, is listed as a student in the Burwell 1848–51 catalogue. There are few mentions of Emily in Hillsborough; evidently she remained at home, at the Howerton House (i.e., Hotel) on W. King Street, to care for her ailing mother after her sisters, Maria and Annie, married. Additional trouble came when her mother was set upon, in a passageway of the hotel and struck a heavy blow on the back of her head and neck. The *Hillsborough Recorder* noted the death on June 13, 1864, of Mrs. Maria M.M. Howerton, wife of Maj. Howerton, in its issue of June 22, 1864.

Emily Howerton apparently did not marry, since scattered surviving letters from her are signed "Emily Howerton." Two Howerton boys, evidently Emily's brothers, William H. Howerton and Albertus W. Howerton, attended the Caldwell Institute in 1848–49, according to the catalogue, printed by Dennis Heartt in 1849. Dr. William H. Howerton married Amanda Koonce, daughter of Calvin Koonce, on June 29, 1858, according to the *Hillsborough Recorder* of July 7, 1858.

## MARIA LOUISE HOWERTON
Hillsborough, North Carolina

Maria Louise Howerton, Emily Howerton, and Annie C. Howerton were the daughters of Maj. Thomas Howerton and his wife, Maria M.M. Howerton, who in the 1850s kept the old Union Hotel in downtown Hillsborough where Mrs. Burwell's music-masters and even an occasional Burwell girl resided. When the hotel burned, Maj. Howerton removed to W. King Street and opened a hostelry, Howerton House, just east of the Masonic Hall.

In the complicated mid-19th century social structure of Hills-borough, the Howerton girls as daughters of a local hotel-keeper might not have been expected to marry into professional or "old" families, but in fact Maria and Annie did.

Two of the girls, Maria Louise and Emily, are listed in the 1848–51 Burwell catalogue, and probably attended the school in 1852 and 1853 or even later. Maria Howerton married Hasell Norwood on January 3, 1856, with the ceremony (conducted by the Rev. Robert Burwell), reception, wedding supper, and dance all taking place at the Union Hotel, fitted out with new carpeting and fresh muslin curtains for the occasion. The Burwells attended, and Mrs. Burwell gave a lengthy and detailed account of Maria's wedding in her weekly letter, dated January 5, to Fanny—the receiving lines in reception room and parlor, the ceremony in "the long dining-room" with Maria's heavy, rich "figured" white silk gown sweeping the muddy floor, the really mag-nificent wedding supper with its separate oyster tables, then the dance at which almost no one "stood up" to dance.

Three parties followed in the next several days; then Hase and Maria began housekeeping in a picturesque old log cabin (still standing) in the vicinity of Indian Hill and his parents' home, Poplar Hill. Hasell Norwood (1827–1911), never well and doomed to chronic nervous disorders, tried teaching school and a number of other occupations. One delightful sketch survives of the Hasell Norwoods' early married life in the old cabin at Indian Hill, written in the 1870s by their brother-in-law, lawyer William H. Bailey (husband of Annie C. Howerton), and entitled, "A Visit to the 'Athens' of North Carolina."

The Hasell Norwoods had four children:

1. Christian Giles; m. Robert Davidson Alexander, Mecklenburg Co.
2. Haselline; m. Robert Ashton Dunn, Charlotte, N.C.
3. Maria Howerton; m. William Bibb Pope, Mobile, Ala.
4. Emily Martin; m. Col. John Chapman Michie, Rockbridge Co., Va.

Family letters indicate that Hasell's nervous and mental difficulties increased with age, and it is uncertain how Maria managed to rear and educate her children. Hasell accepted teaching posts here and there away from Hillsborough. Neither of the Hasell Norwoods appears to be buried in Hillsborough.

Materials in this sketch are from the John Lancaster Bailey Papers, So. Hist. Collection, UNC, Chapel Hill; Mrs. M.A. Burwell's letters, Records Room, Burwell School; W.N. Tillinghast Papers, Ms. Collection, Perkins Library, Duke Univ.; Thomas Hickerson's *Echoes of Happy Valley* (Durham, 1962).

## [ MARY E. JEFFREYS
Caswell County, North Carolina

Mary Jeffreys, who was listed in the Burwell School catalogue, was the daughter of Agnes Wilson Glenn and Judge James W. Jeffreys, and a cousin of schoolmate Victoria Garland. According to the *Hillsborough Recorder* of July 12, 1854, Mary Jeffreys married Littleton Tazewell Hunt in Caswell County. Mary and Tazewell's mothers were sisters. Tazewell was the son of Elizabeth Anderson Glenn and Eustace Hunt. Mary and Tazewell had a son named Glenn Jeffreys Hunt.

Sources include "The Original Bloomsburg—1797," *Record-Advertiser*, June 15, 1972, by Kenneth H. Cook. ]

## [ MARGARET JOHNSON (JOHNSTON)
### Orange County, North Carolina

Mrs. Engstrom's list of Burwell students includes a Margaret Johnson of Orange County. An obituary notice in the *Hillsborough Recorder* of September 15, 1858, records the death of Margaret J. Johnston, 18, of Alamance County at the Concord Female College in Statesville, North Carolina, on September 4. She was the only daughter of her widowed mother and a member of the Presbyterian Church. This may in fact be the Margaret Johnson of the Burwell School. ]

## ELIZA (LIZZIE) ADAM JONES
### May 16, 1839–1911
### Hillsborough, North Carolina

Eliza (Lizzie) Adam Jones (always known in later years as "Miss Lizzie Jones") was the daughter of Dr. Pride Jones and his first wife, Mary E. Cameron Jones. She is listed as a Burwell student in the catalogue of 1848–51 and probably attended the school beginning in 1850 or 1851. Lizzie Jones's special forte was music, and it is likely that most of her time and effort were concentrated on her music lessons in the Brick House.

Lizzie (or Liz, as Mrs. Burwell called her in the popular mode of the day) went to New York for additional music study in 1855–56. Fanny Burwell called on her there, as Lizzie's grandmother, Mrs. Cadwallader Jones, Sr., reported to Mrs. Burwell on January 19, 1856. Wrote Mrs. Burwell to Fanny,

> *I enjoyed Mrs. Jones's visit very much. She is certainly one of the loveliest of old ladies. She told me what a pleasure it was to Liz to have you to go to see her. She thinks Liz will come home in February.*

Lizzie Jones, the music student, eventually became "Miss Lizzie Jones," the organist at St. Matthew's Episcopal Church and the coadjutor with the Rev. Moses Ashley Curtis in developing a superior musical tradition at St. Matthew's. Of many tributes to her musicianship, perhaps that of Bishop Joseph Blount Cheshire in his Centennial Celebration Address on August 24, 1924, is outstanding:

> . . . I remind you of one noble woman . . . your organist for so many years, the faithful co-laborer with Dr. Curtis in creating the high standard of sacred music, which characterized his services; and the perpetuator for so many years after his death of his musical tradition—Miss Lizzie Jones. Omitting only the names of Bishop Green and Dr. Curtis, I doubt if any should be put on a level with hers, in respect to her influence upon the life and work of the parish, as well as on its spiritual side, as in the expression of that life in the worship of the sanctuary . . . I think of Miss Lizzie Jones. In my mind's eye I can see her now, sitting there before the organ, radiant with the light of unaffected goodness and devotion, "the beauty of holiness."

Miss Lizzie A. Jones died in 1911 at the age of seventy-two, according to her tombstone in St. Matthew's Churchyard.

Mrs. Burwell's letters and Bishop Joseph Blount Cheshire's Centennial Celebration Address (Durham, 1925), 35 pp., are in the Records Room, Burwell School.

## FRANCES (FANNY) IREDELL JONES
February 5, 1837– ?
Hillsborough, North Carolina

Fanny I. Jones, listed mistakenly in the 1848–51 catalogue as "Fanny J. Jones," was the daughter of the lawyer Col. Cadwallader Jones, Jr. (1813–99), and Annie Isabella Iredell Jones (1816–97), daughter of North Carolina Gov. James Iredell of Edenton. The younger Cadwallader Joneses purchased Burnside on the eastern edge of Hillsborough on May 27, 1838, but Frances Iredell, their first child, was born on February 5, 1837, before Burnside was acquired. Besides having a most distinguished maternal ancestry, Frances was also the granddaughter of Col. Cadwallader Jones, Sr., and Rebecca Edwards Long Jones of West Hill in Hillsborough. Although many Burwell students had notable ancestries, few could have surpassed that of Fanny Iredell Jones.

Fanny was evidently a student in the late 1840s or early 1850s. She apparently had an interest in music, for Mrs. Burwell mentions in a letter of March 4, 1856, that Dr. Edward Scott has bought "Fanny Jones's piano" for his sister, Billie. Fanny married George W. Erwin, son of John Erwin and Eliza Margaret Chadwick of Glencairn, Greensboro, Alabama, on October 14, 1856, at West Hill, her grandparents' home.

## MARY ALBERTINE JONES
January 4, 1849–March 2, 1907
Hillsborough, North Carolina

Mary Albertine Jones was the daughter of Richard M. Jones (1812–99) and Carolina Jones (1824–99). Richard M. Jones served as sheriff of Orange County from August 23, 1852, to August 26, 1862, and again from August 22, 1864, to July 4, 1865. Mary Albertine Jones was the sister of Dr. Clarence D. Jones (1866–1937). She was a young day pupil at the Burwell School in its closing years.

Mary Albertine Jones married George Nathaniel Waitt (Nov. 7, 1844–May 2, 1925) and became the mother of Carrie Waitt (May 2, 1869–Sept. 9, 1963), who married Dr. John Sanford Spurgeon, dentist. Carrie Waitt Spurgeon resided during her married life in the Burwell School house in which her mother many years earlier had been taught. It is particularly appropriate that the Carrie Waitt Spurgeon Garden adjoining the old Burwell School should be named in honor of the daughter of a Burwell student.

Mary Albertine Jones died in 1907, at age fifty-eight. She and her parents, her husband, her brother, her son, George N. Waitt, Jr. (1888–1920), and her daughter, Mrs. Spurgeon, are all buried in the Hillsborough Memorial Cemetery (the New Town Cemetery).

## MARY CAMERON JONES
July 10, 1843–February 1, 1924
Hillsborough, North Carolina

Mary Cameron Jones was the daughter of Dr. Pride Jones and his first wife, Mary E. Cameron, who died on May 15, 1845. Shortly thereafter Dr. Jones married Martha Ann Cain, and the estate of Sans Souci on the eastern side of Hillsborough became their home. Dr. Pride Jones and his first wife had four children, the eldest of whom was the musician Eliza (Lizzie) A. Jones. Mary Cameron Jones, her sister, was the third child.

Mary Cameron Jones must have entered the Burwell School when she was ten or eleven years of age. According to Mrs. Burwell's letter to Fanny on January 19, 1856, "Mary Jones" had departed the preceding session to go to St. Mary's in Raleigh, but in 1856 returned to the Burwell School, and her delightful, gracious grandmother, Mrs. Cadwallader Jones, Sr., had on a bitter winter's day brought the little girl back.

> . . . about twelve o'clock *Mrs. Jones was announced . . . I love her so much & 'twas such a day for her to come out so . . . I came in & welcomed her truly. She came to bring Mary Jones back to school. She has learned <u>nothing</u> not even Music at St. Mary's.*

But all did not work out smoothly. Mrs. Burwell wrote to Fanny in considerable distress on February 8, 1856:

> *We have had, I suspect, <u>a final difficulty</u> with the <u>Jones</u> children. I wrote you that Mary Jones had come back to school. Mrs. Jones [that is, the second Mrs. Jones, Martha Ann Cain Jones] requested that she should join the class she left a session ago. I told her I was afraid the studies would be too hard for Mary, as the class had progressed steadily, while, according to her own account, Mary had been at <u>St. Mary's</u> learning nothing but <u>idle</u> habits. Well! She joined the class, & sure enough could not recite a single lesson. . . .*

The upshot of this difficulty was that Dr. Pride Jones withdrew his daughter from the Burwell School. Mrs. Burwell added, "I got a very affectionate note from her [Mrs. Jones]. She seems very troubled about it." This is the only occurrence of the kind, however, in the commission's records of the Burwell School. Usually Mrs. Burwell's extraordinary diplomacy could smooth over run-of-the-mill upsets. (The particular lesson that was too hard for little Mary Cameron was an assignment in Smith's *First Lessons in Astronomy*.)

Mary Cameron Jones lived to be eighty-one years old. She died unmarried and is buried in St. Matthew's Churchyard.

## MARY REBECCA JONES
November 10, 1823–December 20, 1878
Hillsborough, North Carolina

Mary Rebecca Jones, always known as Rebecca, was the sixth child of Col. Cadwallader Jones, Sr., and Rebecca Edwards Long Jones. Col. Jones had been a wealthy and successful planter on the Roanoke River before removing to Hillsborough in 1824 and building a new home, West Hill, just outside the town's western boundary. Rebecca Jones was born on November 10, 1823, at Weldon Place on the Roanoke, but her childhood and girlhood were spent at West Hill (no longer standing).

Both of her parents were known as the epitome of hospitality and elegant social graces. Mrs. Jones was described as "regal" and "queenly" and in person extremely beautiful. Little Rebecca grew up in a home noted far and wide for its emphasis on culture and manners.

Rebecca is not listed in the 1848–51 catalogue, which lists relatively few early students. It is likely she attended the school briefly in 1839 or 1840 when she was sixteen or seventeen. Her Reward of Merit, presented to her by Sarah Jane Kollock for saying the multiplication table correctly, was presented to the commission by Mr. James Webb Cheshire. (Miss Kollock, scarcely more than a child herself, was already assisting Mrs. Burwell with routine tasks.) It is probable that Rebecca concentrated on music and drawing.

On November 14, 1843, when she was twenty, Rebecca married businessman Peter Browne Ruffin, son of Judge Thomas Ruffin. The young Ruffins eventually went to live in a pleasant white frame house on W. King Street, where Maj. Allen Jones Davie had lived and which Col. Jones had Capt. John Berry renovate and enlarge for them. It was, in fact, made into an eight-acre estate with a circular entrance drive, a three-story brick kitchen, stone piers on King Street, and a kitchen garden and servants' quarters on the other side of the street.

The Peter Browne Ruffins had eleven children including three sets of twins:

1. Rebecca Edwards, Sept. 15, 1846.
2. Mary Browne (Mim), Sept. 20, 1850.
3. Thomas, Nov. 25, 1852.
4. Susan Browne, Nov. 25, 1852.
5. Cadwallader Jones, d.y.
6. Sarah Jones (Sallie), d.y.
7. Sterling, Dec. 27, 1857.
8. Allen Jones, Dec. 27, 1857.
9. Sarah Jones (Daisy) [twin].
10. Anna Kirkland (Lilly) [twin].
11. Joseph Roulhac.

Rebecca Jones Ruffin died December 20, 1878, aged fifty-six years. Her husband, Peter Browne Ruffin, lived twenty-two years longer, dying on August 5, 1900. Both are buried in St. Matthew's Churchyard.

*Reward of Merit: Miss Sara Kollock presented this to Mary Rebecca Jones for reciting the multiplication table perfectly.*

Reward of Merit was given to the Historic Hillsborough Commissioner by James Webb Cheshire in October 1965.

## SALLY REBECCA JONES
### March 16, 1833–October 29, 1892
### Hillsborough, North Carolina

Sally Rebecca Jones, the ninth child of Col. Cadwallader Jones, Sr. (1788–1861), and Rebecca Edwards Long Jones (1810–81) was born March 16, 1833, at the Joneses' family estate, West Hill, west of Hillsborough. Col. Jones was a wealthy, distinguished man, and his wife was a legend in her own time for her queenly bearing and her charm of person and manner. West Hill was renowned for its hospitality and the graciousness of its owners.

Sally Jones evidently attended the Burwell School for a few years in the 1840s, when she was ten or eleven years old, too young as yet to be sent to the fashionable school in New York, which she would attend later. Sally Jones is not listed in the 1848–51 catalogue, but the Burwells were fond of her and of her lovely mother, and there are various mentions of both of them in letters and accounts.

Annabella (Bell) Norwood wrote her cousin, W.N. Tillinghast, on October 9, 1847 (or 48?), that "Miss Sallie Jones has left school"; and in an undated letter (1849), "I attended a dance on Monday evening at Col. Jones's as Miss Sally is spending her Christmas Holiday at home"; and in still another undated letter of September 22 (1849?): "Miss Sally Jones is back from the Springs . . . she is a perfectly beautiful girl."

Mrs. Burwell herself wrote on January 19, 1856, to her daughter Fanny,

> . . . about twelve o'clock Mrs. Jones was announced. . . . I love her
> so much & 'twas such a day for her to come out so. . . . I came in
> & welcomed her truly. . . . I enjoyed Mrs. Jones's visit very much.
> She is certainly one of the loveliest of old ladies.

Sally Jones evidently lived a fairy-tale girlhood at West Hill. On December 13, 1859, when she was twenty-six, she married Josiah Collins (1830–Feb. 14, 1890) of Edenton and Lake Phelps. This was the fourth Josiah Collins of the wealthy shipping and "Lake Company" family. The Collinses had six children:

1. Mary Riggs, 1861–1912.
2. Josiah.
3. Cadwallader Jones.
4. Rebecca Allen.
5. Lizzie Jones, 1871–1900.
6. Althea.

Sally Jones Collins died at the age of fifty-nine on October 29, 1892. She had been a widow for over two and a half years, for Josiah Collins had died on February 14, 1890. Sally, her husband, and two of their children, Mary Riggs and Lizzie Jones, are buried in St. Matthew's Churchyard, Hillsborough.

*Sally Rebecca Jones Collins, wife of Josiah Collins IV. Oil on canvas, c. 1858.*

Annabella Norwood's letter is in the W.N. Tillinghast Papers, Ms. Collection, Perkins Library, Duke Univ. Mrs. Burwell's letters are in the Records Room, Burwell School.

## ANN (NAN) JORDAN &
## ELIZABETH (BET) JORDAN
Orange County, North Carolina

These two little girls, called only Nan and Bet Jordan by Mrs. Burwell, arrived at the Burwell School in January 1856 and are consequently not listed in the 1848–51 catalogue. They appear to have been twins "so exactly alike" that Mrs. Burwell could not tell them apart. Her January 19, 1856, letter to Fanny in New York describes their arrival with unusual pleasure and enthusiasm, and it is clear that Mrs. Jordan was a valued friend to whom special kindness and attention were due. It seems probable that the Jordans were the family of the Rev. William M. Jordan who in 1848 succeeded to the charge of the little frame Methodist church on E. Tryon Street, just vacated by the Rev. Samuel J. Pearce (see Annie Blount Pearce). Mrs. Jordan thus would have been an old neighbor as well as a minister's wife. A John Jordan is also listed as a student at the Caldwell Institute in 1848–49.

Mrs. Burwell thus described the little Jordans' arrival in her January 19, 1856, letter to Fanny,

> . . . *just as we finished dinner who do you think drove up? Mrs. Jordan with Nan and Bet to put them to school. Now don't you know we were glad—They are the sweetest little creatures I ever saw & so exactly alike that I can't tell them apart—to oblige Mrs. Jordan who you know was a kind friend to you & Nan, Nan has taken them in her own room—They are lying now like two little roses in the little bed by the fireplace—Sally Bridges sleeps on the couch at the foot & Nan & Jenny in the large bed— I felt for Mrs. Jordan as she left them—you know what a trial it must have been.*

It will be observed that the gentle Nannie Burwell in January 1856 thus had four students in her bedroom at the head of the stairs— her two Bridges cousins, Sally and Jenny, and the two little Jordans "in the little bed by the fireplace." The commission has placed a "little bed by the fireplace" in Nan's room in accordance with this letter.

On February 16, however, Mrs. Burwell wrote to Fanny that "Mrs. Jordan sent for the little girls today." It indicates that the Jordans' new charge was not far from Hillsborough, possibly in the northeast section of the county.

Materials in this sketch are from Mrs. M.A. Burwell's letters, the *Catalogue of the Caldwell Institute 1848–49* (Dennis Heartt, 1849), and George Stevenson's notes for a biographical sketch of the Rev. S. J. Pearce (N.C. Div. of Archives & History, Raleigh) —all in the Records Room, Burwell School. (*See also* Annie Blount Pearce.)

## SARA(H) JANE KOLLOCK ("LA PETITE")
November 7, 1826–June 26, 1907
Hillsborough, North Carolina

Sarah Jane Kollock, born November 7, 1826, was one of the famous Kollocks (orig. "de Colloque," a French Huguenot name) of New Jersey. She was the daughter of the Rev. Shepard Kosciusko Kollock, D.D., who in 1818 married his first wife, Sarah Blount Littlejohn of Oxford. Orphaned at an early age and wholly dependent on the uncertain bounty of distant relatives, the little girl, "Cousin Sara," finally found a secure second home and her life's work in her Aunt Mary Goddard Kollock Nash's (Mrs. Frederick Nash's) home on Margaret Lane in Hillsborough.

Sarah Jane was one of the first pupils of the Burwell School, but she seems to have earned her way from the beginning by helping with the smaller Burwell children. Finding the wherewithal to clothe herself was always a problem. The commission owns a copy of her letter of "Saturday 1841" written in pencil when she was fifteen to her "Grandpa," the printer and editor Shepard Kollock, who had married Susannah Arnett:

> *Hillsboro Saturday 1841*

> *Dear Grandpa,*
> *I am very much in need of a great many articles and Aunt Nash has authorized me to draw on the hire of my negroes to the amount of $20. I suppose you have the hire of them of last year by this time. There are a great many necessary articles which I must have and Aunt Nash says she will take the responsibility if Pa [her brother] should object, which she knows he will not do. Aunt Margaret has a very pretty calico frock (the one she made up before*

*I left and which she will show you) and as there is no pretty calico*
*in town, I wish, dear sir, you would take a few dollars more and*
*buy a dress of it for me. Understand, dear Grandpa, 'tis to be*
*taken from the hire of negroes belonging to me, I do not wish you to*
*buy it as I know you cannot afford it or you would do it with*
*pleasure. Please send the dress & money by Cousin H. You see*
*this is a real business note. I have written it on a seperate piece of*
*paper as it is addressed to no eye but yours and intended for no one*
*else to see. Do burn it up immediately.*
    *Your affec. grandchild*

                *Sarah Kollock*

Burwell schoolgirls wore calico frocks in summer, and little
Sarah Kollock needed one.

Sara (she soon dropped the *h* from her name) proved to be an
exceptionally efficient teacher and gradually took on heavier duties until
in 1848 and 1849 she was the fulltime teacher of French and drawing.
Like all the Kollocks, Sara was intellectually keen and perceptive, and
remarkably quick to become angered. (Tradition says that all the
Kollocks had large noses and hair-trigger tempers.) Nevertheless, she
was an excellent French teacher and much liked by her pupils. A letter
of September 27, 1851, from Burwell student Mary H. Pearce to William
H. Tillinghast reports,

> *I expect you will be glad to hear we have changed our French*
> *teacher. Miss Molly Burwell now fills Miss Kollock's place, and is*
> *much more gentle. I never knew how well I loved Miss Sarah, until*
> *now that I am seperated [sic] from her. She is in Oxford, and I*
> *am really anxious to see "La petite" as we called her.*

Although the Burwells could not afford to employ Sara on a
permanent basis, it was clear she had unusual administrative ability, as
she demonstrated later. Her entire education had been at the Burwell
School, and Mrs. Burwell even speculated in 1855 whether it might be
possible for Sara Kollock to take her place. She wrote to Fanny on
November 27, 1855,

> *Sarah Kollock is very anxious to get a position in our school, but*
> *we have none to offer her. I do wish I could retire and let her take*
> *my place, but I suppose that would not do. I must take a hand as*
> *long as there is a school and I have health and strength.*

Sara became both a teacher and a partner with her Nash cousins in the successful Nash & Kollock School venture (she was the Kollock of the title), spending her long life there and continuing to operate a school of her own for small boys even after the Misses Nash died.

Ann Strudwick Nash describes "Cousin Sara's" appearance and temperament in some detail in *Ladies in the Making*. She was red-haired and possessed of a "thunder-and-lightning temper." She was almost a dwarf, and chair legs had to be cut off so that her feet could touch the ground. (Miss Sara's little ladder-back chair that she used for teaching is now on display in the Burwell School.) She was much given to wearing innumerable beads, bangles, and chains, and affected a frizzed, tightly curled hair-dress probably meant to add some height to her tiny figure.

There is a daguerreotype of "Cousin Sara" in the N. C. Collection, Wilson Library, UNC, and a picture of her and her boys' school in Allen A. and Pauline Lloyd's *History of the Town of Hillsborough*.

Sara Kollock died at the age of eighty-one in 1907 and is buried in Hillsborough's Old Town Cemetery near her cousins and partners, Maria J. and Sarah K. Nash.

Materials in this sketch are from Mrs. M.A. Burwell's letters, Records Room, Burwell School; W.N. Tillinghast Papers, Ms. Collection, Perkins Library, Duke Univ.; Ann Strudwick Nash's *Ladies in the Making* (Hillsborough, 1964). Sara Kollock's letter (1841) to her grandfather was the gift of Mrs. Elizabeth Hicks Hummel, Oxford, N.C. (*See also* the Kollock Family Chart accompanying the sketch of Henrietta Holdich and Margaret [Maggie] McLester.)

## ANNETTE ELIZA LINDSAY
Greensboro, North Carolina

Annette E. Lindsay's grandfather Robert Lindsay was one of the pioneers of Greensboro in 1808. He bought a lot for $52 at the northeast corner of Market and Elm streets and built a store there, according to James W. Albright's *Greensboro, 1808–1904*. Robert Lindsay married Letitia Harper, and their son, Jesse Harper Lindsay, married Amelia Ellison of Charleston. Jesse Harper Lindsay and Amelia had two daughters: Sarah (who apparently did not go to the Burwell School and married John Alexander Gilmer [1805–68]); and Annette Eliza, who is listed in the *Burwell School Catalogue of 1848–51*, and married lawyer

Clement Gillespie Wright of Fayetteville on October 10, 1855, in Greensboro (*Raleigh Register,* Oct. 17, 1855). Although Annette Eliza's dates are not available, it would appear that she may have been considerably younger than her sister.

The *Alumni History of the University of North Carolina* (1924 edition) carries this entry on Clement Gillespie Wright:

> *WRIGHT, CLEMENT GILLESPIE     Lawyer*
> *From Bladen co.; Fayetteville; b. Oct. 15, 1824; died in service,*
> *1865; A.B., 1843; A.M., 1853; mem. house of c. 1860;*
> *lieut. col. C.S.A. 66th reg.*

The Wrights had one son, Clement Gillespie Wright of Greensboro, a well-known lawyer, trustee of UNC, and member of the General Assembly, who married Josephine(?) Harris of Greensboro. Their children were

1. Annette, d. June 1965, Southern Pines; m. W. C. Harris of Reidsville.
2. Bernard; m. Mary Louise Everett, Rockingham Co., whose father was W. N. Everett (N.C. Sec. of State for many years).

Information came from Mrs. Cumings Mebane, descendant and namesake of Sarah Lindsay Gilmer, to the late Miss Alice Noble. Mrs. Mebane stated that Mary Virginia Lindsay was not a sister of Annette; to the best of her knowledge they were not related, but there could be a connection. Information also came from Albright's *Greensboro, 1808–1904* (p. 34); *Alumni History of the Univ. of North Carolina,* p. 697.

## MARY VIRGINIA LINDSAY
September 7, 1834–May 5, 1853
Greensboro, North Carolina

Mary Virginia Lindsay, born September 7, 1834, was the daughter of Jeduthun (Jed) Harper Lindsay (1806–81) and his wife, Martha Strange Lindsay of Kentucky (1811– Jan. 13, 1867). Jed Harper Lindsay was an active, substantial, and prominent citizen of Greensboro in the 19th century, according to the following references from James Albright's *Greensboro, 1808–1904*: In 1829 his real estate was valued at

$3,500; in 1839–41 he served as member of the Town Board; in 1840–41 he was listed as owning a saw mill about where the Southern Railway crosses Lindsay Street; in 1856 he was a member of a committee to purchase a lot and erect a new courthouse; and in 1876 he was listed as a member of the first board of directors of the newly organized National Bank of Greensboro.

Nothing whatever is known of his daughter, Mary Virginia, save that her name appears in the *Burwell School Catalogue of 1848–51*, that she died unmarried at the age of eighteen on May 5, 1853 (possibly a victim of some epidemic), and that she is buried in the Lindsay plot in the old First Presbyterian Church Cemetery in Greensboro, now directly in the rear of the Greensboro Museum.

(Note: Mary Virginia Lindsay was not a sister of Annette Eliza Lindsay, also a Burwell student at about the same time, but there may have been some connection.)

Information from Mary Virginia Lindsay's tombstone was collected by Greensboro historian, Mr. A. Earl Weatherly, for the late Miss Alice Noble, Chapel Hill, who collected additional data. Information also is from James W. Albright's *Greensboro, 1808–1904*, pp. 7, 35, 37, 58.

[    **HELEN CALDWELL LONG**
1834–
Hillsborough, North Carolina

Helen was one of the daughters of Osmond F. Long and Frances Helen Webb, whose younger sister, Mary Webb, was one of the first students at the Burwell School, and whose father, Dr. James Webb, was its first patron. Helen followed in the footsteps of many Burwell graduates and became a teacher. She never married and lived with her mother well into the late 19th century. (Her sister, Margaret Taylor, also attended the Burwell School.)    ]

## MARGARET (MAG) TAYLOR LONG
Hillsborough, North Carolina

Margaret (Mag) Taylor Long was the second daughter of Dr. Osmond Fitz Long (Mar. 11, 1808–July 8, 1864), originally of Randolph County, and Frances Helen Webb (Jan. 13, 1810–88), the eldest daughter of Dr. James Webb and Annie Alves Huske Webb of Hillsborough. Margaret Long is listed in the school catalogue as a Burwell School student and was probably enrolled in the late 1840s.

She married Gen. Rufus Barringer of Concord and Charlotte as his third wife. His first wife, Eugenia Morrison, had died in 1858, leaving him with two children, Paul (later Dr. Paul B. Barringer of the Univ. of Virginia) and Anna. Gen. Barringer's second wife was Miss Rosalie Chunn of Asheville who died, leaving one son, Rufus C. Barringer. Gen. Barringer's third wife, Margaret Long of Hillsborough, brought him a third son, Osmond Long Barringer.

The considerable body of written material dealing with Rufus Barringer all testifies to his eminence as a Confederate general, his integrity and faithfulness as a churchman in Charlotte (he founded the Second Presbyterian Church), his probity in politics, and his unswerving devotion as a family man.

*Margaret Taylor Long Barringer.*

Mary Alves Long, a cousin, remarked in her book of family reminiscences, *High Time to Tell It,* that Gen. Barringer was the only member of the entire Long connection who was rich, and that he was as generous as he was rich, educating, supporting, and practically adopting an orphan boy of the large Long family. One provision of Rufus Barringer's will testified in particular to his deep concern and affection for his family: It stipulated that his handsome home in Charlotte should be kept in the Barringer family as a common home for his wife, children, and their descendants for as long as they should desire it.

**BARRINGER, RUFUS**            **LAWYER**
*From Cabarrus co.; Charlotte; b. December 2, 1821; d. Feb. 3, 1895; m. Eugenia Morrison; A.B., 1842; mem. house of commons, 1848; state sen.; 1850; brig. gen. C.S.A.*

Materials in this sketch are from Mary Alves Long, *High Time to Tell It* (Duke Univ. Press, Durham, 1950), pp. 54, 136; S.A. Ashe and others, ed., *Biographical History of North Carolina* (Greensboro, 1905–1917, 8 vols., Vol. I), p. 124; *Our Webb Kin of Dixie,* by W. J. Webb et al. (Oxford, N.C., 1940); *Alumni History of the University of North Carolina* (1924 ed.), p. 36.

# FRANCES ELIZABETH LUNSFORD (c. 1844– ?)
# &
# VIRGINIA LUNSFORD (December 30 1848–July 28, 1881)
Roxboro, North Carolina

Frances Elizabeth Lunsford's granddaughter, Mrs. Bessie D. Beam, sent this information about the two Lunsford sisters to the Historic Hillsborough Commission in a letter dated February 22, 1965:

> *My grandmother . . . was a student [at the Burwell School] about 1856–1857 or maybe earlier. From the dates in her Remembrance Album it seems most of the dates there were 1856. She married Stephen W. Glenn in 1867. Her sister, Virginia Lunsford, was also a student there, but moved to Texas soon after that and married a Mr. Bumpass.*

The Lunsford sisters did not appear in the *Burwell School Catalogue of 1848–51* since it was apparently published about 1851, and they attended the school ca. 1856.

Information was provided by Mrs. Bessie D. Beam (Roxboro, N.C.).

[ Frances Elizabeth (or Elizabeth Frances) and her sister, Virginia, were the daughters of Jesse (Joseph?) A. Lunsford, a wealthy planter, and his wife, Elmira Trotter.

After the Civil War, Virginia married Thomas Halliburton Bumpass, and they moved to Collin County, Texas, where Thomas became a farmer. According to the United States Census of 1880, the Bumpass family was living in Texas and had four living children: Irene A., Horace M., Virginia T., and Walter C. Also living with them was Virginia's father, Jesse.

Virginia died in 1881 and was buried in the Abston Cemetery, Collin County, Texas. Thomas died twelve years later, on March 9, 1893, and was buried beside her.

Frances Lunsford also married after the Civil War. In 1867 she married Stephen W. Glenn. They lived in Roxboro. By 1880, they had five children: Minnie E., Ira T., Myrtle, John A., and Mable C. By 1890, Frances had seven children and Stephen had died.    ]

## ELIZABETH (LIZZIE) PALMER LYNCH
June 26, 1833–December 13, 1918
Hillsborough, North Carolina

Elizabeth (Lizzie) Palmer Lynch was born June 26, 1833, in Hillsborough, the daughter of silversmith (and later Keeper of the Town Clock) Lemuel Lynch (1808–93) and Margaret Palmer, daughter of William and Elizabeth Clancy Palmer.

Lizzie Lynch was probably a Burwell student in the mid- or late 1840s. Her granddaughter, Virginia Epes Feild, recalls that her grandmother used to tell her that on rainy mornings Dr. Burwell would always require excuses for absences. If a girl said it was because of rain or inclement weather, he would always reply, "Well, young ladies, you are neither sugar nor salt. You won't melt!"

Lizzie Lynch married Calvin E. Parish (Feb. 14, 1832–Nov. 20, 1898) in Marion, Alabama, at the home of relatives on March 16, 1859, when she was twenty-five years old. Her husband, affectionately known as "Squire Parish," was an attorney in Hillsborough and later a member of the State Legislature.

The Parishes spent the first few years of their married life in the tiny "saltbox" house, now razed, which once stood near the Gattis Well-House and Masonic Hall but which had originally been a Quaker inn belonging to John Stubbs. Later, they built a house at the northwest corner of Wake and King streets.

*Elizabeth Palmer Lynch Parish.*

The Parishes had four daughters and two sons:

1. Ida*, Apr. 26, 1860–July 14, 1888, d. Clarksville, Va.; m. A.J. Wooton.
2. Harry Lynch*, 1862–1917.
3. Margaret*, Nov. 3, 1864–Oct. 1, 1949; m. Samuel Mallett Gattis.
4. Agnes; m. V.L. Epes, Richmond, Va.
5. Elizabeth (Lizzie) Clancy*, 1872–1914; d. unmarried.
6. Calvin R.*, Sept. 11, 1876–Jan. 17, 1907.

The charming picture of Lizzie Palmer Lynch Parish which accompanies this sketch, made when she was a grandmother, was sent to the Historic Hillsborough Commission by her granddaughter, Virginia Epes Feild, daughter of Agnes Parish, who went to the Nash & Kollock School in the 1880s. Agnes used to say, according to Mrs. Feild, that the cemetery was the only place they were allowed to walk on Sunday afternoons when they were growing up in their deeply Presbyterian home.

Virginia Epes Feild describes her grandmother as "a faithful and devoted member of the Presbyterian Church of Hillsborough, always interested in the affairs of Eagle Lodge (of which her husband was at one time Grand Master), an ardent gardener, a great reader, and a most devoted daughter, mother, and grandmother." She died in Richmond, Virginia, at the home of her daughter, Agnes Parish Epes (Mrs. V.L. Epes) on December 13, 1918, in her eighty-fifth year and was buried in the Parish-Lynch plot in the Hillsborough Memorial Cemetery (New Town Cemetery).

*Buried in the Parish-Lynch plot, Hillsborough Memorial Cemetery

Materials in this sketch are in part from Lizzie Lynch Parish's granddaughter, Virginia Epes Feild (Mrs. James W. Feild), 3314 Alabama Ave., Alexandria, Va., who also supplied the picture.

## [  MARY CAROLINE McCAULEY
c. 1838–June 9, 1859
Orange County, North Carolina

Although a Caroline McAuley is listed among the Burwell School students, nothing is known about her. The obituary of a Mary Caroline McCauley, however, was carried in the *Hillsborough Recorder* on June 22, 1859. She was the twenty-one-year-old daughter of Col. W[illiam] H. and Cornelia Watson McCauley of Hillsborough. She died at the residence of her uncle, Richard Tap[p], of consumption.    ]

## ANNIE McDIARMID
Cumberland County, North Carolina

Annie McDiarmid, who attended the Burwell School in 1855 and 1856, was apparently a younger sister of Catharine McDiarmid, an earlier student at the school. Both girls were the daughters of Daniel McDiarmid, Esq., of Cumberland County, who is listed as a Patron of the School in the *Burwell School Catalogue of 1848–51*. The McDiarmid families of adjoining Robeson, Hoke, and Cumberland counties have long been known as staunch Presbyterians.

Mrs. Burwell wrote to Fanny on a snowy, chilly February 8, 1856: "We expect the Alstons & Annie McDiarmid & the Garretts as soon as the weather is better & they are all Music scholars"; she added, "I must write to Phi Williams and Annie McD___ tonight."

## CATHARINE McDIARMID
August 26, 1836–December 1849
Cumberland County, North Carolina

Catharine McDiarmid of Cumberland, whose name appears in the *Burwell School Catalogue of 1848–51,* was the daughter of Daniel McDiarmid, Esq., a Patron of the School.

The following article appeared in the *Hillsborough Recorder* of December 26, 1849, reprinting a notice in the *North Carolinian:*

> DISTRESSING ACCIDENT—On last Friday week, a young lady, Miss Catharine McDiarmid, 13 years of age, was thrown from a horse, and falling with her breast on a stump, was killed immediately. She was a promising and interesting girl. The accident happened in the upper part of Robeson County.
>
> The name and age correspond with that of an interesting young lady from Cumberland, a pupil at the last session in Mr. and Mrs. Burwell's School in this place—we hope it is not the same.

[    Catharine McDiarmid (Aug. 26, 1836–July 27, 1874) and Ann, her younger sister, were the daughters of Ann Eliza and Daniel McDiarmid, a wealthy planter. Catharine attended the Burwell School from1848–51. She was not killed in a riding accident, as Mrs. Burwell believed, but lived to marry Henry Clay Robinson, son of Eliza Pearce and Dr. Benjamin Robinson, who moved to Fayetteville in 1805 from Vermont. Henry Clay was a grandson of Anne McNeill and the Rev. Angus McDiarmid, who had emigrated from Edinburgh, Scotland, in 1793.

In the United States Census of 1860, Catharine and Henry Clay Robinson were listed with three children: Eliza Wright, Lucy, and Henry McDiarmid (1860–1939). By 1870 Catharine, presumably a widow, and her children were listed with her parents. She died in 1874, a few days after the death of her daughter, Eliza Wright. Catharine and Eliza Wright are buried at the Cross Creek Cemetery in Cumberland County.

Catharine's son married Mary Faison Hill on February 24, 1886, and left many descendents.

Nothing is known about Catharine's sister, Ann, who is shown in the 1850 census—a year after the Robeson County accident.    ]

[    **FLORA McKAY** (c. 1834– ?)
Memphis, Tennessee
**&**
**ISABELLA McKAY**
Cumberland County, North Carolina

Flora and Isabella McKay could well have been cousins. Both names are found in the family of Neill McKay of Cumberland County, whose will of August 18, 1830, names a wife, Flora, and a daughter, Flora Isabella, and a son, Neill. The young Neill may have been the Rev. Neill McKay, patron of the Burwell School, about twenty years later. Flora McKay from Memphis, Tennessee, may have been the daughter of Neill's brother, John.

The *Fayetteville Observer* of July 2, 1850, carried the marriage announcement of an Isabella McKay, daughter of the late Dr. Edward

McKay, and M. McRae of Robeson County. Robeson adjoins Cumberland County. This Isabella McKay may have been the Burwell student. ]

[   **MARGARET McKEITHEN (McKEITHAN)**
c. 1835– ?
Cumberland County, North Carolina

Margaret McKeithen (spelled McKeithan in the *Burwell School Catalogue of 1848–51*) was the daughter of a well-to-do planter, James McKeithen. Listed in his household in the U.S. Census of 1850 were his wife, Julie C., and their four children, all in their teens: John C., Margaret, James R., and William R. Margaret was born about 1835. Nothing more is known of her.   ]

**MARGARET (MAGGIE) McLESTER**
September 3, 1842–August 1, 1921
Hillsborough, North Carolina

Margaret (Maggie) McLester was the daughter of Scots merchant William Kirkland's child, Phebe (1811–44), who married [Nelson] McLester (?–1850) of Columbia, Georgia. The little girl came very early as an orphan to her grandfather's great brick manor house, Ayr Mount, in Hillsborough and spent the whole of her long life there. Margaret McLester is listed in the *Burwell School Catalogue of 1848–51*; she therefore must have enrolled in 1850 or 1851 at the age of eight or nine. The little girl probably walked in each morning from Ayr Mount, possibly with an older Kirkland, Susan Mary Kirkland, who also walked in later years from Ayr Mount to the Nash & Kollock School. So far as is known, this was the only schooling Maggie McLester received.

Adopted by John U. Kirkland at Ayr Mount, she devoted the whole of her long, useful life to his family. She seems to have become the pattern of the "maiden aunt" to absolute perfection. Although she never married, the name "Maggie McLester" is not forgotten—a number of loving friends named their children for her (e.g., Margaret McLester Strudwick, who married Thomas May Van Planche).

Ann Strudwick Nash has left this thumbnail sketch of Maggie McLester in her book, *Ladies in the Making*:

> *[At] Ayr Mount . . . it [the maiden aunt] was Miss Maggie McLester who busily darned the socks and bound up the wounds of the lively little Kirklands. Pleased by the prospect of a changed scene, she accepted Aunt Maria's [Maria Nash's] offer [to become a companion to the Nash & Kollock School], and was soon established in the niche from which matrimony had so suddenly removed her predecessor. Miss Maggie was good company and a good housekeeper, but possessed of a will and a temper quite as determined as Cousin Sarah's. Naturally, when the two came together under one roof there was daily conflict, a source of amusement and sometimes of dismay to those of us whose purpose it was to occupy a position of strict neutrality.*

Mrs. Nash does not say so, but each of the proponents was a Burwell girl, an orphan who had had to learn to fend for herself. It is interesting that each should have confronted the other in the old Margaret Lane household (see Sara[h] Jane Kollock).

To earn her living after losing her ample inheritance invested in Confederate bonds, Miss Maggie became housekeeper in a series of families. She died unmarried at the age of seventy-nine on August 1, 1921. She is buried in the Kirkland family cemetery at Ayr Mount in the shelter of a great deodar cedar. A rough fieldstone marks her grave. A dozen years ago (about 1967) one could discern the letters, "Maggie McLester," but these have been eroded away.

*Maggie McLester.*

Information is from Ann Strudwick Nash, *Ladies in the Making*, pp. 130–31.

## SALLIE (SALLY) ALSTON MANGUM
January 6, 1824–October 14, 1896
Orange County, North Carolina

Sallie (Sally) Alston Mangum, born January 6, 1824, was the eldest child of Willie Person Mangum and Charity Alston Cain Mangum of Walnut Hall, north of present-day Durham. Although the site of Walnut Hall is now in northern Durham County, it was in Willie P. Mangum's day in the northeastern corner of Orange County. U.S. Sen. Willie P. Mangum, it has been observed, probably came closer to the U.S. presidency than any other resident Tar Heel. Throughout the Tyler administration Mangum was president pro tem of the Senate. His wife, Charity Alston Cain, was the daughter of the wealthy Orange County merchant and planter, William Cain.

Sallie Alston Mangum was undoubtedly a great favorite with her parents. They always referred to her in letters as "dear little Sallie" or "dear little lambe," and Sallie's letters to each of them after her marriage are filled with the tenderest affection and the most extravagant endearments. Sallie's sisters were Martha Person (Pattie) and Mary; she also had a brother, William Preston, killed in the Civil War.

Sallie attended at least four schools. For a short time, she was a day student at a country school near Walnut Hall. In 1834 and 1835 she attended the Hillsborough Female Academy on E. Tryon Street, then under the superintendency of the Rev. William M. Green. During this period she seems to have lived with her uncle Priestly H. Mangum and his wife, Rebecca, in the house that once stood diagonally opposite the Graham home, Montrose.

In February 1836, Sallie and one or more of her sisters went to the Franklin Academy at Louisburg, operated by Mr. and Mrs. John B. Bobbitt, and remained there at least until October 1838.

Sallie was sent in the spring session of 1839 to the relatively new Burwell School; and on March 11, 1839, her father wrote to her,

> . . . I am much pleased to perceive evidence of great improvement in your writing; & trust, My dear, that not only in that, but in all respects you will make all reasonable efforts to improve your time—No acquirement or valuable accomplishment is attainable, save only by perseverance & toilsome effort. . . . Present my best wishes to Mr. and Mrs. B.

In June Sallie came home for a vacation and thought of bringing a friend with her. She wrote to her father on June 9, 1839,

> ... Mrs. Burwell says that the session will close on Friday morning, we will not say any lessons on Friday; she says if you will come after me I can go Friday after two o'clock, please come after me. I expect that Miss Harriet Johnston will come home with me, if you can send her back conveniently in a week. Mrs. Burwell expects to start Monday after school breaks up for Petersburg. We began last week to review our studies, we will have six weeks vacation. Please come after me.

On December 5, 1839, Sallie Mangum received one of Mrs. Burwell's informal "certificates" of satisfactory work:

> Sally Mangum's attention to her studies merits the approbation of her friends. I hope her Father will examine her and judge of her improvement for himself. Her deportment has been good.
> Decr 5th 1839                                M.A. Burwell

The year, 1839, appears to be the only year Sallie spent at the Burwell School, although her sister Martha attended the academy on Tryon Street in 1840. In January 1841, Willie P. Mangum agreed that Sallie might stay at home:

> —I rec'd. Sally's letter this morning, and I am willing she may remain at home, if she will read _attentively_ Rollins History and use the Gazetteer a book of Wm. Cain's, so as to understand _Heathen Mythology_, the names of _persons_ & _places_ &c. . . . I shall write to Petersburg to buy Sally a Pianno, & will write you on the business & when to send to the Depot for it.

In 1851, Sallie married Col. Martin Washington Leach, a planter from Randolph County, according to the Mangum Papers:

> Colonel Leach bought for his bride a handsome carriage lined with red velvet and drawn by a pair of white horses. They planned to live in Hillsboro and they did live there for a while. He soon found it necessary, however, to move to Randolph County, where his business interests were and where was located his plantation which was called "Lansdowne." With Sallie Leach her family sent "Aunt Polly," a young white woman who was her personal maid and who remained with her as long as she lived. The family loved

*"Aunt Polly" dearly and she in turn loved them and came to admire Colonel Leach so much that she asked to be buried at his feet, which request was carried out. It is said... that Colonel Leach owned the second largest number of slaves [in Randolph Co.].*

The Leaches had four children:

1. Marie Alma, 1854–1926; m. Julian Augustine Turner.
2. Sallie Mangum, 1857–1934; m. Dr. Stephen Beauregard Weeks.
3. William Preston, 1858–62.
4. Annie Preston, 1865–1942.

Sallie Alston Mangum Leach died on October 14, 1896, at the age of seventy-two. She is buried in the Mangum family graveyard at Walnut Hall, as is her daughter Annie Preston Leach. Walnut Hall, itself, burned on Christmas Eve 1933.

*Sallie Alston Mangum Leach.*

The photo of Sallie A. Mangum and other information were supplied by Sallie's grandson, Mr. Mangum Weeks, an original member of the Historic Hillsborough Commission. The photo was made from a daguerreotype "taken" shortly after Sallie's marriage, according to Mr. Weeks. References above are to the *Papers of Willie Person Mangum*, ed. Henry Thomas Shanks, 5 vols., N.C. Dept. of Archives & History, Raleigh, 1950–1956 ( Vol. III, pp. 2, 10, 27, 88; Vol. V, p. 760).

# MARTHA F. MEBANE
Orange County (Yanceyville), North Carolina

Martha F. Mebane, daughter of the Honorable Giles Mebane
(1809–99), Orange County planter and statesman, and Mary Catherine
Yancey Mebane, is listed as a student in the *Burwell School Catalogue of*
*1848–51* and was probably enrolled at the Burwell School in 1850 or
1851. The catalogue also lists the Honorable Giles Mebane as one of the
Burwell School's References and Patrons.

The *Alumni History of the University of North Carolina* (1924 edition)
contains this sketch of former Lt. Gov. Giles Mebane (p. 423):

> *MEBANE, GILES*      *Farmer*
> *Orange co.; b. Jan. 25, 1809; d. June 3, 1899; m. Mary*
> *Catherine Yancey, 1837; A.B., 1831; lawyer; mem. conv. 1861;*
> *mem. house of c. 1844–48 and 1854–58; state sen. 1862–64;*
> *speaker of sen. 1862–64; trustee UNC 1846–68; lieut.-gov.*
> *1862–64; Presbyterian.*

# MARY (MOLLIE) E. MEBANE
Bertie*, North Carolina

Mary (Mollie) E. Mebane of Bertie was evidently a student at the
Burwell School in the 1850s. Mrs. Burwell wrote to her daughter Fanny
in New York on January 19, 1856,

> *She [Mrs. Jordan] told me that Molly Mebane's mother is dead,*
> *died of cancer about a month after Mollie left here. She left Mollie*
> *that place & everything in the house & on the farm just as it*
> *stands—I expect Molly will soon marry—*

Mary (Mollie) Mebane was the daughter of Dr. Alexander Wood
Mebane of Bertie County. The progenitor and statesman of the Mebane
family was Alexander Mebane, according to the Mebane family sketch in

John Wheeler's *Reminiscences and Memoirs of North Carolina and Eminent North Carolinians*. He was born in Pennsylvania, November 26, 1744, and died July 5, 1795. He married first Mary Armstrong of Orange County and second Miss Claypoole of Philadelphia. This first Alexander Mebane, a well-known political figure and member of the U.S. Congress, had several children: James, William, Dr. John A. Mebane of Greensboro, et al.

Dr. Alexander Wood Mebane was a son of William Mebane and a grandson of the first Alexander Mebane. He was born in Orange County, liberally educated, graduated in Philadelphia, and settled in Bertie County on the Chowan River where he became one of the successful, enterprising men of the area. He was "a man of unblemished reputation, faithful to every duty, active and energetic in every good work." In 1829 and 1830 he was elected a member of the House of Commons and in 1833, '34, '35, and '36 he was in the Senate. In 1848 he was a candidate for Elector on the Cass ticket [Democratic candidate for President]. This was his last public effort.

His wife was Mary Howe, "a lady of fine estate," by whom he had several children. Two sons, William A. Mebane and Julius A. Mebane of Bertie, attended the Caldwell Institute in Hillsborough in 1848–49 according to the institute's catalogue. Mary E. Mebane, always called Mollie, was evidently named for her mother.

Mrs. Burwell's prophecy that Mollie would soon marry was correct; the *Raleigh Register* of December 30, 1857, carried the notice of the marriage on December 16, 1857, of Mollie E. Mebane of Bertie County to John Pool of Elizabeth City. *Alumni History of the University of North Carolina* (1924 edition) carries this sketch of the Hon. John Pool:

> *JOHN POOL*              *Lawyer*
> *b. June 16, 1826; d. Washington, D.C. Aug. 16, 1884; A.B., 1847; mem. conv., 1865; state sen. 1856–58 and '64–65; U.S. sen. 1868–73; trustee UNC 1864, 1868.*

*Bertie, according to William S. Powell's *North Carolina Gazetteer* (Chapel Hill, 1968), p. 40, was "a former town in Bertie County. Inc. 1939 and merged with the town of Windsor in 1959. Known earlier as Rosemont."

Some data in this sketch was contributed by the late Miss Alice Noble. Mrs. Burwell's letter to Fanny is in the Records Room, Burwell School. Information also is from *Alumni History of the University of North Carolina* (1924 ed.), p. 499, and John Wheeler's *Reminiscences and Memoirs of North Carolina and Eminent North Carolinians*, p. 331.

## ELIZA N. MITCHELL
Chapel Hill, North Carolina

In a letter of January 26, 1846, Annabella Norwood states that there are only fourteen pupils in the Burwell School and that only two of those are from out of town— the daughters of Prof. Mitchell and Dr. George Moore (see Rebecca Moore). Mrs. Burwell listed "Rev. E. Mitchell—Chapel Hill" as one of the school's Patrons in the *Burwell School Catalogue of 1848–51.*

Prof. Elisha Mitchell, born in Connecticut, was a Yale man and had been a tutor there after his graduation. He was a scientist of remarkable distinction and signal accomplishment, second perhaps only to Pres. Caldwell on the UNC campus. The eldest of his four daughters, Mary Mitchell, herself a prodigy of learning, had married lawyer Richard J. Ashe and moved to Hillsborough in January 1846. A letter from Mrs. M.A. Burwell to her friends Mary A. Kirkland and Susan Kirkland visiting in Fayetteville noted in mid-January 1846,

> *Mr. or rather Mrs. Richard Ashe has gone to housekeeping in the "Yellow House" [i.e., the James A. Cheek-Houston Walker House]. She came up from Chapel Hill & went to fixing while he was in Wilmington—he came night before last. She & her sister Miss Mitchell [Miss Eliza N. Mitchell] have been so in confusion that no one has called on them. They will be ready to receive visitors next week I hear.*

Another Mitchell daughter, Ellen, married Dr. J. J. Summerell of Salisbury (c. Dec. 1844), and became the mother of Hope Summerell Chamberlain who wrote *Old Days in Chapel Hill.*

Eliza N. Mitchell, who would have been the younger Mitchell daughter attending the Burwell School in 1846, like all the Mitchell children, would have been educated at home to read Greek and Latin by sight at eight years old or earlier (see Rosaline Brooke Spotswood), and her other basic skills would have been comparable. Mrs. Burwell may have found it difficult to have absorbed an Eliza Mitchell into her usual classes. Whether Eliza's sister Margaret Eliot ever attended the school is problematical. It is uncertain also how long Eliza attended the school.

On November 20, 1852, Eliza N. Mitchell married Richard S. Grant at the Elisha Mitchell home in Chapel Hill near the west gate of the campus (see Orange County Marriage Bonds). Dr. Alexander Wilson of Hillsborough performed the ceremony. Mr. Grant died early, as did the Grants' only child, a little boy, Richard Mitchell Grant, aged four years, seven months, very suddenly of diphtheria on October 17, 1862. His original grave was moved from the rear of the Mitchell house (no longer standing), and he is now buried near the Mitchell obelisk in Sec. II of the Old Chapel Hill Cemetery.

These two deaths were utterly crushing blows to the young wife from which it seemed she might not recover; but eventually she and her sister Margaret began a school for girls in Oxford, North Carolina; later they removed to Statesville where their elder sister, Mary Mitchell Ashe, finally joined them after Richard Ashe's death in Bakersfield, California. For a time their Statesville school was known as Simonton Female College, but its name was later changed to Mitchell College, and it appears always to have been most favorably known. Today, the school, a junior college, has changed its name again and is known as Mitchell Community College.

Cornelia Phillips Spencer wrote of her beloved old friend Margaret Eliot Mitchell in 1904,

> *. . . now sole survivor of Dr. Mitchell's family . . . a woman of highest character, and one of the excellent ones; my old friend, my good comrade, what shall I do without her warm sympathy, her clear good sense, her uncompromising faith in the unseen. . . . Since Mrs. Grant's death, she has lived in her own house in Statesville, North Carolina, a useful, secluded life, hampered of late years by cataract in both eyes. Her oldest sister, Mrs. Richard Ashe [Mary Mitchell] died in California. . . .*

Eliza N. Mitchell, together with her sisters, left a college of their own making behind them, the only Burwell School girl to have accomplished such a feat.

Sources include Marriage Bonds of Orange Co., p. 49; Records of the Chapel Hill Cemetery; Hope Summerell Chamberlain, *Old Days in Chapel Hill* (Chapel Hill, 1926), pp. 28–29, 314, 237; Cornelia Phillips Spencer, *Selected Papers* (Chapel Hill, 1953), p. 310. Annabella Norwood's letter is from the W.N. Tillinghast Papers, Ms. Collection, Perkins Library, Duke Univ.

## BARBARA MARIA MONTGOMERY
### Alamance County, North Carolina

Barbara Maria Montgomery, listed as Maria Montgomery in the *Burwell School Catalogue of 1848–51* and apparently always called Maria, was the younger sister of Dr. Daniel Archibald Montgomery who married Josephine Berry, also a Burwell student. Maria, who must have attended the school in the late 1840s, was the daughter of U.S. Congressman Dr. William Montgomery (1789–1843) and his second wife Sara (or Sarah) Albright. The third of their ten children was Dr. Daniel Archibald Montgomery; the ninth was Maria. Since Dr. William Montgomery, Maria's father, died in 1843, her brother Daniel became her sponsor at the Burwell School and is consequently listed in the school's published list of Patrons in the catalogue. Nothing is known of Maria at the Burwell School; she must inevitably have known the Berry sisters well, but it is possible that Capt. John Berry and Dr. William Montgomery would have formed political acquaintance independent of other considerations.

Some materials in this sketch are from Sallie W. Stockard, *History of Alamance County* (Raleigh, 1900), pp. 112, 114, 115. (*See also* Josephine Berry.)

## JULIA REBECCA MOORE
### Chapel Hill, North Carolina

Julia Rebecca Moore of Chapel Hill, always called Rebecca, was the daughter of "old" Dr. George Moore, whose family home was in Pittsboro and who was allied by descent and marriage with some of the oldest families of the Cape Fear. Dr. Moore had established a medical practice and a second home in Chapel Hill. He purchased the old Maj. Pleasant Henderson dwelling with its satellite buildings at the corner of Henderson and Franklin streets (where the U.S. Post Office building stands today) and lived there with his family, including sons Duncan, William, and Hugh, and daughter Rebecca.

Most local reminiscences refer to him as "Old Dr. George Moore." [Kemp] Battle's *History of the University of North Carolina* describes him as a quiet man of considerable distinction:

> *The physicians of the place [Chapel Hill] were notable men. The leaders were Johnston Blakely Jones and George Moore. Both were of distinguished lineage. . . . [Dr. Moore was] of the blood of Governor James Moore of South Carolina, and of Governor Sir John Yeamans. . . . Doctor Moore was a silent, reserved man, the soul of truthfulness and honor; a good physician, but without the genius of his partner [Dr. Jones]. He gave the impression that he did not know what fear was. He had great respect for religion, often attended church, but did not become a member.*

Rebecca was apparently the Moores' youngest child and was enrolled in the Burwell School for the spring term of 1846. Annabella Norwood of Hillsborough, writing Burwell School news to her cousin William N. Tillinghast in Fayetteville, reported on January 26, 1846,

> *Mrs. Burwell has only fourteen scholars and only two of them that do not reside in this place; they are Professor Mitchell and Dr. George Moore's daughters.*

The *Burwell School Catalogue of 1848–51* lists Rebecca Moore's name. Rebecca apparently met a medical student, Thomas R. Emery of New Bern, in 1855, and her marriage to him on June 10, 1856, in Chapel Hill was announced in the *Raleigh Register* of June 25, 1856. The *Alumni History of the University of North Carolina* (1924 edition) lists the following:

> *EMERY, THOMAS R.*          *Physician*
> *New Bern; s. 1855–56*

At least three major events occurred in Rebecca Moore Emery's life the following year, 1857: Her father died; her first child was born; and her father's old home in Chapel Hill burned to the ground.

Mrs. Robina Norwood, visiting her daughter Mrs. Andrew Mickle in Chapel Hill, wrote to her daughter Jane Tillinghast in Fayetteville on April 2, 1857,

> *Old Dr. George Moore . . . died on Monday last after a short illness. His funeral had it been here would probably have exhibited a very affecting scene . . . but he was carried to Pittsboro' where most of [his] Relations had been interred. Mr. Mickle, Dr. Wheat*

*& several Students attended the Body Yesterday morning to Pittsboro'. I believe two of his sons, Drs. Wm. & Duncan, were all of his own family that were at home. Poor Mrs. Moore had been sometime at Newberne with her daughter Rebecca who was expecting to be confined & the intelligence of his danger could not & did not reach her in time. . . .*

Seven months later, on November 2, Mrs. Norwood, still in Chapel Hill, wrote to Jane,

*Old Dr. Moore's house was burnt down & so completely on fire before people were alarmed (being accustomed to Bell-ringing & all sorts of noises in the night) that it was impossible to save it. . . . Dr. Duncan & his wife boarded with Miss Nancy H[illiard] . . . & the rooms in the old house were rented to students . . . the wind which was very strong providentially blew hard in the opposite direction to the buildings otherwise a great part of the village must have been burnt. . . .*

According to preserved deeds, Mrs. Thomas R. Emery retained possession of her father's home lot in Chapel Hill for many years.

Sources include the W.N. Tillinghast Papers, Ms. Collection, Perkins Library, Duke Univ.; *Alumni History of the University of North Carolina* (1924 ed.), p. 185; and Kemp Battle's *History of the University of North Carolina* (vol. I, pp. 608–09).

## BETTIE S. MORRIS
### Hillsborough, North Carolina

Bettie S. Morris was almost certainly the daughter of tavern-keeper Robert F. Morris, who advertised in the *Hillsborough Recorder* of January 14, 1847, that he had recently purchased Hillsborough House, lately occupied by James Jackson (i.e., the famous old Faddis Tavern). Morris claimed several years' experience in tavern-keeping and promised the quality and standards of his table, bar, and stables would be high. His ad stated he would be prepared by February Court 1847 to accommodate all callers.

Successive *Recorder* ads (July 12, 1847; Jan. 13, 1848) announced that Robert F. Morris's tavern, "situated near the Court House, well known as Faddis old stand," had been "thoroughly repaired and fitted up." An ad of January 27, 1848 (dated as of Apr. 26, 1847), stated that Morris had "opened a Variety Store North of the Courthouse and one door east of Long, Webb & County, where he will be pleased to see the public generally, but particularly his old friends who so liberally patronized him when a pedlar. He has on hand a stock of Dry Goods and Groceries, Confectionaries, Cigars, Chewing and Smoking Tobacco, and in fact a little of almost everything. . . ."

Morris's Variety Store, in the old building in front of Faddis Tavern and flush with E. King Street, was known for decades as the Store and Bar Room. An ad dated July 12, 1847, published in the January 27, 1848, issue of the *Recorder,* advised, "Call at Morris's, if you want good liquors," and advertised "genuine French Brandy, Imitation Do., Holland Gin, Jamaica Rum, Port & Madeira, Rye Whiskey, and One Tierce London Porter first rate—Also Bacon and Lard, Corn Meal and Flour."

A fire in the early morning of March 7, 1848, did considerable damage to Morris's stables, but all the horses were saved. On March 7, 1855, William McCauley announced in the *Recorder* that he had taken charge of Robert F. Morris's "Public House." Morris served from 1868–70 on Orange County's first Board of County Commissioners.

[ Robert Morris realized the great opportunities available in the new community of Durham after the building of the North Carolina Railroad in the mid-1850s. He moved to Durham and opened the first hotel opposite the new train station, at the same time becoming a pioneer tobacco manufacturer. Although he sold his factory to John R. Green in 1858, he and his son Edward W. with William H. Willard incorporated another tobacco manufacturing company in 1866. He early acquired land in Durham and its environs, which proved a lucrative investment. ]

Bettie S. Morris is listed in the *Burwell School Catalogue of 1848–51* and presumably was a student in the late 1840s, about the time of her father's purchase of Faddis Tavern. She would have been a day student residing with her family at the tavern. The Thomas B. Morris listed as a student in the *Catalogue of the Caldwell Institute 1848–49* (printed by Dennis Heartt) would likely have been Bettie S. Morris's brother.

Bettie S. Morris married John A. Cox on December 9, 1852, according to the Orange County Marriage Bonds. The Rev. Robert Burwell officiated.

## VIRGINIA MOSELEY
Tallahassee, Florida (Catalogue)
Centerville, Florida (Memory Album)

Virginia Moseley, whose name appears in the *Burwell School Catalogue of 1848–51*, was the daughter of the first governor of Florida, William Dunn Moseley (1795–1863), whose biographical sketch in the *Alumni History of the University of North Carolina* (1924 edition) reads,

> *WILLIAM DUNN MOSELEY*
> *Lenoir co.; b. 1795; d. 1863; A.B. 1818; A.M. 1821; tutor UNC 1817; state sen. 1828–38; pres. sen. and lieut. gov. 1832–36; mem. gen. assem. Fla., 1840; first gov. Fla., 1845-49.*

According to Battle's *History of the University of North Carolina*, it was Moseley who verified some of the background of the Davie Poplar, earlier called "the Old Poplar," and it was Moseley's famous letter of 1853 which described the early village of Chapel Hill in such accurate detail that a map could be drawn of it in 1977 and published by the Chapel Hill Historical Society.

The fifty-eight-year-old Moseley noted in his 1853 letter that he was then "living the life of a hermit" in his distant home, "worn out with old age, his six children all grown but one," and that he was still rejoicing over the successes of the university.

It is not remarkable that Moseley should have elected to send his daughter Virginia back to be educated in an area he knew so intimately and loved so well. No references to Virginia at the Burwell School have as yet come to light except her name in the 1848–51 catalogue and her signature, "V. Moseley, Centerville, Florida," in Mary Bailey Easley's Memory Album (1852), now preserved at the Burwell School. These dates indicate that she spent at least two years at the school, and it would appear also that she had become a member of the Halifax, Virginia, group of girls.

Data for this sketch is from the *Alumni History of the University of North Carolina* (1924 edition), p. 445, and Kemp Battle's *History of the University of North Carolina* (2 vols., 1907, 1912): Vol. I, pp. 271–73, Vol. II, p. 37.

[ **CATHERINE A. MURCHISON** (c. 1834– ?)
&
**MARGARET MURCHISON** (c. 1836– ?)
Cumberland County, North Carolina

Catherine and Margaret were the daughters of the wealthy cotton manufacturer Duncan Murchison (1801–70) of Cumberland County. In the United States Census of 1850, Duncan and his wife, Catherine D. Wright (1808–83), were listed with their children, among them Catherine A. and Margaret, who were recorded as having attended school in the last year. ]

## JULIA MURPHY
November 12, 1834–September 7, 1852
Sampson County, North Carolina

Julia Murphy, born November 12, 1834, was the daughter and second child of Archibald Murphy (May 30, 1805–Feb. 2, 1858), younger brother of Patrick Murphy, Esq., and his wife, Ann Meredith Murphy (b. Feb. 9, 1818). Archibald and Ann Murphy appear to have remained on his father Robert Murphy's farm near Tomahawk, North Carolina. Patrick Murphy had married the daughter of well-to-do William (Billie) A. Faison (who was said to own 30,000 acres and 402 slaves), and it was a happy arrangement for Julia Murphy to accompany her first cousins, the twins Mary Bailey and Susan Moseley Murphy, to Mrs. Burwell's school in Hillsborough. There was only a few months' difference in the girls' ages, and their Sampson County backgrounds were similar.

Julia's name is listed in the *Burwell School Catalogue of 1848–51*, and she arrived with her cousins in mid-July 1848 to enroll for the autumn session, which opened July 17. The preserved letters of the twins mention Julia who "sends her love" or goes "down street" with

Sallie Grice and Amelia Faison. Presumably Julia remained at the school for two years as the Murphy twins planned to do.

In 1852 Archibald Murphy and his family moved to Tennessee; Julia Murphy, not quite eighteen years old, died on September 7, 1852.

Information is from *Williams and Murphy Records* (Raleigh, 1949), pp. 201–02; and from three letters of Mary Bailey and Susan Moseley Murphy, written from the Burwell School in 1848 and given to the commission by Mrs. J.M. Saunders, Chapel Hill, N.C.

### MARY BAILEY MURPHY (June 23, 1834– ?)
### &
### SUSAN MOSELEY MURPHY (June 23, 1834– ?)
#### Sampson County, North Carolina

Mary Bailey Murphy and Susan Moseley Murphy, twin sisters born on June 23, 1834, were the daughters of Patrick Murphy, Esq., and Eliza Ann Faison Murphy who lived on Cuwhiffle Plantation in Sampson County, the name Cuwhiffle (also spelled Quwhiffle) being variously attributed to Gaelic and to Indian origins. The Murphys' post-office address was Taylor's Bridge, Sampson County.

Patrick Murphy, Esq. (May 9, 1801–Nov. 15, 1874), the son of Robert Murphy and Mary Bailey, was largely a self-educated man and a prominent lay Presbyterian. He is listed in the Burwells' catalogue as one of the Patrons of the School. (See biographical sketch appended to this article.) Patrick Murphy had a number of brothers and sisters, one of whom, Archibald Murphy, was the father of Julia Murphy, who attended the Burwell School with her twin cousins, Mary Bailey and Susan Moseley Murphy.

Eliza Ann Faison Murphy, the mother of the twins, was the daughter of William (Billie) Faison and Susan Moseley Faison. She, too, came from a large family, and the commodious Patrick Murphy home at Cuwhiffle seems to have been permanently filled with an assortment of nieces, nephews, aunts, and orphaned cousins.

Attending the Burwell School with the Murphy twins besides their cousin Julia Murphy were a youthful aunt, Mary Amelia Faison, and an orphaned cousin, Sarah (Sallie) Grice. These five girls from

Cuwhiffle and its immediate vicinity, all kin in some degree, formed a happy (sometimes homesick) Sampson County group. The twins were fourteen years old when they arrived at the Burwell School to enroll for the fall session beginning Monday, July 17, 1848. This was the year when Capt. John Berry was enlarging the Burwell house, and the school had removed to crowded temporary quarters in the Parks-Hasell House diagonally northwest across Union Street.

An invaluable, completely charming letter, written jointly by the twins to their mother on Saturday, July15, 1848, before school opened on Monday the 17th, was made available to the commission by Susan Rose Saunders, Susan Moseley Murphy's granddaughter. In it the two girls give an uninhibited estimate of their new surroundings and new companions in Hillsborough. (A copy of the letter is appended to this sketch.) Susan Moseley remarks, "Mr. Burwell's house will not be done in 2 weeks. 8 of us sleeps in a room together now but we will not when the house gets done."

Mary Bailey sent her "Dear Ma" this thumbnail sketch of Mrs. Burwell and the school:

> *Mrs. Burwell is very particular with everything we wash up the dishes if we choose to if not we need nott to we have to make up our bed and fold up our night gown very neatly every morning if we dond do it we will get a erors mark when we get up from the table we have to set back our chair our food is very common we have for supper light bread and butter and for breakfast nearly the same we are just like a family we talk to [word omitted] just like we would our mother every night she goes in our room and kiss us all we girls kiss another. . . .*

Susan's acute attack of homesickness was probably typical of the feelings of many a student leaving home for the first time:

> *I donot like to stay here atoll I think to much about home but I cannot help it. Sometimes I feel like my heart would break. It appears like I have been here 5 months allredy I never wanted to see home so bad in my life. . . . tell him (Pa) if he donot send for me I will go in the stage for I cannot stand it I must go home if I have to walk. . . .*

Mary Bailey Murphy married Dr. Joseph Dickson Pearsall

(b. Dec. 8, 1829) of Sampson County, a surgeon in the Confederate army at Fort Fisher. Their four children were

1. Patrick Murphy, b. Aug. 28, 1858.
2. Joseph Dickson, b. Feb. 3, 1860.
3. Jere Robert, MD, b. July 15, 1861.
4. Kate J., b. Dec. 1, 1863.

Susan Moseley Murphy married Erasmus Hervey Evans (b. Mar. 31, 1830) of Cumberland County. Their four children were

1. Mary (Mollie); second wife of William Waller Martin.
2. Eliza Faison, Dec. 26, 1858–Jan. 19, _____ .
3. Erasmus Hervey II, b. July 27, 1861.
4. Susan Murphy, b. Apr. 10, 1863.

The dates of the twins' marriages are not known, nor are the dates of their deaths.

Eliza Ann Faison Murphy died in September 1862, and the burden of family care fell upon Lou Murphy, a younger daughter who attended the Nash & Kollock School for a time. After his wife's death, Patrick Murphy married a second time.

Biographical Sketch of PATRICK MURPHY, ESQ.

*PATRICK MURPHY (1801–1874): son of Robert Murphy and Mary Bailey, was born on his Father's farm near Tomahawk, May 9, 1801. He attended Grove Academy and was largely self-educated. He studied law, was admitted to the Bar and practiced for a time in New Hanover County, which he represented in the House of Commons in 1829. He moved to Taylor's Bridge Township, Sampson County, and in 1833 married Eliza Ann Faison, and erected a large two-story home on Quwhiffle Creek, where he raised a large family. The original home still stands and is known as the Amos J. Johnson place. In 1838 he was appointed Clerk and Master of the Equity Division of the Superior Court of Sampson County, a position he held for more than twenty-five years. He represented Sampson County in the lower branch of the General Assembly during the War years of 1864 and 1865. He was a prominent layman of the Presbyterian Church, and was one of the first elders of Shiloh Presbyterian church in 1832, parent of the Clinton Presbyterian church. In 1859 he was instrumental in the organization of the Oak Plains Presbyterian church, in*

*Taylor's Bridge Township; and it was in the home of Patrick*
*Murphy in Wilmington, to which town he moved after the War,*
*that the Wilmington Presbytery was organized November 21,*
*1868. He died November 15, 1874 and is buried at Oak Plains*
*Church, Samson County. An oil portrait of Patrick Murphy,*
*presented by his grand-son, Charles Williams, of Jacksonville,*
*Florida, hangs in the Superior Court Room at Clinton.*
—*John A.* Oates, Story of Fayetteville and
the Upper Cape Fear

Letters of Mary and Susan Murphy to their mother:

*July15<sup>th</sup> 1848*

*My Dear Ma,*
*I have taken my seat to the writeing desk to write you a few*
*lines to let you know how we are coming on. Mrs. Burwell will*
*open school Monday she put us in the very first class we are in the*
*class with Fanny Burwell she is a little girl about eleven years old*
*but she ought to know a heap she has been to school long enough.*
*Miss Burwell has 12[?] boarders and she expect 4 more she got*
*a new one yesterday she came from Brunswick 4 miles from*
*Wilmington. I like Mrs. and Mr. Burwell very much I like*
*Hillsboro tolerabley well Mrs. Burwell is very particular with*
*evrything we wash up the dishes if we choose to if not we need nott*
*to we have to make up our bed and fold up our night gown very*
*neatly every morning if we dond do it we will get a erors mark*
*when we get up from the table we have to set back our chair our*
*food is very common we have for supper light bread and butter and*
*for breakfast nearly the same we are just like a family we talk to*
*[Mrs. Burwell] just like we would our mother evry night she goes*
*in our room and kiss us all we girls kiss [one] another every night*
*before we go to sleep they wul be a episkiple fair as of this month*
*Mrs. Burwell and all of the girls will go I recon we cant go enny*
*wheres with out Mrs. Burwell go with us their is to be a show here*
*as of this month. I dont know where we will go or not but I recon*
*not ther is a male school about a quarter of a mile from Mr*
*Burwell. they are passing a bout the house all the time Mr Burwell*
*don't allow them to go to his house they went last session but they*
*will not come this session Miss Burwell has a daught[er] as large*
*as I am I have been to prayer meeting since I have been up here*
*Mrs. Burwell has 34 scholasrs she has some very smart ones to*

*Sally and Amelia sends their love to you kiss Marry and Lou for
me I remain your affectonate daughter*

*Mary B Murphy*

*P S My Dear Ma
As this is our writing day I will write to you I donot like to stay
here atall I think to much about home but I cannot help it
Sometimes I fell like my heart would break. It appears like I have
been here 5 months already I never wanted to see home so bad in
my life I cannot stay here any longer than next winter nohow but
Pa says I shall stay untill I am done here tell him if he donot send
for me I will go in the stage for I cannot stand it I must go home
if I have to walk my legs has not got well yet tell Laura she must
be smart and work hard Kiss all of the children for me and tell
them I wish I was their to kiss them myself tell Sarah Monks I
wish she was here with me Tell her I will try and write soon
When you write tell me where to direct my letter to her when you
write tell me when you got home from grand Pa's Tell Sarah I
think of her often Tell Grand Ma I will write soon I expect she
is staying with you yet I cannot say no more about home for I have
cried enough over this to stop I want to get a work box to keep my
thread in Mrs Burwell wont let us keep our trunk they cost $1 ½
when you write tell me whether I must get one or not send us some
seals Mr Burwell's house will not be done in [?] weeks 8 of us
sleeps in a room to gether now but we will not when the house gets
done I am not agoing to take Music lessons but sister will I recon
Uncle Jo called to see us yesterday Bet Holmes came this morning
I think she is [a] great deal pirtier than she was when I saw her I
cannot tell you so much about the school I do not think of any
thing e[l]se but how all of us has writing home today There are 5
Newbern girls and 5 Sampsons girls give my love to Mrs and Mr
Eeger and kiss Jimmy for me I was in such a hurry that I cant
half write I will write more and better next time I do not expect
you can redd it give my love to all I remain your affectionate
daughter*

*Susan M Murphy*

Three letters of Mary Bailey Murphy and Susan Moseley Murphy were given to the
Historic Hillsborough Commission by Susan Moseley's granddaughter, Susan Rose
Saunders (Mrs. J.M. Saunders). The marriage records of the twins is from the *Williams
and Murphy Records,* by Robert Murphy Williams (Raleigh, N.C., 1949), pp. 170 ff., 182
ff. *Williams and Murphy Records* contain these photographs: Cuwhiffle (facing p. 229),

Eliza and Patrick Murphy (facing p. 188), and Mary Bailey and Susan Moseley Murphy (facing p. 169). The biographical sketch of Patrick Murphy is in John A. Oates, *The Story of Fayetteville and the Upper Cape Fear* (Charlotte, N.C., 1950), p. 679. The late Miss Alice Noble of Chapel Hill assisted in collecting much of the information in the article. (*See also* Amelia Faison, Sarah [Sallie] Grice.)

# EMMA NEWKIRK
June 5, 1837–October 17, 1883
New Hanover County, North Carolina

Emma Newkirk was born June 5, 1837, in New Hanover County, the daughter of Bryan Newkirk, a man of considerable wealth, and Margaret Hawes Newkirk.

Emma was a frail young girl. When she went to the Burwell School (c. 1848) she was accompanied by a slave girl since her parents felt she was too delicate to go alone. It is thought that she majored in music. She is mentioned briefly by name in a letter by Mrs. M.A. Burwell dated January 19, 1856, but there is no surviving record of her in her student days, save her name in the *Burwell School Catalogue of 1848–51*.

On December 29, 1854, at the age of seventeen, Emma married Erskine McKoy (originally McKay). Her marriage evidently came almost immediately following her departure from the Burwell School. The couple, who had seven children, went to live on a plantation in Cumberland County, where they owned a number of slaves.

Erskine McKoy fought in the Civil War and died a few years after the war. According to family records, Emma Newkirk McKoy owned a considerable store of jewelry and silver. Near the end of the war, when she saw Union soldiers approaching her home, she took steps to save a few of her valuables. She tied some of her jewelry in a rag and tossed it into some litter on the floor. Two pieces of this jewelry were inherited by her descendant, great-great-granddaughter Mrs. Jo Ann Meacham McAllister.

Another Civil War anecdote concerning Emma is told by her great-granddaughter Mrs. Ethel Parker Wray. Mrs. Wray recalls that the resourceful Emma, hearing that Union soldiers were approaching her neighborhood, had her hams taken from the smokehouse and hung under the planks of the bridge over which the soldiers would cross.

After her husband's death Emma taught music. She lived near Fayetteville and drove a horse and buggy to teach students in their homes. Emma died at the age of forty-six in Cumberland County on October 17, 1883. She and her husband are both buried at Old Bluff Presbyterian Church near Wade, North Carolina, in Cumberland County.

Two of her chairs, matching "fancy chairs" with spindle backs, probably from her parlor in the McKoy home on the Cumberland County plantation, have been given to the Burwell School restoration by Mrs. McAllister and her late mother Mrs. Frank Meacham (Emma's great-granddaughter). Emma's chairs are now in the parlor of the Burwell School.

*Emma Newkirk in her forties, dressed in "widow's weeds."*

Material in the above sketch was contributed by Mrs. J. Malcolm McAllister, 2525 Wake Dr., Raleigh, N.C., and Mrs. David L. Wray, 510 Dixie Tr., Raleigh, N.C. The picture, contributed by Mrs. McAllister, was made from a pastel portrait. (Note: Mrs. Frank Meacham, Emma's great-granddaughter and a loyal friend of the Burwell School, died in the summer of 1980.)

# ANNABELLA (BELL) GILES NORWOOD
July 2, 1831–May 29, 1914
Hillsborough, North Carolina

Annabella (Bell) Giles Norwood and her younger sisters, Robina and Margaret, were students at the Burwell School. They were the daughters of lawyer John Wall Norwood (Jan. 29, 1803–July 24, 1885) and Annabella Giles Norwood (May 31, 1805–Mar. 28, 1876). Their grandparents were Judge William Norwood and Robina Hogg Norwood of Poplar Hill, and William Giles and Anabella Fleming Giles of St. James Parish, Wilmington.

Annabella Norwood, who developed into a delightful and lovable girl, pretty and charming, apparently entered the Burwell School when she was but a child as one of its first students. Her sisters Robina (Rob) and Margaret (Mag), born in 1835 and 1838, came along proportionately later. It is rather surprising that the Norwood girls attended the Burwell School at all, for their grandmother, Mrs. Robina Hogg Norwood, deeply disapproved of Mrs. Burwell's practice of using Milton's *Paradise Lost* simply for parsing.

Bell Norwood, however, seems to have been a well-adjusted Burwell girl. The W.N. Tillinghast Papers contain a dozen of her newsy, bright letters to her Tillinghast cousins about activities at the school. She wrote to her cousin William in Fayetteville on January 26, 1846,

> *They have sixty-nine scholars in the Caldwell Institute. Mrs. Burwell has only fourteen scholars and only two of them that do not reside in this place; they are Professor Mitchell and Dr. George Moore's daughters.*
>
> *The streets of Hillsboro' are nothing but mud . . . I might say a foot deep. The stage drivers say they never saw the roads in such a state but once before. . . . I see nothing but books from morning 'til night. I rise early in the morning and get my lessons, go to school at nine and that is directly after breakfast these times. On Tuesdays & Thursdays after school I take my drawing lessons. On Mondays and Wednesdays after school I write my composition for the next day. Friday evenings we have a working society so you see I don't have much spare time.*

On January 18, 1847, she commented wryly to William about Prof. Bingham's sending her cousin Eliza to the Edgeworth School in Greensborough, ". . . one who has always been so much opposed to boarding schools as her father to send her to one."

*You have no idea how very literary Hillsborough has become, & if the coming generation are not all able to spell, read & write, it will not be because there are no schools in the place, their being only ten....*

On June 14, 1847, she mentioned the social events at the end of the session:

*The young people here have been quite gay for the last month; we had four parties. You know Dr. Wilson and Mrs. Burwell do not like their scholars to attend parties during the session, but at the last part of it we always manage to get round them.*

A month later, on July 13, 1847, she relayed the news of the new session:

*Mrs. Burwell will have quite a large school for Hillsboro'. She is looking for Mat Williams every day. Susan Webb (I expect you saw her down at Uncle Bingham's) is going to her and boards here. She is a very stout girl & quite a pleasant companion for me. So I'll recommend her to you. You must come up and see her.*

*I shall now have as much as I can possibly do for I am going to take drawing & French lessons from Mr. Martino, Mrs. Burwell's music teacher. He takes Daguereotype likenesses & can take his Camera Obscura & double it up so as not to contain more space than a square foot; he will then take the legs & fix them so that they can be used as a walking stick & goes about & takes views. Mr. B. intends taking him on the "Indian Hill" to take that beautiful view.*

An undated letter (1849?) from Bell, as she had begun to sign herself, describes a Christmas vacation:

*What kind of Christmas have you spent? I dont believe I ever knew one to pass more heavily. I was by myself & was not very well. Last Tuesday I spent at Miss Carry Heartt's, Wednesday at Mr. Burwell's & Thursday at Grandma's & by that time I was* *pretty well worn out. I attended a dance on Monday evening at Col. Jones' as Miss Sally is spending her Christmas Holiday at home. I was too good a <u>Presbyterian</u> to dance as you might know, but enjoyed myself very much as a spectator. We had two parties at the end of the Session both of which I attended—There are very few girls in Hillsboro' at this time & no gentlemen that I know of except a few Chapel Hill students. . . .*

Annabella's school years, indeed most of her life, were shadowed by her mother's terrible illness, which involved excruciating pain so great that it drove Mrs. Norwood to long periods of insanity. Sometime in 1848 or 1849, another cousin, young Benjamin R. Huske of Fayetteville, met Annabella. Ben Huske took an AB at UNC in 1850, opened a successful school for boys in Hillsborough, and on December 4, 1851, married Annabella Norwood at Poplar Hill. The next few years were undoubtedly the brightest and happiest of Annabella's life.

The young Huskes had four children:

1. Benjamin Norwood, b. 1853.
2. Anna Bella.
3. Thomas Webb, 1856–1931.
4. Elizabeth Anderson.

Maj. Benjamin R. Huske of the 48th N.C. Troops was mortally wounded in an engagement near Petersburg and died of erysipelas near Richmond on July 15, 1862. Annabella with four small children to support returned to live at Poplar Hill.

Inevitably she thought of opening a seminary for girls and using her Burwell School education. The new school, Mrs. Huske's School, was in operation for the autumn session of 1863. Her successive ads in the *Hillsborough Recorder* are minimal, however, obviously the most economical ones possible, giving no hint of her curriculum. Her tuition charge for the Spring session of 1864 was $35 in advance, for the Fall session $60 in advance, and for the Spring session of 1865, $100 in advance. Her ads through 1866 do not mention tuition. How much longer Mrs. Huske's School continued is difficult to say. There was the competition of the new Nash & Kollock School as well as of Mrs. V. A. Blackwood's (Virginia A. Fuller's) School.

Maj. Huske (Oct. 28, 1829–July 15, 1862), his wife, Annabella, and their son Thomas Webb Huske (Aug. 1, 1856–Feb. 8, 1931) are all buried in the Norwood section of the Hogg-Hooper-Norwood walled enclosure in Hillsborough's Old Town Cemetery. At the time of her death on May 29, 1914, Annabella had been a widow for fifty-two years. Her tombstone reads,

*ANNABELLA GILES NORWOOD*
*HUSKE*
*Beloved wife of Benjamin*
*Robinson Huske*
*b. July 2, 1831*
*d. May 29, 1914*

Materials are from the W.N. Tillinghast Papers, Ms. Collection, Perkins Library, Duke Univ.; Old Town Cemetery Records; *Hillsborough Recorder,* N.C. Collection, Wilson Library, UNC, Chapel Hill; and Ruth Blackwelder, *The Age of Orange* (Charlotte, 1961).

## MARGARET (MAG) YONGE NORWOOD
February 20, 1838–January 15, 1925
Hillsborough, North Carolina

Margaret (Mag) Yonge Norwood, born February 20, 1838, was the sixth child and youngest daughter of eminent lawyer and State Sen. John Wall Norwood (Jan. 29, 1803–July 24, 1885) and Annabella Giles Norwood (May 31, 1805–Mar. 28, 1876). Her grandparents were Judge William Norwood and Robina Hogg Norwood of Hillsborough, and William Giles and Anabella Fleming Giles of St. James Parish, Wilmington. Margaret Yonge Norwood was named for her great-aunt, Margaret Giles, sister of William Giles, who married Dr. Philip Yonge on April 13, 1830, according to Kellam-McKoy's St. James Parish Historical Records, 1737–1852. Mrs. Yonge appears to have been almost a second mother to the Norwood girls.

Margaret Yonge Norwood attended the Burwell School in the 1850s and seems in her school days to have been generally known as Mag. She lived over the Eno River with her large family in the old family home, Poplar Hill, built by James Hogg. There are many passing references to her in Burwell student letters, and her name appears in various Burwell keepsake albums, but there is no sustained description of her as a young girl. She appears to have been subject to colds and small indispositions on various occasions. "Mag Norwood has been sick this week," wrote Mary H. Pearce on November 1, 1851, to her cousin, W.N. Tillinghast, "but Rob said she was a good deal better, & would be able to come to school next week."

Margaret developed into a tall, stately, most impressive woman, such a person as her grandmother Robina Hogg Norwood must have been in her prime. She lived on at Poplar Hill with her bachelor brother, James Hogg Norwood (1839–1912), famous for breeding fighting cocks ("the Norwood War Horses"), until it was decided in 1891 to sell the old place to industrialist Julian Shakespeare Carr. Margaret Norwood, then fifty-three years of age, moved to the Occoneechee Hotel (Colonial Inn). Since she was a spinster, numerous letters to her exist. One such group was reprinted by the late Prof. Thomas Felix Hickerson in his *Echoes of Happy Valley,* which includes a collection of Joseph C. Webb's Civil War letters to Norwood ladies, including "Cousin Mag."

In her later years Margaret Norwood became known as something of an amateur historian, especially where Hillsborough and family history were concerned. One of her letters, attached to this sketch, is so immensely valuable that it has become a major source of historic information. Preserved in the John De Bernière Hooper Papers, the letter, dated April 20, 1905, gives accounts of 1) the Nash-Hooper House; 2) the "Rye Patch" (i.e., the ground between the Nash-Hooper House and the cemetery); 3) the private cemeteries to the west of Lot 98 (the original Old Town Cemetery), sold from the Hooper (Watters) estate after 1846; 4) a sketch of the Hooper private burial plot and of the adjoining Norwood plot; and 5) an eye-witness account (her own) of the opening of the Signer's grave [the disinterment of Declaration of Independence signer, John De Bernière Hooper], which she attended as a representative of the family. The letter is solid proof of Margaret Norwood's extraordinary sense of history.

Margaret Yonge Norwood died unmarried at the age of eighty-seven and is buried in the Norwood plot in the Old Town Cemetery beside her father and mother.

*Hillsboro April 20th 1905*

*My dear Cousin,*

*I am owing you an apology for my delay in answering your letter of March 29th; but as writing is not a thing I often do easily I will not waste my strength in explanations—I was in Durham, quite sick just then, and later there was such confusion in the house, on account of preparations for the removal of my nephew's* family to a new home at Duke that I could not contribute to ancient history. Now to answer your questions—

William Hooper died in the house now standing, on the property adjoining the Presbyterian Church—The garden was at the back of the house to the north. On the east side of the residence, between the yard and churchyard, was a cultivated lot—When Mr. Hooper died a burial lot was laid off in the N. E. corner of that lot, & he was interred in it—it was enclosed by a substantial wall which is still standing in excellent condition—this wall must have been built some years later and my grandmother shared the expense, the agreement being that the two families should own it jointly. Aunt Watters sold a strip the width of that lot extending to the street, it was divided & resold as private lots—The Watters and Norwood lot was like this—I have written you of the building of the inner wall, indicated by the double line. About 22 yrs. ago this wall had become insecure, and my father, with your Mother's consent, had it removed, but it can still be traced, i.e., the foundtion line. The ground within the enclosure is covered with ivy.

The old Hooper home was bought by Gov. Graham several years after the burning of his own house during the war, & was his place of residence during the remaining years of his life—it is still owned by Judge A.W. Graham. The house now standing, and also an office in the yard, are the same that W.H. occupied.

Now as to the Convention—It must have been as yr. Gr. Father wrote—the present Pres. Ch. Building was erected, I think, in 1819—it is the only one ever built here—it is about on the site of the Ch. of England church which was burned. The whole community united in building a church—in which services were held by ministers of all denominations for several years. Then the Pres. had increased so in strength as to employ a minister regularly—and they were given possession of that church at a valuation covering value of site & cost of building—payment of ¼ of this am't to be made to each of the other denominations as in time their churches came to be erected; meanwhile when their ministers came they held services in that church. And so it is that the Pres. Ch. stands where the Epis. Ch. would naturally be. It was a good many years before the Episcopal Church was built.

Robert Hogg was brother to James Hogg, I am not sure about Thomas—will try to find out.

Henry Hyrn Watters was a Colonel—& commanded a regt. in the battle of Cowpens. The family do not know the name or

162

number of his regiment. Mr. Watters thinks he can get dates of his uncle Henry's birth & death from a bible in his sister's possession. So you can yet hope for that—Carrie Strudwick did not know. They tell me he served in the navy for ten years—then resigned & took charge of his plantation on the Cape Fear. The title General was from his rank in the Militia service.

Helen Hogg married William Hooper June 26$^{th}$ 1791—She married Joseph Caldwell August 17$^{th}$ 1809—

The *only* Hooper grave in the cemetery *here* is that of William Hooper, Signer of the Declaration of Independence.

I do not know the dates of birth or death of his son William, nor his burial place.

I do not think your Uncle Thomas died in Hillsboro, I would have been told of his grave, as my parents were both warmly attached to him. The only unmarked grave in the enclosure is that of a Scotch woman whom my grandmother befriended through a long illness.

So I think the wife of the Signer must have died and been buried elsewhere; for the same loving & dutiful daughter who marked her father's grave would not have neglected to respect her Mother's last resting place.

When the Signer's grave was opened and all that could be identified as fragments of the body had been secured by Dr. Schenck, I did suggest replacing first the dust from the bottom of the grave, as that was truly what remained of the body interred. Then Dr. S. turned and was careful to have it properly done.

The mound was made as a newly made grave, and I at once had it turfed; there was delay about the return of the tombstone from the battle-ground after the monument was erected, but it has been replaced, and the appearance of the grave now is just what it was before being opened.

I think it most probable that your Uncle Thomas died & was buried in Fayetteville, that was his home during his married life. But the *fact* is he died in Chapel Hill, Nov. 22$^{nd}$, 1828. Uncle Joe remembers it as a little child, & thinks the body was interred at Hillsboro, so his burial place is yet a mystery as the grave cannot be found there or at C.H. or Fayetteville.

The slab that covers Wm Hooper's grave is marble, dark with age—Sometime I will copy the inscription for you. I've a "turned ancle" that disables me at present. The stone rests on brick pillars about a foot high, horizontally of course. I do not know where I *could find a copy of Dr. Alderman's address—I never had the pleasure of reading it.*

*Mrs. Strudwick and Mr. Watters say that Hyrn is the proper spelling of the name.*

*Dear Cousin, I would love so to see you, I wish you would come to Hillsboro—for I think you would find it pleasant here—and I'm not such a meek christian as to wait willingly till I get to heaven to enjoy things that I might as well have here. So please when you must move again consider this place. We were all interested in the Alderman Installation.*

*Where is dear Cousin Helen now? And how is Julia getting on?*

*I hope your dear children are well & prosperous—that you may have at least that comfort in the great trial of separation from them.*

*It is late & I must close—*

*Lovingly as ever yours,*
*Margaret Norwood*

Materials in this sketch are from Old Town Cemetery Records; Thomas Felix Hickerson, *Echoes of Happy Valley* (Chapel Hill, 1962), pp. 70–78; St. James Parish Hist. Records, 1737–1852; W.N. Tillinghast Papers, Ms. Collection,, Perkins Library, Duke Univ.; and John De Bernière Hooper Papers, So. Hist. Collection, UNC, Chapel Hill.

## ROBINA (ROB) NORWOOD
July 18, 1835–December 24, 1919
Hillsborough, North Carolina

Robina (Rob) Norwood, born July 18, 1835, was the second daughter and fourth child of Hillsborough lawyer John Wall Norwood (1803–85) and Annabella Giles Norwood (1805–76) of Wilmington. The Norwood home was the James Hogg home known as Poplar Hill on the south bank of the Eno. All three Norwood girls, Annabella, Robina, and Margaret, attended the Burwell School as day students.

Robina or Rob, sometimes called Robbie, probably entered the school in 1849 or 1850. All student references to her express warm friendship and genuine admiration for the lively schoolgirl Rob.

Miss S.C. Ray wrote to John A. Tillinghast, July 1, 1851,

*What is Rob doing with herself? Is she as lively as ever? Tell her I*
*say she must conclude to go to school next session, that I cannot do*
*without her in the French class.*

Mary H. Pearce on November 1, 1851, mentioned to her cousin
William Tillinghast Rob's ambitious program for self-improvement,
something Mrs. Burwell championed vigorously for every girl:

> *I think Rob will be an uncommonly smart young lady if she*
> *continues in her present course for she devotes a regular part of*
> *every day to reading, another to practising on the piano, a third*
> *to sewing, and then, she says, has a plenty of time to take exercise*
> *and enjoy herself in any way she pleases. I think this is a sure way*
> *of improving herself.*

The Historic Hillsborough Commission now owns a handsome
white centerpiece with a graceful design of convolvulus vines and
flowers beautifully embroidered by Rob, proof that her program
achieved results.

*Robina Norwood Webb.*

On November 16, 1854, at the age of nineteen, Rob married her
cousin Thomas Webb (Nov. 2, 1827–May 29, 1894), the youngest son

of Dr. James Webb and Annie Alves Huske Webb. Both young people were direct descendants of Scotsman James Hogg: Robina through her grandmother, James Hogg's youngest daughter, Robina Hogg Norwood, and Thomas Webb through his mother, Annie Alves Huske Webb.

Thomas Webb had graduated from UNC in 1847 with an AB, and he also took an MA in 1851. He has been described as a handsome young man, very well read, and extremely able. For a few years the young couple lived at Poplar Hill; eventually Thomas Webb formed a law partnership with his father-in-law, John Wall Norwood. The firm of Norwood & Webb established itself in a handsome columned Greek Revival office (now gone) on Court Street and did a flourishing business throughout the countryside.

About 1860 the Thomas Webbs moved to the old Webb-Long House at 117 E. Queen Street, part of which had once been Miss Mary W. Burke's log schoolhouse. Nine children were born to them, seven of whom survived to adulthood:

1. Margaret Taylor, Sept. 22, 1855–1939; m. Andrew D. Mickle.
2. John Norwood, May 25, 1858–1934; m. Katherine Pratt.
3. Annabella Giles, Sept. 10, 1860–Feb. 8, 1935; unmarried.
4. Benjamin Huske, July 6, 1863–July 7, 1866.
5. Alves, Dec. 24, 1865–1924; m. Cora C. Girdler.
6. James H., Aug. 23, 1868–May 23, 1927; m. Annie Hudgins Bond.
7. Thomas H., Mar. 5, 1871–1939; m. 1) Isabella D. Graham, 2) Louise Cross Robson.
8. Robin, May 24, 1874–Mar. 27, 1941; unmarried.
9. Eliza Plumer, Oct. 29, 1876–Mar. 26, 1877.

Throughout the Civil War Thomas Webb did arduous service for the highly essential North Carolina Railroad of which he was president. The Red Cross established itself in the Norwood & Webb Law Office, and Thomas Webb served also as Treasurer of the Soldiers' Fund. In the 1870s he suffered a severe paralytic stroke, possibly caused in part by the heavy duties of the Civil War years. At the same time his wife, Robina, was immobilized with inflammatory rheumatism. For eighteen years Thomas Webb was an invalid. He died at the age of sixty-seven on May 29, 1894. Robina lived to be eighty-four and died on

December 24, 1919, twenty-five years after her husband. Both are buried in the Webb-Long plot in the Old Town Cemetery, as are four of their children: Annabella Giles, "Bennie," Robin, and Eliza Plumer. Another son, James H. Webb, is buried in St. Matthew's Episcopal Churchyard.

Materials in this sketch are from the W.N. Tillinghast Papers, Ms. Collection, Perkins Library, Duke Univ.; Hillsborough Cemetery Records; and a biographical sketch of Thomas Webb by Mena F. Webb. The picture of Robina Norwood Webb was contributed by Miss Louise Webb, Concord, N.C.

## SARAH (SALLY) E. NUNN
### 1838– ?
### Orange County, North Carolina

Sarah (Sally) E. Nunn was the granddaughter of the well-known Orange County pioneer settler William Nunn, Esq., originally from Dobbs County, North Carolina, who took out an early land grant north of Hillsborough, owned a tavern (Nunn's Tavern) on Lot 26, opposite the first courthouse, and served as one of Hillsborough's first Town Commissioners. His first wife was Elizabeth Loftin; his second was Elizabeth (Betsy) Copeland of the Hawfields, who later became the famous, long-lived "Betsy Nunn" of Chapel Hill tavern fame. William Nunn's children by his second wife included David H., Hugh, Ilai W., Sally, and Edith (Edy).

Sarah (Sally) E. Nunn, the Burwell School student, was the eldest child of Ilai W. Nunn (b. 1793) and Emily Stuart Barbee Nunn (b. 1815), daughter of William and Shastria Barbee, and granddaughter of early settler Christopher ("Old Kit") Barbee. Sally Nunn, therefore, was descended from two of Orange County's best-known pioneer figures.

Ilai W. Nunn was known about the countryside as a violinist and something of a dancing-master. The Nunns lived north of Chapel Hill in the Nunn's Mountain area. The 1850 census lists the Ilai W. Nunn family thus:

Ilai W. Nunn—age 57, farmer, $3,075. property,
   born Orange Co.
Emily Nunn—age 35
Sarah Nunn—age 12
William Nunn—age 10
Willis Nunn—age 8
Laura Nunn—age 5

All the Orange County Nunns have traditionally been Presbyterians, and the Burwell School would for various family reasons have been the logical place for Ilai Nunn to have sent his daughter. Sally was probably a student there ca. 1850 or 1851. Her name appears in the 1848–51 catalogue as "Sally Nunn . . . Orange."

On October 26, 1857 (when Sally was nineteen years old), a marriage bond was recorded for Sally E. Nunn and dentist David A. Robertson (witnessed by D. C. McDade and J. B. McDade). On November 10, 1865, David A. Robertson undertook to purchase, for $3000, Lot 78 and two portions of Lot 77 on E. Queen Street together with the one-story dwelling-house long known as "Old Yaller," which the Robertsons briefly occupied. Paul C. Cameron came to the Robertsons' rescue when they found they could not meet their obligations, and in 1868 they deeded the property to Cameron, who renovated it thoroughly and then advertised it in the *Hillsborough Recorder* of November 18, 1874:

### FOR SALE

*In the Town of Hillsboro, a neat well-built Cottage of 6 rooms with fireplaces, Kitchen, Servants' House, Stables, Garden, and Well. The health and high grade of Schools make this a most desirable location to a person desirous of educating sons or daughters.*

The house was later markedly enlarged to become known as the James A. Cheek or Houston J. Walker House.

The *Recorder* carried notices of Dr. David Robertson's dental practice for many years. Descendants still live in Hillsborough.

Information for this sketch is from Marriage Bonds of Orange Co., p. 298, and 7th Census of U.S., 1850, Orange Co., N.C. (No. 105).

## ELIZA PALMER
Hillsborough, North Carolina

Eliza Palmer was the daughter of James M. Palmer of Hillsborough and Sophia Lutterloh Palmer, daughter of well-to-do Gen.
Charles Lutterloh of Chatham County. James M. Palmer was one of
the three sons of the widow Mrs. Mary A. Palmer, who died on December 7, 1840. (Her tombstone in St. Matthew's Episcopal Churchyard
bears only one line, however, "Mother of J.M. Palmer.")

James M. Palmer was popular and well-liked in the Hillsborough
community. He was chosen as a Town Commissioner in 1835 and held
various positions of trust; but he seems also to have had a talent for
losing money in ill-starred ventures. One of these, a newspaper scheme,
seems fortunately to have come to nothing. In 1843 he announced plans
to publish a new area paper, to be called the *Orange Democrat,* as soon
as 250 subscribers were secured; but there is no record that an issue
ever appeared.

In 1846 the Palmers purchased and moved into the charming
Carleton Walker House on Lot 19 at 173 W. Margaret Lane. Sophia
Lutterloh was a member of a large family who lived lavishly and easily,
and it is clear that the James M. Palmers lived considerably beyond their
income from the beginning.

Eliza Palmer probably enrolled in the Burwell School as a day
pupil in the late 1840s or early 1850s. Her name appears in the *Burwell
School Catalogue of 1848–51.* She undoubtedly took courses in music, since
her pianoforte is listed in legal records. On January 12, 1856, Mrs. Burwell wrote to her daughter Fanny in New York: "Eliza Palmer has gone
to St. Mary's, to be <u>polished,</u> I suppose."

Even as early as 1853 Gen. Lutterloh had to come to the
Palmers' financial rescue. Deeds books in the Orange County Register
of Deeds office preserve ample evidence of all the financial juggling
necessary to secure the house and lot on Margaret Lane "to the sole
and separate use of the said Sophia Palmer." Virtually all of James M.
Palmer's property, including his daughter Eliza's "Pianoforte," was
conveyed in trust to his brother Nathaniel J. Palmer of Caswell County.

James M. Palmer served as postmaster for four years from
August 27, 1853, to September 16, 1857, and as mayor from May 1856
to June 2, 1857. Financially, however, he was walking a tightrope during

these years, for Nathaniel J. Palmer had died in 1854, and his heirs and executors were settling his estate. By July 30, 1865, James M. Palmer and his wife were living in Wayne County, North Carolina, and on that date conveyed their former home on Margaret Lane to James S. Watson.

It is interesting to speculate on the contrast Eliza Palmer must have observed daily between her extravagant home life and the Presbyterian simplicity of the Burwell School regime. (Note: The Palmers' house on Margaret Lane is included today in the Historic District and the National Register as the Walker-Palmer House.)

Sources include Orange Co. Courthouse records: DB 32, 48 (Jan. 29, 1846); DB 34, 249 (Nov. 1, 1852); DB 34, 246–49 (Mar. 21, 1853); DB 34, 344 (Sept. 13, 1853); DB 34, 309–10 (Sept. 15, 1853); Will of Nathaniel J. Palmer, Caswell Co., probated Jan. term 1855; DB 35, 148–49 (Apr. 5, 1856); DB 37, 124–25 (July 30, 1863); and Mrs. Burwell's letters, Records Room, Burwell School.

## JANE REBECCA PARKER
August 18, 1839–March 30, 1869
Hillsborough, North Carolina

Jane Parker, as she is entered in the *Burwell School Catalogue of 1848–51*, was orphaned almost at birth. She was the daughter of the William Nelsons' only child, Jane Rebecca Nelson (Apr. 18, 1819–Sept. 8, 1839), and David Parker, Jr. (1814–Nov. 11, 1841). Her mother died a few weeks after Jane's birth and is buried in Hillsborough's Old Town Cemetery in one of the three crypts behind the Presbyterian church. Her young father, who came from the Bahama (or Round Hill) community near Flat River, died on November 11, 1841, aged twenty-seven, when Jane was a little over two years old.

Jane appears to have been reared by her Hillsborough grandparents, William and Elizabeth Nelson, and perhaps by her great-aunt, Jane Nelson, who lived nearby. William Nelson, appointed Jane's legal guardian, was a dry goods merchant in Hillsborough whose name appears in various partnerships, but whose character is something of a puzzle. When Jane's grandmother, Elizabeth Nelson, died at the age of fifty-one on July 10, 1850, the little girl was nearly eleven years old.

It is possible that her grandfather could have sent her to the Burwell School as early as 1845 or possibly even earlier, but it seems clear she was always a day student. The Nelson & Parker Account Book, Vol. 6, in the Southern Historical Collection, UNC, records money paid to Robert Burwell for "Miss Jane R. Parker" in August 1851, and the 1850 census records that she was then living in William Nelson's household.

In 1854, however, her grandfather entered into a partnership with John C. Shields to operate the Alpha Woolen Mills on the Eno River some six miles downstream from Hillsborough, and it may be that he maintained a small house there. At any rate Jane Parker made a new friend, Julia Shields, and fell in love with a young man, Robert Harrison Harris, actually a first cousin once removed, from Bahama.

Although nothing is known of Jane's relationship with her Presbyterian grandfather, the fact is that on the morning of August 7, 1856, she mounted a horse behind Robert Harris at Eno and rode off on the spur of the moment, without any clothing, save the garments she had on, to be married at South Lowell by the Rev. John A. McMannen. Six days later she sent this letter to her friend Julia Shields:

*Aug. 13th 1856*

*Dearest Julia*

*As I promised to write to you I will fulfill my promise for never can I forget your kindness to me and I ever will remember you with the warmest love for I believe that you are my friend. After I left you Thursday morning I thought about you a great many times. We got to Mr. McMannens about 1 oclock and were married there by Mr. Mc then we come on home and have been to see some of our friends. There has been a meeting going on at South Lowell for 2 or 3 days. I have attended evry day with the dresses of one or two of my friends and also a bonnet which is loned. I tell you Sunday I cut a shine with my white swiss dress and black lace mantle and white hair bonnet. I walked as large as if they were mine but no one did not know any better. The camp meeting is going to be at New Bethel soon it commences the 29 of this month you must be sure to come and tent with us I would be so glad to see you. It is cloudy and raining here to day we will make something to eat down here I think for it has been raining yesterday and today in a hurry last night it poured all night. I am as happy as possible love Mr. Harris better than ever but I can hardly say Mr. Harris yet I never knew how good I loved him till now yes I love him too well but no better than he loves me he sends his best respects to you. You*

*must be sure to come down as I want him to get better acquainted
with you for I know you will like each other. Julia please send me
my clothes put them all in my trunk as they are scattered about
Becky has got some of them please pack them all up and send them
to me send me both my bonnets you can put them in the same Box
and I will do as much for you some day give the keys to Mr.
Parrish as he will bring my clothes to me. You must burn this as
soon as you read it for I am in such a hurry I do not know hardly
what I am writing but you must excuse it this time and I will do
better next time do not let any person see this letter. You must be
sure to write often and come to the Camp Meeting. Give my love to
all and tell them to come. Be sure to send me all my clothes.*

*Your affectionate Friend
Jane R. Harris*

Whatever the reason for Jane's elopement, she did enclose a
brief impersonal note to her Grandfather Nelson on the fourth page
of Julia's letter.

*Jane Rebecca Parker Harris.*      *Robert Harrison Harris.*

Jane and Robert Harris eventually settled in a small house (still
standing) at the end of Jock Rd., Bahama. They had three small boys by
the time the Civil War began:

1. David D., Aug. 24, 1857–Apr. 8, 1932.
2. W. Henry, Mar. 10, 1859–Dec. 9, 1886.
3. Charles, 1861– ?

Jane's picture, taken about this time and owned by her granddaughter, Mrs. Clifton Ball, shows her, as researcher Jean Bradley Anderson remarks, to be "a pretty young woman with a steely and determined look in her eyes, a direct and forthright gaze."

Jane died of pneumonia on March 30, 1869, when she was twenty-nine years old. She is buried in Mt. Bethel Cemetery at Bahama with Robert (who died in 1892) beside her in an unmarked grave, and two of their sons, David and Henry, to her left.

Materials were collected by Jean Bradley Anderson (Mrs. Carl Anderson) of Cabe Ford Rd. who interviewed Jane Parker's granddaughter, Mrs. Clifton Ball of Bahama, and acquired copies of Mrs. Ball's pictures of Jane and Robert. The commission has in its files a 19-page account of the Harrises, written by Mrs. Anderson. Jane Harris's letter is in the John Couch Papers, Ms. Collection, Perkins Library, Duke Univ.

## MARIA L. PARKS
Hillsborough, North Carolina

Maria Parks appears to have been the daughter of James R. Parks (Feb. 23, 1812–Feb. 10, 1902) and his wife, Maria A. Parks (Sept. 6, 1815–Feb. 17, 1895), also the parents of

1. David C., 1834–1917.
2. Charles M., 1841–1922.
3. William F., 1850–1915.
4. Annie, 1857–1931; m. D.C. Parris.

David C. Parks and his brother Charles were much involved in the purchase of Hillsborough lots and the renovation of various houses, including the former Burwell School. Maria L(ouisa?) Parks may have been born c. 1836 or 1837 and would have attended the school in the closing years of the forties and early fifties. The Orange County

Marriage Bonds (p. 355) list her marriage to W. B. Routon (Wilson B. Rowton) as having been issued on January 24, 1860, and her marriage by L.K. Willie (bondsman and J.P.) as having taken place the same day. George Laws witnessed the ceremony.

## ANNIE BLOUNT PEARCE
### 1842– ?
### Hillsborough, North Carolina

Annie Blount Pearce was born apparently in Virginia in 1842. She was the daughter of the Rev. Samuel Pearce, a native-born Englishman of either Berkshire or Truro in Cornwall (sources differ). Pearce was born about 1809, came to the United States at an early age, lived in Virginia, became a Methodist minister (in the 1830s?), and married a North Carolinian named Mary Blount, who was two years his senior. Their daughter Ann (or Annie) was born in 1842 shortly before the Rev. Pearce was appointed to the Hillsborough charge (i.e., to the frame First Methodist Church on E. Tryon Street).

In 1848 the Rev. Pearce appears to have given up his pastorship in favor of the Rev. William M. Jordan and to have embarked on several money-making ventures of an academic nature. He advertised in the *Hillsborough Recorder* on December 20, 1848, that he was opening a school "in that pleasant dwelling known as the residence of the late Mrs. Watters" (i.e., the Nash-Hooper House) and that he would accommodate a few boarders. His school, it might be conjectured, may have been run on the lines of Mrs. Burwell's well-known school to which the Pearces sent their daughter, Annie. *Burwell School Catalogue of 1848–51* carries Annie Pearce's name, and she may have been enrolled there in 1850 (when she was only eight) or any of the years immediately thereafter. It seems likely that she attended her father's short-lived school in 1848 and 1849 and thereafter attended the Burwell School.

The Rev. Pearce was interested in maps and globes, and as early as 1852 began to plan a map of North Carolina, which was published in 1857 with Wm. D. Cooke, but with only Cooke's name on it. Rev. Pearce "after 10 years of toil and expense" published his own map as "Pearce's New Map of the State of North Carolina" in 1866. There were also other impressions in 1871, 1872, and 1873 (under Alfred Williams's name). It is worth noting that Charlotte and Raleigh papers, in obituaries of the Rev. Pearce published on January 1, 1879, praised his map as the best ever done of North Carolina.

Annie Pearce was listed in the 1860 census as a teacher, aged seventeen, although there is no indication as to where she taught. On January 20, 1863, at the age of twenty-one, she married as his second wife Hillsborough speculator James W. Turrentine. He purchased for his bride Lot 30 and the comfortable home on it, now known as Seven Hearths. He aided in buying the house next door on Lot 29 as a home for the Pearces. The lot was bought in Mary A. Pearce's name to protect it from Rev. Pearce's debts. On April 15, 1870, the Pearces sold their home to the Thomas D. Tinnen family and left Hillsborough. Rev. Pearce died in Charlotte of paralysis at the age of sixty-nine on December 25, 1878. James W. Turrentine continued his speculations in Hillsborough properties for a number of years. There are no marked graves in Hillsborough for James W. and Annie Blount Pearce Turrentine.

Data in the above sketch is from the *Hillsborough Recorder* (June 12, 1861 [shows death of first wife]; Jan. 28, 1863); Orange Co. Deeds Books; biographical notes on Samuel Pearce, by George Stevenson, N.C. Div. of Archives & History; and Orange Co. Marriage Bonds.

## MARY (HUSKE) PEARCE
Fayetteville, North Carolina

Mary (Huske) Pearce of Fayetteville was a student at the Burwell School in 1851 and perhaps earlier, but did not return for the spring session of 1852. Two of her surviving letters, preserved in the W. N. Tillinghast Papers, picture a warm-hearted, highly intelligent girl, bent on improving herself as Mrs. Burwell urged all Burwell girls to do.

Her letter of September 27, 1851, written from the Burwell School to her cousin William Tillinghast, states that they cannot get "novels or tales" to read at the Burwell School, so she has turned to reading history, "Maria Antoinette, for example."

> *I believe you have an idea that I do not take exercise enough, so I will try to clear myself on that point by telling you—that on each of*

*these cool mornings, while some of the girls were huddling around the fire, I have been running up and down the hill several times, which kept me warm the whole day. And when it is too warm for that, I always take exercise in the evening by walking about.*

*We now have to write compositions every week, and I know you would feel sorry for me, if you knew how difficult it is for me, especially as we have to write something imaginative, and I am nearly exhausted of subject, substance, and everything else.*

*Cousin Ben Huske has thirteen scholars. Armstead [sic] Burwell goes to him, and is always very careful about preparing his lessons, getting to school on time, &c. He says, "Mr. Huske makes us walk a chalk line"; and I believe he is generaley considered as being pretty strict.*

*I expect you will be glad to hear we have changed our French teacher. Miss Molly Burwell now fills Miss Kollock's place, and is much more gentle. I never knew how well I loved Miss Sarah, until now that I am seperated [sic] from her. She is in Oxford, and I am really anxious to see "La petite" as we called her.*

Mary adds that she has received a little pen-knife (in Sarah C. Ray's bundle) which she presumes is a gift from W.N.T.:

*All the Fayetteville girls are well and in good spirits, Lucy Gilchrist sends her <u>love</u> to you, and Sarah her <u>respect</u>.*

> *Your affectionate cousin,*
> *Mary H. Pearce.*

Another letter of November 1, 1851, to William Tillinghast describes Robina (Rob) Norwood's self-improvement program with considerable admiration:

*. . . I had the pleasure of seeing Miss Bell and Rob Norwood, Miss Bell Young [Yonge], and Cousin Ben Huske last night. They were invited to hear the girls play, and seemed to be in fine spirits. Miss Bell N___ looked very pretty, as usual, and Rob was as lively as ever. I am much pleased with Miss Bell Young's [Yonge's] appearance and think she must be a very fine young lady. Mag Norwood has been sick this week, but Rob said she was a good deal better, & would be able to come to school next week. I think Rob will be an <u>uncommonly</u> smart young lady if she continues in her present course for she devotes a regular part of every day to reading, another to practising on the piano, a third to*

*sewing, and then, she says, has a plenty of time to take exercise*
*and enjoy herself, in any way she pleases. I think this is a sure*
*way of improving herself.*

*We took a walk of about two miles the other evening to see*
*the <u>railroad</u>, which I know you will be glad to hear, is progressing.*
*They have a considerable way raised to the same height, though*
*a great deal more work is necessary to make it sufficiently even.*
*It runs through Mr. Norwood's wheat field, where the young wheat*
*is just peeping above the ground, and we left it at the foot of a*
*tremendous hill, which it seems almost impossible to cut down,*
*though I hope industry and perseverance will be able to effect it.*
*The road is now as solid as our Plank-Road, so planks would not*
*be necessary had we the Hillsboro clay, which you see is of <u>some</u>*
*perceptible use, after all. The Hillsboro people seem to take a good*
*deal of interest in the work; a good many were walking upon it,*
*while we were there—more young men indeed, than I thought the*
*town afforded, and I believe, they expect it to be finished in three*
*years. Cousin Ben [Huske] made a promise last night of giving*
*the boys holyday, <u>when</u> the railroad whould be finished, and seemed*
*to consider it a very safe one, but Armstead Burwell,*
*I believe, thought himself certain of it in a very short time.*

*We had a picnic on the mountains, some time ago, though I*
*think it was since I wrote to you. We were assembled in the school-*
*room as usual, not even suspecting we were to have holydays, when*
*Mr. B. entered and told us we could go to the mountain, if we*
*wished. I can tell you we quickly concluded, (as one of the girls*
*remarked) that "unexpected pleasures were better than unknown*
*quantities," and joyfully assented. We spent a delightful day—*
*took our dinner, sitting on the grass around the Mountain Spring*
*—quite romantic. Was it not? We went to the Panther's Den,*
*which I suppose you have often visited. You remember the dripping*
*rock near it. I think it is beautiful—more so than I can express—*
*indeed the whole scenery is lovely.*

William Tillinghast wrote from Fayetteville to his brother John
at Oaks on February 2, 1852,

*I suppose Sister told you that Miss S___ Ray had gone to Cheraw*
*[to her "Uncle Coit's"] and that Mary P[earce] had remained in*
*Louisburg. We are all very sorry to lose our belles; but it is so*

*much better for Mary to be away from home (how miserable a situation)—*

Mary Pearce's "miserable situation" appears to have been that her brother(?) Tom Pearce had become mentally deranged. The Tillinghast Papers mention also a Mr. Samuel Pearce and "Cousin Nan" Pearce who may or may not have been Mary's parents (letter of Sept. 6, 1850, from Thomas H. Tillinghast to John H. Tillinghast, Bethmount [Oaks], Orange County.). The Tillinghast Papers indicate that Mary Pearce finished school at Louisburg, North Carolina, with flying colors.

Materials are from the W.N. Tillinghast Papers, Ms. Collection, Perkins Library, Duke University.

## MARGARET (MAG) POINTER (or PORTER)
Person County, North Carolina

Margaret (Mag) Pointer of Person County attended the Burwell School during the Spring Session of 1856 and perhaps longer. Mrs. M.A. Burwell's letters to Fanny contain a few fleeting mentions of her. On February 4, 1856, she wrote,

> *Since I wrote three girls have come Hariet Brooks, Miss Williams & Miss Pointer—these last are very nice girls. Cornelia Williams is the image of Mary Jefferies—only prettier. Mag P__ has only one eye—but is smart & seems amiable & lady like.*

On February 16, 1856, Mrs. Burwell wrote to Fanny,

> *The girl who stopped Music is that Miss Pointer with one eye. She took three lessons & could not learn the notes, got discouraged & quit very much to Mr. Hunt's delight, I believe.*

Note: There is a possibility that this student's name was Margaret Porter. Mrs. Burwell's handwriting is sometimes puzzling when she was tired and very cold. (*See also* ___ Horner.)

## MARY ANNE PRIMROSE
### September 13, 1826–February 1, 1916
### New Bern, North Carolina

Mary Anne Primrose, born in New Bern on September 13, 1826, is one of the very early documented Burwell students. She was always called by her full name, Mary Anne, since "Mary" and "Anne" were both established family names. Her forebears were early settlers of Bath and New Bern. She was the daughter of Robert Stuart Primrose, born in Kilmarnock, Scotland (b. Oct. 15, 1782; d. Dec. 6, 1856, New Bern), and Anne Stephens Primrose (b. Mar. 12, 1802, New Bern; d. Apr. 13, 1863, Salisbury—she had refugeed in Salisbury with her daughter-in-law when Federal forces occupied New Bern).

Two of Mary Anne's brothers married Burwell School girls: Robert Stuart Primrose (Jr.) married Sarah (Sally) Attmore; and Cicero Stephens Primrose married Mary Snead Chapman.

Mary Anne, then aged fourteen, was evidently in attendance at the Burwell School for the fall session of 1840 which began on July 13 (*Hillsborough Recorder,* June 11, 1840), for Robert Primrose's name is given for the first time as a reference in the *Recorder* advertisement of May 20, 1841. Moreover, two extremely valuable letters to Mary Anne survive—one from her father, dated August 14, 1841; the other from her grandfather, Marcus Cicero Stephens, dated November 7, 1841. Both letters are concerned with the theory of women's education, but that of Stephens is remarkable for its judgment and balance.

Mary Anne was a dark-eyed, serious-looking girl. She came to the school just when the new frame schoolhouse was being completed to the north of the Burwells' dwelling house and was perhaps one of the early students to have occupied it. Her granddaughter, the late Miss Alice Noble, wrote to the present compiler in 1965,

> *Mary Anne was undoubtedly talented and the training she received in school must have been thorough and inspirational. Her needlework was exquisite and her painting showed real ability—particularly china painting. Many surviving pieces of her handiwork are treasured by descendants.*

According to her grandfather's letter, Mary Anne took lessons in music, drawing, and French, besides her regular studies, so that many of her hours would have been spent in the Brick House. After his careful letter, Marcus Cicero Stephens added this note: "Learn to play and sing 'Highland Mary.' It is the sweetest thing I ever heard and should we ever meet, it will be the first tune I shall call for."

On November 18, 1850, at the age of twenty-four, Mary Anne Primrose married Albert Morris Noble (b. Amelia Co., Va., Dec. 20, 1823; died in Selma, N.C., July 11, 1903). Their son was the well-known educator and UNC professor Marcus Cicero Stephens Noble. Mary Anne also reared an orphaned niece, Mary Ellis (Min) Primrose. On November 18, 1900, Mary Anne Primrose and Albert Noble celebrated their golden wedding anniversary with an elaborate dinner-reception attended by many friends. On this occasion two granddaughters, one of whom was Alice Noble, wore dresses made from frocks in the trousseau of their grandmother Mary Anne Primrose.

*Mary Ann Primrose Noble.*

Mary Anne died in Selma on February 1, 1916, aged ninety years. She had been a widow since 1903.

Robert Stuart Primrose, a stern Scotsman and Presbyterian, wrote this letter from the Primrose home in New Bern to Mary Anne, enrolled in the Burwell School:

*August 14, 1841*

*Dear Daughter:*

*Your favor of the 2d Inst. annexing Mr. and Mrs. Burwell's report of your progress was duly received, and I assure you that it gives us all great pleasure to have received one so favorable and so much to your credit. We were aware of your deficiencies in grammar, but being fully satisfied, that ere another report is received, you will overcome this by your assiduity and attention to your studies. The only other part of your report that I will notice is that of disobedience, which is very small, but my dear child I sincerely trust by your future good behavior to your kind teachers that that word will not again be in any future report.*

*We are happy to hear that you have got well of your slight indisposition and that you will continue to enjoy your health, as any indisposition alarms your mother not a little, but any necessary complaint it is proper that you should inform us, for it is not to be expected that you will find at a boarding school all those little comforts which a father and mother can give you when at home, and it is your duty as well as your interest to keep all your clothes and books in regular and good order, and to consult your teacher, Mrs. B, about your clothes and even if she does scold I would be apt to fully excuse her for a dozen of rampant young girls would at times set the mildest temper a <u>scolding</u> so you must make allowance for they are doing everything for your advancement in knowledge which is to be hoped will be for your good, for you are told in your grammar that "modesty is a quality that highly adorns a woman," and it ought to begin with girls (say modestly) so we hope you will try to excel in your studies, and your general deportment to all, and let others do as they please, and beware of the idle and no care-girls, rather cultivate the acquaintance of the studious and intelligent girls from them you may learn something, but from the idle you can gain nothing—*

*Write regular once a fortnight for if you miss it causes great uneasiness with your mother, —I am*

*Dear Daughter*
*Your afft. Father*
*Robert Primrose*

Letter from M. C. Stephens, then of Quincy, Florida, formerly of New Bern, to his granddaughter, Mary Anne Primrose, while she was attending the Burwell School:

*Quincy, Fla., Nov. 7, 1847*

*My dear Child:*

*Your letter dated 27 Sept. at Hillsboro has been duly received, and gave me great satisfaction. As you are the only daughter of your parents it follows as a natural consequence that they are the more anxious for your improvement, and your letter to me affords the assurance that you will not neglect the opportunity now presented. You tell me you are taking lessons in music, drawing and French besides the usual studies, all this is very well a young woman ought to perfect herself in all the accomplishments she can, that she may in the first place render herself interesting and agreeable to others and moreover possess internal resources of pleasure and amusement in those moments of listlessness and apathy to which we are all more or less subjected.*

*While however you bestow all needfull attention to these accomplishments, don't neglect the higher branches of education— study History, Geography, and some of the best ethical writers with care and attention—this will greatly add to your stock of ideas, and enable you when occasion serves to take part in a rational conversation for nothing is so insipid as some young ladies I have seen, they have been asked to sing and play on some instrument or to exhibit their drawings to the visitors after doing which they retired to their seats and sit mumchanced until some dandy of a beau sidles up to them and talks of the weather or last ball or some such frivolities. Generally speaking, the women have not been treated with Justice by the male sex. It is true the rougher walks of life have very properly been destined to men, and the knowledge necessary for such purposes is also the peculiar study of man. But if the woman be inferior to the man in bodily strength, her mind is equally vigorous as his. The records of ancient and modern History set this matter beyond doubt and I have known several instances in private life where women have exhibited full as much courage, prudence and strong sense as any men in like circumstances.*

*The fact appears to be this, the men have entered into a kind of conspiracy to keep the women in the background—a prejudice has been excited against their improvement beyond a certain limit—the women have been cowed if I may so term it—for should she in her remarks on any subject of conversation show any superiority of intellect, she is instantly denounced as a bas bleu or blue stocking, and is avoided in a measure by both men and women. How ungenerous! It is true, there are fools of both sexes, who frequently annoy the company with scraps of learning, which they happen to pick up, the men are called pedants, the women blue stockings. I don't wish you to become the latter—store your mind well with useful knowledge and use such knowledge with prudence and discretion. A man may possess great bodily strength but it would be folly in him to rush into the streets and throw down everyone he might meet, merely to show his strength.*

*As I said above, gather as much usefull information as you can, increase your stock of ideas, and exercise a due discretion, and depend on it, tho' fools may shun you and make malicious remarks, your society will be sought and valued by persons of discriminating minds. Another thing I wish to inculcate, don't imagine that when you quit school, your improvement is finished, far from it—you then become your own instructress—the discipline of the Academy teaches you the use of the tools—points out the different routes of knowledge—from that moment all depends on your own industry and discretion. . . .*

*God bless you my dear Grandchild*

*M.C. Stephens*

*P.S. Learn to play and sing "Highland Mary." It is the sweetest thing I ever heard and should we ever meet, it will be the first tune I shall call for.*

The foregoing letter was received in Hillsborough by Mary Anne Primrose on Nov. 16, 1841. The photograph of Mary Anne Primrose and much of the data are from the documented Primrose family files of the late Miss Alice Noble, who also supplied the two 1841 letters of Robert Stuart Primrose and Marcus Cicero Stephens. (*See also* Sarah [Sally] Sitgreaves Attmore; Mary Snead Chapman.)

## SARAH C. RAY
### Fayetteville, North Carolina

Sarah C. Ray's letters, some of which are preserved in the W. N. Tillinghast Papers, indicate that she attended the Burwell School in 1851, but that she spent the spring session at her "Uncle Coit's" home at Rose Hill, near Cheraw, South Carolina. It seems probable, therefore, that her name may have been Sarah Coit Ray.

It was Sarah C. Ray, apparently, who influenced, Uncle Coit to send her cousin Elizabeth Coit to the Burwell School in January 1852. [Elizabeth died there on June 4, 1852.] Sarah's letters reflect good humor and vitality (evidently she was a charming girl), but not the perception and observation of a Mary Pearce. She wrote to John Tillinghast: "What is Rob [Norwood] doing with herself? Is she as lively as ever? Tell her I say she must conclude to go to school next session, that I cannot do without her in the French class."

Another letter from Sarah, still at her Uncle Coit's at Rose Hill, on February 28, 1852, to John Tillinghast, indicates her interest in the social life of her cousins and friends:

*I hear sad complaints of the weariness of study and their inability to fix their minds this session from many of my school friends, particularly the ones from Cumberland. By the way I heard from Cattie [Kate Murchison] a few days since. She says she is gratified that you desire to visit H—and if you will come to Mrs. Burwell's she will contrive to open the parlor door for you. She also desired her love when I wrote. But I suspect you have visited that attractive town before this, as I knew very well the reason you were so indifferent, was, that you had heard that the watered silk still graced Cumberland.*

Various Tillinghast letters indicate that Sarah C. Ray had caught the interest of young William N. Tillinghast. There is no indication that she returned to the Burwell School after the autumn session of 1851.

The *Raleigh Register* of April 6, 1859, reported Sarah Ray's marriage on March 29 to Archibald Graham in Cumberland County.

Letters from Miss Ray to John Tillinghast are from the W.N. Tillinghast Papers, Ms. Collection, Perkins Library, Duke Univ. (*See also* Elizabeth Coit, Mary H. Pearce.)

## [ SUSAN MARY RUFFIN
### January 6, 1827– September 18, 1851

Descended from two prominent North Carolina families— the Ruffins and Kirklands—Susan Mary Ruffin was the tenth of Chief Justice Thomas Ruffin and Annie M. Kirkland's fourteen children. She was born in Hillsborough on January 6, 1827, according to her mother's Bible. However, she lived most of her life in what is now Alamance County, after her parents moved in 1829 to Hermitage Plantation on Great Alamance Creek.

Her father, Thomas Ruffin, was the son of Sterling Ruffin and Alice Roane, both from prominent Virginia families. He began his legal career as a politician, then became an Orange County judge, and later a North Carolina Supreme Court justice. He retired from the bench about 1860, but continued to play an important role in local and state politics.

Thomas and Annie sent Susan to the Burwell School, where many of their friends' daughters (e.g., Frances Holt) also attended.

Susan married John W. Broadnax on October 17, 1848. Their marriage was announced in the *Hillsborough Recorder* on October 25, 1848: "Married—John W. Broadnax of Rockingham County, to Susan M. Ruffin, dtr. of Thomas Ruffin, in this county Tuesday 17th inst. by Rev. Dr. Dame."

Three years later, Susan died. Her obituary was printed in the September 24, 1851, edition of the *Hillsborough Recorder:* "Died—Mrs. Susan Mary Broadnax, wife of John W. Broadnax, dtr. of Chief Justice Ruffin, of Congestive fever the morning of 18th inst. at the residence of Robert Broadnax in Rockingham County, North Carolina. Not 3 years a wife. Left 2 infant children."

The two children were daughters. Susan's sister Alice moved into the household after Susan's death and cared for the children.    ]

[    **BETTIE SANDERS** (March 1, 1840–August 10, 1900)
&
**LAURA SANDERS** (1842–66)
Johnston County, North Carolina

Bettie and Laura Sanders were the daughters of Ransom Sanders (1787–1844), a planter and descendant of early 18th century settlers in what became Johnston County, and his second wife, Sarah Campbell (Jan. 17, 1814– ?). She was a daughter of James Campbell. Ransom Sanders was the son of Reuben and grandson of Hardy Sanders. The girls' names were actually Sarah Elizabeth and Lauretta W., but they were always called Bettie and Laura, as they were at the Burwell School, which they attended in 1856, the year before it closed.

In 1861 Laura married William S. Long of Caswell County, but she died at the age of twenty-four, perhaps in childbirth. Bettie married in 1868 the UNC graduate and physician Farquard Campbell Smith (May 8, 1839–Nov. 2, 1919), perhaps a relation on her mother's side. Farquard Smith's mother was Sarah Slocumb Grady and his father was another Farquhard (more usual spelling) C. Smith, a wealthy planter before the war and large landowner in Cumberland County where his ancestors had been among the earliest settlers on the Upper Cape Fear

River. Farquhard, senior, inherited from his father Lebanon Plantation where the Civil War battle of Averasboro took place. The house is now a historic site because of its Civil War use as a military hospital.

After Bettie and Farquard's marriage, they lived with her mother in Johnston County, probably because by then she was her mother's only surviving child. Bettie's brother Edwin had been killed in the war (as had many of Farquard's brothers) and her sister Laura was also dead. They eventually moved to Harnett County (formed from Cumberland in 1855) where his family land then lay. There he carried on an extensive medical practice for some fifty years. Family records give their children's names as Ross, Edwin, Laura, Douglas, Farquhard, Jane, and Bettie, who died as an infant in 1881. Farquard's and Bettie's graves lie with hers in Sardis Presbyterian Cemetery in Cumberland County.

Sources include the U.S. Census, 1850, 1860, 1870, Johnston Co., N.C.; U.S. Census, 1860, 1870, Harnett Co., N.C.; *The Heritage of Harnett County, North Carolina*, v. I (1993); *The Heritage of Johnston County, North Carolina* (1985); Sanders family information from John L. Sanders, Chapel Hill, N.C. ]

## EMMA JANE SCALES
November 26, 1835–March 8, 1904
Rockingham County, North Carolina

Emma Jane Scales was one of the handful of Burwell students who established and operated schools successfully. Her great-niece, Mrs. Irvin Jensen, wrote of Miss Emma Scales's background,

> *Emma J. Scales was born in Reidsville, November 26, 1835, the daughter of Dr. Robert [H.] Scales and Jane Watt Bethel Scales, died March 8th, 1904. She never married, had a brilliant mind and was active and attractive. Her brother, Governor Alfred Scales, frequently sought her advice. She owned and operated the Reidsville Female Academy (later Reidsville Seminary) for many years, very successfully. She was considered somewhat eccentric, kind, and most generous; she kept her philanthropies unknown as much as possible. She has many great-nieces and nephews living in Reidsville, Winston-Salem and Greensboro, one of whom is her namesake—Emily Preyer (Mrs. Richardson).*

John Wheeler's *Reminiscences and Memoirs of North Carolina and Eminent North Carolinians* gives this note concerning the forebears of Gov. Alfred Moore Scales:

> *Alfred Moore Scales [the brother of Emma] was born November 26, 1827 at Engleside, the old homestead in Rockingham Co. He is the son of Dr. Robert H. Scales, who married Jane W. Bethell. His grandfather, Nathaniel Scales, was for several years a member of the Legislature; his wife was named Annie Allen. The maternal grandfather was General William Bethell, also a member of the Legislature; his wife was Mary Watt.*

The *Alumni History of the University of North Carolina* gives this sketch of Gov. Alfred Moore Scales:

> *SCALES, ALFRED MOORE*         *Banker*
> *From Rockingham co.; Greensboro; b. Nov. 26, 1827; d. Feb. 9, 1892; s. 1845–46; LL.D. 1889; co. sol. of Rockingham co.; lawyer ; mem. house of c. 1852–56, 1866–69; mem. U.S. Cong. 1857–59 and '75–85; pres. elector, 1860; gov. 1885–89; brig. gen. C.S.A.; trustee, U.N.C. 1856–68.*

When Emma was a student at the Burwell School (apparently about 1849), most of her brother's distinctions and accomplishments still lay in the future. It seems likely that she met members of the Samuel W. Hughes family about this time. Sometime later Emma was to invite Samuel Wellwood Hughes's remarkable daughter, Miss Annie Savalette Hughes (Sept. 3, 1851–July 5, 1932), to become her co-principal in her Reidsville Female Seminary venture, thereby uniting the teaching traditions of two successful schools, the Hughes Academy and the Burwell School. Annie Hughes was seventeen years younger than Emma Scales, but she had been educated by her father in the old thorough-going way. The late Samuel Hughes of Hillsborough presented the Historic Hillsborough Commission with an 1885 flyer advertising the Reidsville Seminary. It lists Miss Scales and Miss Hughes as "Principals" of the seminary with one assistant, Miss Annie B. Scoffin. It is noteworthy that Miss Scales, like Mrs. Burwell, put special emphasis on spelling, reading, writing, and composition, but also offered Latin, French, and piano in an otherwise-Spartan curriculum. She even offered a special separate course in Mrs. Burwell's favorite book, Archbishop Richard Trench's *The Study of Words*.

Miss Emma Scales died on March 8, 1904, at the age of sixty-nine, and Miss Annie Hughes returned to Cedar Grove to take over the Cedar Grove Academy. The Reidsville Seminary had flourished for nearly half a century.

*The Reidsville Female Seminary.*

Biographical details in this sketch were contributed by Mrs. Sara Irvin Jensen, Reidsville, N.C.; the late Miss Alice Noble of Chapel Hill; and others. The late Mr. Samuel Hughes of Hillsborough contributed the flyer on the Reidsville Female Seminary. Information also is from *Alumni History of the University of North Carolina* (1924 ed.), p.547, and John Wheeler's *Reminiscences and Memoirs of North Carolina and Eminent North Carolinians,* p. 386.

## FRANCES (FANNY) A. SELLERS & ROSA SELLERS
### Sampson County, North Carolina

The Historic Hillsborough Commission to date possesses only a few scraps of information about the Sellers girls of Sampson County. Frances A. Sellers's name heads the list of students in the *Burwell School Catalogue of 1848–51*, and "Fanny S. of Clinton" signed her name on May

24, 1850, in Rob Norwood's autograph album, thus giving a definite date of when Fanny attended the Burwell School and suggesting that the Sellers family lived in or near Clinton. Rosa Sellers appears to have been a younger sister who attended the school somewhat later than Fanny.

Mrs. Burwell in a letter of February 8, 1856, to her daughter Fanny in New York deplored the way rumors get started and mentioned Rosa Sellers:

> *It just shows how people can get the wrong end of a story. Nothing tho' seems unaccountable to me since the "Brown ribbon" story\* the late Frank Sellers told of Rosa's being so abominably treated here as to excite the compassion of_____[page torn].*

"The late Frank Sellers" may have been Rosa's father or brother. No other mentions of the Sellers girls have been discovered.

\*A tale to the effect that Burwell students were required to wear brown ribbon bands around their necks to save laundering white collars.

## MARGARET SHEPARD
### New Bern, North Carolina

Margaret Shepard of New Bern, who attended the Burwell School in the late 1840s and is listed in the 1848–51 catalogue, was a student of exceptionally distinguished ancestry.

Her great-great-grandfather was Gov. Richard Dobbs Spaight, Sr. (1758–1802), who married Mary Leach, ca. 1795. Their son was Gov. Richard Dobbs Spaight, Jr. (b. New Bern, 1796–Nov. 2, 1850), governor of North Carolina from 1835 to 1837 and Margaret Shepard's great-grandfather. Gov. Spaight's daughter, Margaret, married Judge John Robert Donnell, judge of the North Carolina Superior Court from 1819–36 and UNC trustee for thirty-five years.

One of the Donnells' five children, Mary Donnell, married the Hon. Charles Biddle Shepard of New Bern (Dec. 5, 1808–Oct. 31, 1843). Charles B. Shepard took an AB at UNC in 1827 and received an MA in 1830. He served in the North Carolina General Assembly, 1832–33, and was a member of the U.S. Congress from 1837 to 1841. Charles

Biddle Shepard and Mary Donnell Shepard had two daughters: Margaret Shepard, who attended the Burwell School in Hillsborough and married Samuel S. Nelson, and Mary Shepard, who married James A. Bryan.

Information is from John Wheeler's *Reminiscences and Memoirs of North Carolina and Eminent North Carolinians* (Columbus, Oh., 1884), p. 139; and *Alumni History of the University of North Carolina* (1924 ed.), pp. 558, 582.

## ___SMITH
## & ___SMITH
## & FANNY SMITH
### Caswell County, North Carolina

Fanny Smith of Caswell County signed Robina Norwood's autograph album on May 24, 1850, and therefore may be assumed to have been enrolled in the Burwell School at that time. Her name also appears in the 1848–51 catalogue. She appears to have been the daughter of Richard Ivy Smith of Caswell, who took an AB at UNC in 1820.

Richard J. Smith, Esq., of Caswell is listed as a trustee of the Caldwell Institute in its *Catalogue of the Caldwell Institute 1848–49,* printed by Dennis Heartt, and it seems likely that the *J* is a misprint for *I,* a common error in Heartt's early catalogues. Thomas McGehee Smith of Milton, possibly Fanny's brother, was a Caldwell Institute student in 1848–49 when Fanny Smith was probably at the Burwell School.

On March 4, 1856, Mrs. Burwell wrote to her daughter Fanny,

> *Two new boarders have this moment come Fanny Smith's sisters nice <u>little</u> girls—so Farewell. . . .*

On March 10, she wrote,

> *The last girls who came Fanny Smith's sisters are just as good as she was—but tho' they are all <u>good</u> I find plenty more than enough to do.*

The commission has no further records of the Smith sisters of Caswell County.

Mrs. M.A. Burwell's letters are in the Records Room, Burwell School. Other information is from *Alumni History of the University of North Carolina* (1924 ed.), p. 577.

[ **ISABELLA SMITH** (1830–53)
&
**BETTIE SMITH** (1836–75)
&
**JULIA SMITH** (1835–94)
Cumberland County, North Carolina

Three Smith girls from Cumberland County are listed in the *Burwell School Catalogue of 1848-51,* but are otherwise unidentified. It seems likely they belonged to the prominent Smith family that settled early in the 18th century on the Upper Neuse River and then established itself along the Upper Cape Fear before the American Revolution.

Isabella and Bettie are names found in the family of Farquhard Campbell Smith (1801–71) of Lebanon Plantation. His daughters Isabella and Elizabeth E. were of the right ages to have been Burwell students in the late 1840s and early 1850s, respectively, and Elizabeth did use the nickname "Bettie." It appears on her grave marker. These sisters had a cousin Julia Smith (1835–94), eldest child of Farquhard's brother William Turner Smith, living in the same neighborhood and of the right age to be the third of the unidentified trio.

The probability that these Smith girls' were Burwell students is strengthened by the fact that Dr. Farqu[h]ard Campbell Smith, one of Isabella's and Bettie's nine brothers, married Bettie (Sarah Elizabeth) Sanders, another Burwell School student.

Isabella Smith attended Floral College near Red Springs, North Carolina. An uncharacteristically terse notation in the Smith family archive reports that she "died at graduation" at age twenty-three. There is no portrait or photo of her. All she left were several inscribed books, one of which still has a flower pressed within it. She is buried in a family cemetery near the site of a ferry that was operated by the Smiths from colonial times until near the end of the 19<sup>th</sup> century.

In her late twenties, Bettie Smith was living at Lebanon Plantation with her three surviving sisters and their youngest brother, as the Battle of Averasboro raged through Smithville in March 1865. The house itself was used as a field hospital during the battle and later as the headquarters of Union Gen. Henry W. Slocum. Bettie's sister Janie, who was eighteen years old at the time of the battle, wrote a famous account of the family's ordeal as Gen. William T. Sherman's army passed through Smithville.

In 1866, Bettie married Raiford Robeson, a Bladen County native who practiced medicine in Cumberland County. They were married in Bluff Presbyterian Church, which Bettie had attended from childhood, and made their home nearby. They had one child, Bessie, who died before age thirty unmarried. All three are buried at historic Bluff Presbyterian Church cemetery.

It is known that Julia J. Smith was for a while a student at St. Mary's School in Raleigh, which does not preclude her having spent a year or more at the Burwell School during the course of her schooldays. At least two other Burwell School students also went to St. Mary's School—Eliza Palmer and Mary Cameron Jones. (The latter returned to the Burwell School after a year, reportedly having learned nothing.)

Julia married Isaac Henry Williams in 1857. They had no children. Widowed while still a young woman, Julia returned to her mother's home and again became part of the life of Smithville, helping to memorialize Confederate battle casualties buried on family land in Chicora Cemetery, beside what is now N.C. Highway 82. Julia was co-founder of the group that acquired the property from her Uncle John. Julia herself is buried in the old family cemetery beside the Cape Fear.

Both Lebanon Plantation and the William T. Smith house still stand, as does Oak Grove (built about 1793), the birthplace of William and Farquhard Smith. The William T. Smith house, built in 1834, is now a state transportation museum. Only Lebanon, built in 1825, remains in the Smith family. It is on the Historic Register of Historic Places for its architecture and because the Battle of Averasboro was fought there.

After Bettie's death, Raiford Robeson married her sister Janie. After Janie's death, he married Julia Smith's younger sister Sarah. ]

*Bettie Smith Robeson.*

*Bettie's brother, Farqu[h]ard Campbell Smith.*

Information for this sketch and the photographs are courtesy of Gene Smith, Lebanon Plantation, Dunn, N.C.

## LOU SMITH
Fayetteville, North Carolina

Lou (Louella? Louisa?) Smith of Fayetteville, who was a Burwell student in 1855 and 1856, was apparently the daughter of Archibald Aaron Tyson Smith of Fayetteville who took an AB at UNC in 1831 and an AM in 1838.

Lou Smith, according to Mrs. Burwell's several mentions in her letters to Fanny in 1855 and 1856, seems to have been highly regarded by the Burwell family and to have had an especially friendly, affectionate relationship with Fanny. Lou Smith may have been at the Burwell School as early as 1852, for Mary Bailey Easley's autograph album contains an entry simply signed "Lou."

On December 29, 1855, Mrs. Burwell wrote to Fanny in considerable dismay,

> . . . *today Lou Smith wanted to know [in her letter] if it was a fact that we would take no more boarders, as such was the report in Fayetteville. Now what do you think will come next . . . she says she is coming back to school next session—spoke of having had a letter from you.*

On February 4, 1856, Mrs. Burwell wrote,

> *Lou Smith & Bettie Carrington have just been in to say Goodnight. They stood & talked so long that now I must hurry to a close. I sent them to Nan [Burwell] to look up some Jelly & Cream & I expect they will bring me some. Will you have some?*

On March 4, Mrs. Burwell notes at the end of a long letter,

> *Lou Smith has just come in sends love to you & says you owe her a letter.*

Evidently, Lou had known Fanny very well before her 1855 departure to New York to study music, and Lou was a prime favorite with the Burwell family.

The quotations above are in Mrs. Burwell's letters, Records Room, Burwell School. Data is also from *Alumni History of the University of North Carolina* (1924 ed.), p. 571.

## MARY SMITH &
## SARAH SMITH
Granville County, North Carolina

Mary and Sarah Smith of Granville County appear to have been the daughters of the Rev. Samuel Henry Smith of Granville who took his AB at UNC in 1821. Sarah Smith was a student at the Burwell School in 1845 (but is not listed in the school catalogue).

A letter of January 17, 1846, from Mrs. Burwell to her friends, the Misses Susan and Mary A. Kirkland, then visiting in Fayetteville, mentions Sarah as a student in the fall session of 1845:

> *Neither Sarah Smith nor Lavinia Allston have returned . . .*
> *we do not expect Lavinia but still think Sarah may come, as her*
> *Father said she would. People are so fickle "now a days" that we*
> *never know when we expect scholars.*

Mrs. Burwell's letter is owned by Mrs. Samuel Simpson Kirkland of Ayr Mount. Data is also from *Alumni History of the University of North Carolina* (1924 ed.), p. 577.

## JENNY (or JENNIE) SPEED
Granville County, North Carolina

Jenny (or Jennie) Speed of Granville County was a boarding student at the Burwell School in the spring session of 1852. Jenny's roommate, Elizabeth Coit of Cheraw, South Carolina, wrote to her sister on May 29, 1852,

> *Our session will soon be out. . . . five of our boarders went off this*
> *morning. two of them were my roommates Jennie Speed and Mary*
> *Wortham. . . .*

Both girls were from Granville. The Speed family was well known in northern Granville; Mary Wortham appears to have lived near Warrenton.

When Mrs. Burwell attended Maria Howerton's large wedding at the Union Hotel in Hillsborough on January 3, 1856, in the company of Mrs. Edmund Strudwick, she felt some coolness from Jenny Speed, which she mentioned in a letter to Fanny:

> *Jenny Speed was there waited with Mr. Hall. She did not come to speak to Mrs. S[trudwick]or myself, & Mrs. S. said she should not go to her, but I thought if there was any unkind feeling she might have it all to herself so I went up and spoke to her, but got only a very cool return, poor child.*

Mrs. Burwell noted in the same letter that "Mr. Speed, her father was very polite, came across the room to speak to me." Jenny, it would appear, was serving as a hostess or assistant of some sort at the Howerton-Norwood wedding supper and obviously resented some earlier incident that had involved both Mrs. Strudwick and Mrs. Burwell.

It may be that the early departure of Jenny Speed and Mary Wortham was extremely fortunate, since their roommate, Elizabeth Coit, died on June 4 in the 1852 epidemic.

Nothing further is known of Jenny (or Jennie) Speed.

Elizabeth Coit's letters (originals) and Mrs. Burwell's letters are from the Records Room, Burwell School.

## [ NANNIE (ANNA) TAYLOR SPEED
### 1836–1909
### Granville County, North Carolina

Nannie (Anna) Taylor Speed was the daughter of Francis E. Young and Dr. Edward Speed of Granville County. She was the first cousin of Jennie Speed. Like Jennie, Nannie attended the Burwell School in the 1850s.

The *Hillsborough Recorder* of November 24, 1858, reported her marriage: "Married—Addison Mangum to Nannie Taylor Speed, dtr.

of Dr. E. Speed of Orange County at South Lowell by Rev. Dr. Deems, 9th inst." Addison Mangum was the son of Ellison G. Mangum. Addison became a captain in the C.S.A., according to his tombstone.

According to the United States Census of 1870, Addison and Nannie had six children: Lily, Lizzie, Fanny, Nannie, Addison, and Grace. Also listed as residing in the Mangum household were Nannie's brother, Dr. Edward Speed, and various domestic servants.

Addison and Nannie lived in the Flat River area of what is now Durham County where Addison practiced law. His law office still stands on the grounds of the old homestead.

Addison died in 1907, and Nannie in 1909. They are buried in the Capt. Addison Mangum Cemetery on the east side of Lake Michie. ]

## ROSALINE (ROSA) BROOKE SPOTSWOOD
January 17, 1836–August 9, 1901
Petersburg, Virginia

Rosaline (Rosa) Brooke Spotswood of Petersburg, Virginia, was a closely related member of Mrs. M.A. Burwell's own family, the Spotswoods. She was the daughter of Dandridge Spotswood (b. 1789), a younger brother of Mrs. Burwell's beloved Aunt Bott (Susan Catharine Spotswood Bott), and of his wife, Catherine Brooke Francisco (b. 1801), daughter of the legendary strong man of the Revolution, Peter Francisco (1760–1831). Rosa was by direct descent a great-granddaughter of Gov. Alexander Spotswood, Kt. (1676–1740), the Royal Gov. of Virginia for twelve years (1710–22). Her father's marriage on October 29, 1818, to Catherine Brooke Francisco thus united two of Virginia's spectacular but diverse legends.

Mrs. Burwell was Rosa's cousin, a great-great-granddaughter of Gov. Alexander Spotswood, a situation which teacher and pupil undoubtedly resolved with finesse. Rosa's arrival at the Burwell School in Hillsborough in 1844 is described by her daughter, Ann Spotswood Strudwick Nash, in her book, *Ladies in the Making*: "My mother, eight years old and already studying Virgil, arrived there by stage coach from her home in Petersburg, Virginia." Ann S. Nash further mentioned to the present compiler that her mother together with other little girls in pinafores used to delight in rolling over and over down the long grassy incline to Churton Street, thus wearing out their pinafores prematurely and marking them with grass stains. So far as is known, Rosa Spotswood remained at the Burwell School throughout her entire course of study.

*Rosaline with her stepson, Robbie.*

Another Spotswood cousin wished to attend the school in 1856, but there was no available space. Mrs. Burwell wrote regretfully to Fanny on January 19, 1856,

> *Eliza Spotswood is very anxious to come here to school but Cousin Wm. says they cannot afford it. I do wish we had room we would send for her to come at once & let pay come when it could or never—it seems to me so all important that girls should have educations to qualify themselves to help themselves.*

Rosaline Spotswood on November 13, 1860, married, as his second wife, lawyer-planter Frederick Nash Strudwick (June 27, 1833–

July 29, 1890), son of Dr. Edmund and Ann Nash Strudwick, whose first wife had been Mary Burwell (d. July 3, 1859).

The Frederick Nash Strudwicks apparently settled down on the Strudwick plantation in Marengo County, Alabama. Rosa's first child, Kate Spotswood, was born in 1861 but died in 1865. Her tombstone in the Arcola Cemetery reads, "Kate Spotswood Strudwick, dau. of F.N. & R.B. Strudwick, died Arcola, Alabama, Sept. 22, 1865, in the fourth year of her age."

Eventually the Strudwicks came home to Hillsborough and settled at Meadowside (now the site of Daniel Boone Amusement Park), a 132–acre plantation purchased on February 6, 1872, for Rosaline Strudwick by her brother, William Francisco Spotswood of Petersburg, Virginia. The Strudwicks had one surviving child, Ann Spotswood Strudwick (Aug. 5, 1878–Sept. 20, 1969), a librarian and author (*Ladies in the Making*)—who was the second wife of lawyer-historian Frank Nash, later the Assistant Attorney General of North Carolina

Ann S. Nash gives a charming picture of life at Meadowside in *Ladies in the Making*. She also gives a brief insight into her mother's character:

> *. . . her dark eyes sparkled . . . the spirit of fun was part of her charm. "Darling," she said, "do not on any account suggest it [that there should be dinnertime prayers at the Nash & Kollock School]. I am sure that the only reason our blessed aunts fail to have family prayers for dinner, is that the possibility has not yet occurred to them.*

Rosaline Spotswood Strudwick, her husband, her daughter, Ann S. Nash, and Ann's husband, Frank Nash, all lie buried near each other in the Hillsborough Memorial Cemetery (the New Town Cemetery).

Information is from Genealogy and Letters of the Strudwick, Ashe, Young and Allied Families, compiled by Betsy Lawson Strudwick et al., 1971; Ann Strudwick Nash, *Ladies in the Making* (Hillsborough, 1964), pp. 14, 86; Mrs. M.A. Burwell's letters, Records Room, Burwell School; and *Colonial Families of the United States*, pp. 496–99. The photo of Robbie and his stepmother was given to the commission by Robbie's daughter, the late Mary Strudwick Berry of Greensboro, N.C. (*See also* Mary [Mollie] Susan Burwell.)

## ELIZA STEDMAN
### Fayetteville, North Carolina

Eliza Stedman of Fayetteville, listed in the *Burwell School Catalogue of 1848–51*, was apparently the sister of the Rev. James Owen Stedman of Fayetteville, who is listed in *Alumni History of the University of North Carolina* (p. 590) as having taken an AB degree in 1832. It is more than likely that after graduation he either taught or served a charge in the Hillsborough area; for on November 25, 1836, the *Hillsborough Recorder* published an announcement of the marriage on November 8, 1836, of the Rev. James O. Stedman and Margaretta B. Herbert, daughter of Isaac Herbert.

The 1848 catalogue lists the Rev. James O. Stedman of Wilmington as a Patron of the school. The Stedman family was well known in Fayetteville as substantial, devout Presbyterians. The Rev. Stedman evidently served as sponsor for his sister Eliza's attendance at the school.

## JANE ELLEN STEVENS
### November 28, 1823–April 7, 1909
### Sampson County, North Carolina

Jane Ellen Stevens must have been one of the very early students at the Burwell School. Jane Ellen was the daughter of Charles Stevens (1773–Aug. 21, 1845) of Clinton, Sampson County, and his second wife, Catherine Henry Stevens (Oct. 10, 1790– June 20, 1878) of New Hanover County, who married in 1821.

Jane Ellen's granddaughter, Annie M. Sutton, has supplied all of the information about Jane Ellen:

> *Her father lived on a plantation several miles from Clinton,*
> *Sampson County, and had a home in Clinton for winter living. . .*
> *I remember that she played the piano very well and spoke French*

*. . . . I have a copy of her father's wedding gift to her—a Xerox copy from the Courthouse—a number of slaves. Jane Ellen Stevens was married to Mr. James Kerr of Kerr, N.C., on June 5, 1845 [only a scant three months before her father's death].*

*. . . I have a picture of her taken probably in 1906, when I remember her, also a picture of a portrait of her and one of her husband painted soon after their marriage. I also have a picture of her home which is still standing at Kerr. She is buried there and the inscription on her stone reads:*

*JANE ELLEN STEVENS KERR*
*b. Nov. 28, 1823*
*d. Apr. 2, 1909.*

Mrs. Sutton's files give the following data on Jane Ellen Stevens's grandparents: James Henry (1750– Nov. 25, 1816) and Mary Murphy Stevens (1762–Feb. 25, 1819). "They lived near Kerr which was then in New Hanover, now Sampson County," Mrs. Sutton writes. She also lists William Stevens as a grandparent, but adds, "I have no other records of Wm.; there are probably records in the Courthouse in Clinton as he was the original settler there."

Information for the above sketch is from Mrs. Ivey James Sutton of Wilmington, N.C.

## ELIZABETH (LIZZIE) STEVENSON
### New Bern, North Carolina

Lizzie Stevenson of New Bern is listed in the *Burwell School Catalogue of 1848–51*, but research has thus far not located her with certainty.

Martin Stevenson, Sr., of New Bern is mentioned in records and reminiscences as one of the skilled mechanics and artificers of New Bern. His name occurs in connection with the construction of fine buildings, dwellings, and offices in which a good deal of ornamentation was called for.

Martin Stevenson's Will (1849) mentions a grandson, George S. Stevenson, whose Will (dated Aug. 7, 1858, probated 1861) names his "beloved wife Elizabeth J[erkins?] Stevenson" and Alonzo T. Jerkins as his trustees. There is no mention of a daughter, but it seems possible that Lizzie Stevenson, the Burwell student, might have been the daughter of George S. and Elizabeth J. Stevenson and the great-granddaughter of New Bern's master builder Martin Stevenson, Sr.

A single mention of Lizzie Stevenson at the Burwell School has come to light: Susan Murphy of Cuwhiffle Plantation, Sampson County, mentions in a letter to her father, Patrick Murphy, Esq., in a letter dated April 1849 that "Liza Stevenson is sick now." Lizzie, or Liza, was therefore a student in the spring of 1849 and apparently well known to the Murphys of Cuwhiffle.

Miss Elizabeth Vann Moore, Craven Co. researcher, supplied the information about the Stevenson Wills at the Craven Co. Courthouse. Susan Rose Saunders (Mrs. J. M. Saunders, Chapel Hill) supplied the information from Susan Moseley Murphy's letter.

## NARCISSA J. UNTHANK
? –March 6, 1873
Greensboro, North Carolina

The Quaker Unthank clan came early to the Core Sound region of North Carolina and then migrated west to Guilford County before the Revolution. They settled in the Kernersville–Oak Ridge area and may have attended a small Quaker meetinghouse there. They were well connected, and present-day Quakers know of the family and regard them highly.

Because of the Revolutionary disturbance, the Unthanks gradually left Guilford County for Indiana. There are apparently no Unthanks in North Carolina today, although many descendants by marriage still live in the Greensboro area.

Early settlers in Greensboro were Joseph and John Unthank. Allen Unthank, son of Joseph, in 1774 married Jemima Hunt. The Allen Unthanks had nine children, one of whom, William, married Rebecca Holt on March 3, 1820.

The Holts had various connections with Hillsborough—

e.g., on November 15, 1830, Joseph Norwood wrote to his sister Jane Tillinghast in Fayetteville that "Mrs. Unthank is to set off in the morning." This was in 1830, seven years before the opening of the Burwell School. It was, however, probably the Holt-Webb-Norwood connection that brought Narcissa Unthank to the Burwell School some years later.

It may be that William and Rebecca Holt Unthank were the parents of Narcissa (an unlikely name for a Quakeress). The *Greensboro Patriot* furnishes documentary proof of the later years of Narcissa's life:

| | |
|---|---|
| *Sept. 12, 1853* | *Narcissa Unthank married* |
| | *Jas. R. McLean* |
| *Apr. 12, 1871* | *Died–James R. McLean* |
| *Mar. 6, 1873* | *Died–Narcissa J.,* |
| | *w. of Hon. J. R. McLean* |
| *Aug. 7, 1875* | *Died–Willie, s. of Hon. J. R. McLean* |

[　　In a family history, *The McQuiston, McCuiston and McQuesten families, 1620–1937*, Narcissa (incorrectly named there Marcissa) and her brother, Rufus, are listed as the children of William Unthank and Sarah McCuiston of Greensboro. It also records Sarah's death on August 8, 1840, and her burial in the Quaker burying ground in the Guilford College Churchyard.

Sarah's death may explain why, according to the United States Census of 1850 for the So. Division of Guilford County, Narcissa and Rufus were living with the physician John A. Mebane and his wife, Cecelia F., probably close relations of Rufus and Narcissa. Dr. Mebane, originally from Orange County, was the son of Alexander Mebane, a Hillsborough politician. Dr. Mebane's nephew, Dr. Alexander Wood Mebane, sent his daughter Mary Mebane to the Burwell School in the 1850s, which may explain why Narcissa Unthank also attended.　　]

Much of the data in the foregoing note was collected by the late Miss Alice Noble of Chapel Hill. Joseph Norwood's letter of Nov. 15, 1830, is in the W.N. Tillinghast Papers, Ms. Collection, Perkins Library, Duke Univ.

# [ EMILY VANDERFORD
c. 1839– ?
Hillsborough, North Carolina

Emily Vanderford was the daughter of Sarah Williams and William Vanderford, a blacksmith in Hillsborough during the mid-19th century. She possibly married William B. Thompson in Guilford County, North Carolina, in 1864.    ]

# ISABELLA BROWN VENABLE
&
# MARTHA ELIZABETH VENABLE (1833–77)
Granville County, North Carolina

These two Burwell School students, Isabella Brown Venable and Martha Elizabeth Venable (1833–77), were the two youngest children of the Hon. Abraham (or Abram) Watkins Venable and Isabella Alston Brown Venable of Brownsville near Oxford, North Carolina. Both girls are listed in the *Burwell School Catalogue of 1848–51* and the Hon. A.W. Venable is also listed as "one of the gentlemen who have patronized the School."

Abraham Watkins Venable was born at Springfield, Prince Edward County, Virginia, October 14, 1799, and died February 19, 1876, at Brownsville, Oxford, Granville County. In 1824 he married Isabella Alston Brown, daughter of Thomas Brown, MD, originally of Scotland. Dr. Thomas Brown inherited by right of entail his family estate Auchlachen, Lanarkshire, Scotland, and returned there in 1838. A.W. Venable and his wife, Isabella Alston Brown, in the same year removed from Prince Edward County to live at Brownsville

A.W. Venable had taken an AB from Hampden-Sydney College in 1816, studied medicine for several years, took an MA at Princeton in 1819, and was admitted to the bar in 1821. There followed a long, distinguished political career: Venable was a Presidential Elector in 1832 and 1836; member of U.S. Congress in 1847, 1849, 1851, 1853; and representative of the Granville District, North Carolina, to the Congress of the Confederate States when Richmond was the seat of government. He was a staunch friend of John C. Calhoun. He was an elder of the Presbyterian Church for over fifty years and a member of the Board of Trustees of Hampden-Sydney College.

The Venables of Brownsville (related only distantly to the Venables of Chapel Hill) had five children, of whom Martha and Isabella, the Burwell students, were the fourth and fifth respectively:

1. Thomas Brown, Maj. C.S.A., d. June 23, 1894; m. Jan. 12, 1854, in Oxford, Cordelia Kingsbury.
2. Mary Grace; m. Richard Venable Daniel.
3. Dr. Samuel Frederick, Capt. C.S.A.; m. 1) Gertrude Henderson of La.; 2) Mary Tennent of Charleston.
4. Martha Elizabeth (1833–77); m. 1) Samuel Venable Morton —no children; 2) 1865, Robert Alston Hamilton (1818–88), two children.
5. Isabella Brown; m. Capt. Stephen Taylor Martin, Presbyterian minister. Six children:
   1. Annie Belle.
   2. Abraham Venable, Prof. Presbyterian College, S.C.
   3. Martha Alexander; m. Geo. L. Burr, Cornell Univ.
   4. Stephen Taylor, Jr., d. 1899, aged 27.
   5. Edward Vernon, d. aged 5 yrs.
   6. Grace Vernon; m. Geo. L. Walker.

The fact that Martha and Isabella Venable were sent to the Burwell School in Hillsborough placed a special stamp of approval on the school. The list of Patrons had always been impressive. The Hon. A.W. Venable's name was listed second only to the Hon. William A. Graham's.

Information on the Venable family is from Elizabeth Marshall Venable, *The Venables of Virginia* (1925), printed exclusively for the family (Chap. XII, pp. 149–51, "Abram Watkins Venable of 'Brownsville,' Granville Co., N.C. and his Descendants"), generously loaned by Louise Venable Coker (Mrs. W.C. Coker) of Chapel Hill to the late Miss Alice Noble.

# CHARLOTTE ISABELLA (BELLA) WADDELL
Hillsborough, North Carolina

Charlotte Isabella (Bella) Waddell was the daughter of Col. Haynes Waddell (son of John Waddell and Sallie Nash, daughter of Gen. Francis Nash) and his wife, Mary Fleming Waddell (daughter of Mary Hooper Schaw and James Fleming). Bella Waddell thus inherited a whole galaxy of fine old colonial names in both her maternal and paternal backgrounds. Unfortunately, Col. Haynes Waddell was a well-known spendthrift, who left his family to shift for themselves almost entirely. Mary Fleming Waddell is apparently the "Mrs. Waddill" who did sewing fairly regularly—and cheaply—for Burwell girls, charging only $1.00 for making a summer muslin dress. Bella had at least one brother, later the Rev. De Bernière Waddell, but the lives of the Haynes Waddell family were known to the community to be bleak and narrow.

On January 19, 1856, Mrs. M.A. Burwell wrote to her daughter Fanny, then studying music in New York,

> *I forgot to tell you that Bella Waddell is coming to school to us this session. I do feel for them—poor Mrs. Waddell has seen so much trouble. Bella you know is a remarkably intelligent girl.*

Although Bella enrolled in the spring session of 1856 that was broken by Fanny Burwell's death and funeral, one hopes she continued her schooling throughout 1856 and 1857. Bella married her mother's cousin, George William Mallett Hooper (1839–83), son of George De Bernière Hooper and Caroline Eliza Mallett, and had seven children, most of whom were given the old Hooper and Mallett family names:

1. Elizabeth Fleming.
2. Emma Thurston.
3. Charlotte Isabella.
4. Charles Mallett.
5. Caroline Mallett.
6. Juliet De Bernière.
7. George Beatty; m. Jessie L. Scott.

Mrs. Burwell's letters are in the Records Room, Burwell School.

# MARIA E. WADDELL
1832–Mar. 5, 1853
Hillsborough, North Carolina

Maria E. Waddell, born in 1832, was the only daughter of the Hon. Hugh Waddell (1799–1878), eminent Hillsborough lawyer, prominent in state government, who lived in Twin Chimneys at 168 W. King Street and maintained a law office (not standing) in the extreme northeast intersection of W. King and N. Wake streets.

*Alumni History of the University of North Carolina* contains this entry on Hugh Waddell:

> *HUGH WADDELL          LAWYER*
> *From Hillsboro; Wilmington;*
> *b. Mar. 21, 1799; d. Nov. 2, 1879 ['78?]; A.B.,*
> *1818; mem. N.C. House of Commons; 1828;*
> *state sen., 1836; and 1844–46; pres.*
> *senate, 1836; lieut. gov. 1836.*

Maria E. Waddell is listed in the 1848–51 catalogue, but there are no mentions of her in any letters or remembrance albums that have yet come to hand. It is probable that she was enrolled from about 1846 to 1850. A notice in the *Hillsborough Recorder* of January 12, 1853, reports her marriage to John C. Badham on January 4, 1853. (The Badhams were a firm of commission merchants in Edenton, who may have operated a branch office in Hillsborough.) An obituary clipping preserved in the Heartt-Wilson Papers notes that Mrs. Maria E. Badham, only daughter of the Hon. Hugh Waddell and wife of John C. Badham, died, aged twenty [or twenty-one?], on March 5, 1853, in New York City. One supposes that the Badhams were still on their wedding trip.

Materials are from *Alumni History of the University of North Carolina* (1924 ed.), p. 639; Heartt-Wilson Papers, So. Hist. Collection, UNC, Chapel Hill; *Hillsborough Recorder,* Jan. 12, 1853, N.C. Collection, Wilson Library, UNC, Chapel Hill.

# MARGARET (MAG) ISABELLA WALKER
December 27, 1824–1904
Hillsborough, North Carolina

Margaret Isabella Walker had a far more romantic and picture-esque life than most of the girls at the Burwell School. She was the daughter of Carleton Walker (Jan. 5, 1777–Oct. 12, 1840) and his third wife, Caroline Mary Mallett Walker (Mar. 5, 1789–Nov. 20, 1862), and the granddaughter of such early colonial figures as Peter Mallett, Robinson Mumford, and the Woodhouse and Walker families of Northumberland. Her father, Carleton Walker, had been born in Northumberland near Alnwick Castle but emigrated to America at an early age with his mother, Mrs. Jane Woodhouse Walker. Handsome Carleton Walker had the reputation for marrying beautiful wives, and making and losing fortunes. His first wife, Maria(h) Moseley (d. Oct. 1802), brought him a son, John Moseley Walker, and the valuable Moseley Hall estate of 3000 acres on Cape Fear. His second wife, Sabina T. Legare of Charleston (married in 1804), lived but a short time. His third, Caroline Mary Mallett of Fayetteville, brought him eleven children and the old Mallett property on Margaret Lane in Hillsborough where the Carleton Walkers lived for nearly twenty years.

Margaret Isabella was one of twins born on December 27, 1824, at the old Mallett home in the Haymount section, Fayetteville. Her twin was named John Moseley, to replace the first much-loved John Moseley Walker of Moseley Hall who had died, at the age of twenty-two, two months before, on October 28 in Hillsborough.

In or about 1823 the Carleton Walkers, in depleted financial circumstances, returned to Hillsborough and built the charming little Walker-Palmer House still standing on Lot 19 on W. Margaret Lane. Carleton Walker lived well, and the family brought two valued cooks and a collection of other indoor and outdoor servants from Moseley Hall as well as valuable family silver.

In her eightieth year, Margaret Isabella Walker wrote her "Reminiscences." In it she tells of going to three schools in Hillsborough: Miss Burke's, where as a "quaint little figure" (five years old) in a bib she took a prize for reading Beatty's *Hermit* with long *a*'s; Episcopal Academy on Tryon Street, where she quite fell in love with the gentle Miss Maria Spear; and the Burwell School, which she attended briefly in the spring of 1841.

> *The girls of the first class had completed algebra, but being more fond of arithmetic than any other study, I gladly joined the class. One day after our class had been sent to their seats for failing to solve several problems, I worked at them until I saw "light," and promptly showed my class-mates my solution. When Dr. Burwell gave me the highest mark, and the other members complained of their lower marks, he said, "you all asked to go to Mag Walker's desk to be shown." Dear children, you must excuse Grandma for relating this incident as this was the proudest day of my life.*

In 1842 Mrs. Caroline Mary Mallett Walker and her children left Hillsborough permanently. Buried "near the wall" of St. Matthew's Episcopal Church were Carleton Walker, his mother, Mrs. Jane Woodhouse Walker, John Moseley Walker of Moseley Hall, and an infant Sophia Woodhouse Walker.

In 1852 Margaret Isabella Walker married as his second wife a German teacher Johann Hieinrich D.C.F. Weber, and they removed to Tennessee. Her Reminiscences mention her children and grandchildren. Prof. Weber died on May 17, 1878, but Margaret Isabella Walker Weber died at age eighty in 1804.

## THE CARLETON WALKER FAMILY

*CARLETON WALKER, son of James Walker and Jane Woodhouse*
>> *b. Jan. 5, 1777, at Wooler, Northumberland*
>> *d. Oct. 12, 1840, Hillsborough.; buried at St. Matthew's*
> *m. 1) Maria(h) Moseley, December 24, 1801, Wilmington, N.C.*
>> *d. Oct. 1802*
>> *John Moseley Walker*
>>> *b. Oct. 1802*
>>> *d. Oct. 28, 1824, Hillsborough; buried at St. Matthew's*
> *m. 2) Sabina T. Legare, Mar. 20, 1804, Charleston, S.C.*
> *m. 3) Caroline Mary Mallett, June 11, 1807, Wilmington*
>> *b. Mar. 5, 1789, Fayetteville*
>> *d. Nov. 20, 1862; buried Old Mallett Family Cemetery in Fayetteville, N.C.*

*a) Carleton, b. Wilmington, d.y.*

*b) Sarah Jane*
 *m. Edward J. Hale, May 24, 1828*
 *buried Greenwood Cemetery, N.Y.*

*c) Eliza Henrietta*
 *m. Robert C. Belden, May 21, 1835*
 *buried Beatty Graveyard, Bladen Co., N.C.*

*d) James Woodhouse, d .y. (5 years);*
 *buried Rock Rest, Chatham Co., N.C.*

*e) Mary Pearson*
 *m. 1) Thomas H. Byrne, July 18, 1842,*
  *St. .John's Church, Fayetteville*
 *m. 2) William J. Adams, buried Montgomery, Ala.*

*f) Dr. Peter Mallett Walker*
 *m. Margaret Lane (dau. Levin Lane),*
  *Apr. 24, 1845*
 *buried Wilmington, N.C.*

*g) Caroline de Bernière ("De Bernière")*
 *b. Mar. 11, 1820*
 *m. Dr. Wm. P. Mallett of Fayetteville,*
  *Oct. 25, 1841, in Hillsborough*
 *d. Aug. 24, 1900; buried Old Chapel Hill*
  *Cemetery*

*h) Margaret Isabella (twin)*
 *b. December 27, 1824, at Old Mallett Home in*
  *Haymount, Fayetteville*
 *m. (as his second wife) John Heinrich David Carl*
  *Friedrich Weber, 1852 (d. May 17, 1878)*
 *d. 1904*

*i) John Moseley (twin)*
 *b. December 27, 1824*
 *m. Eliza Jane Gibbs*
 *d. Aug. 1894; buried near church at Blowing Rock;*
  *now in Oak Dale Cemetery, Wilmington*

*j) Catherine Burke*
 *m. John A. Hanks, buried Pittsboro, N.C.*

*k) Sophia Woodhouse, d y.; buried St. Matthew's*

---

The foregoing genealogical information is from the Walker Family Bible, given in Margaret Isabella Walker Weber's "Reminiscences," a 37–page typescript now in the So. Hist. Collection, UNC (listed as #1951), p. 18. Margaret Isabella was presumably buried in Tennessee.

# _____WATKINS
## & ELIZABETH (LIZZIE) WATKINS

The Watkins sisters, students in 1855, appear to have been the granddaughters of Samuel Venable Watkins of Farmville, Virginia, who was a UNC student in 1814–16. Mr. Watkins and Mr. Robertson Owen of Halifax County, Virginia, seem to have come to Hillsborough for their daughters about the same time in November 1855.

On December 29, 1855, Mrs. Burwell wrote to Fanny,

> *Lizzie Watkins is not coming back, is going to Warreton* [sic].
> *Maria Nash saw her mother last week, she said she was more than satisfied with Lizzie's improvement here in every thing but Music, & that she was only sending her to Warreton* [sic] *on that account. Maria told her we were going to have a first-rate teacher—she said "that was said before" so you see how Maj. Z's & Mr. Vampill's unfaithfulness is effecting* [sic] *us, but I do not feel anxious. . . .*

On January 2, 1856, Mrs. Burwell wrote that the Watkins' transfer to Warrenton had been accomplished: ". . . Lizzie Watkins & her sister have gone to Warrenton to learn Music."

Mrs. Burwell's letters are in the Records Room, Burwell School.

## CAROLINE (CARRIE) J. WATTERS
May 15, 1835–June 25, 1914
Wilmington, North Carolina

Caroline (Carrie) Watters was the youngest child of Joseph H. Watters and his second wife, Julia Hall, and therefore a member of an old and numerous Cape Fear family. Caroline evidently came to the Burwell School (opposite to Dr. Edmund Strudwick's home) in the late 1840s since she was only seventeen when she married twenty-two-year-old William S. Strudwick on September 14, 1852.

William S. Strudwick attended UNC between 1849 and 1851 and was probably "reading" medicine with his father when he married Caroline Watters. The young couple moved into a single bedroom at Dr. Strudwick's house. When Mary (Molly) Burwell in 1854 married Frederick Nash Strudwick, William's brother, and also moved into the crowded Strudwick house, the two brides could give each other companionship. Mrs. M.A. Burwell's letters of 1855 indicate, however, that each girl needed and wanted her own home.

*Caroline Watters about the time of her marriage.*

Eventually in the early 1860s Carrie and her growing family removed to Tusculum, south of Hillsborough, where the Rev. John Knox Witherspoon and his family had seen so much tragedy (see sketches of Denah and Mary Nash Witherspoon). Tusculum, however, burned in 1871 or 1872, and the Strudwicks left Hillsborough for a time to venture a medical practice in Wadesboro with Dr. Edmund Ashe. In 1887, Edmund Strudwick of Norfolk and Richmond, the Strudwick's eldest child, who had, surprisingly enough, become a wealthy business man, bought the old Josiah Turner home on Churton Street, enlarged it, modernized it, landscaped the 5-acre grounds, and set up a trust for his mother and three unmarried sisters.

Dr. Strudwick died in 1907, and the trust was terminated in March 1911, and the grounds were subdivided and sold. The house and well-house remain much as they were; the office had already been considerably altered.

The Strudwicks' nine children were,

1. Edmund, b. Apr. 17, 1854; m. Ann (Nannie) Daves Hughes, New Bern.
2. Ann Nash, Feb. 29, 1856–Aug. 16, 1938.
3. Mildred Watters, Nov. 14, 1857–Apr. 12, 1860.
4. William Watters, Nov. 9, 1859–Oct. 6, 1893.
5. Julia Elizabeth, Apr. 6, 1862–1939; m. William B. Meares (1854-1933).
6. Joseph Watters, May 3, 1864–Oct. 28, 1882.
7. Shepperd, Nov. 15, 1868–December 27, 1961; m. Susan Nash Read (June 24, 1875–Jan. 15, 1960).
8. Mary Nash, June 22, 1874–December 24, 1944; m. Thomas M. Arrasmith (Sept. 6, 1869–July 9, 1938).
9. Margaret (Maggie) McLester; m. Thomas May Van Planche.

Dr. William S. Strudwick became a most popular country doctor in the Hillsborough area, and he was virtually the official (and unpaid) doctor at the Nash & Kollock School. He was exceedingly improvident, however, and apparently often forgot to collect fees, record debts, and so on—a circumstance which accounts for the home in trust set up by his son Edmund Strudwick.

The picture of Carolina Watters shows a confident young lady with a taste for pretty frocks and jewelry, and with no inkling of the difficult life ahead of her. Caroline Watters Strudwick died on June 25, 1914, aged seventy-nine years. She is buried in the Hillsborough Memorial Cemetery (New Town Cemetery) with other members of the Strudwick family.

The picture of Carolina Watters was given to the Historic Hillsborough Commission by Mary Exum Shepherd (Mrs. Grant Shepherd).

## ANNE H[USKE] WEBB
? –1891
Greensboro', Alabama

Anne (or Annie) Huske Webb of Greensboro', Alabama, was
the second child of Dr. James Webb's eldest son, Dr. Henry Young
Webb (1808–78) and Maria Dickson Webb, whom he married in 1832.
Henry Webb had first removed to Alabama with the intention of
becoming a planter, but returned to Hillsborough and took a course of
medical training with his father before removing to Alabama a second
time and establishing his medical practice in Gadsden.

The extensive James Webb Papers contain the following records
of payments to Robert Burwell for Anne Webb's tuition from 1841
through 1845 (four receipts). Presumably, throughout this period she
had lived at her grandfather's capacious yellow frame house on E.
Queen Street and had attended the Burwell School as a day student:

*Received of Dr Webb twelve dollars for Anne Webb's tuition the
present session.*
*Feb. 27th 1841*          *R. Burwell*

*Dr. James Webb*          *To R. Burwell Dr.*
*1842        To Tuition of Anne H. Webb        $15.00*
*July 4th     Rec'd payment of J. Webb jr. & Co.*
*July 16, 1842*          *R. Burwell*

*Dr. Webb*          *To R. Burwell Dr.*
*May 23, 1844     Tuition of Anne Webb     $15.00*
*Deduct paid last session*          *2.50*
                                  *$12.50*

*July 30, 1844*          *Received payment*
                        *R. Burwell Dr.*
*Rec'd of James Webb*
        *Anna Webb's Tuition, 1845*
        *August 3rd, 1844          R. Burwell*

Anne (or Annie, as she seems always to have been called) thus
attended the Burwell School as a regular student from spring 1841

apparently through 1845, with a deduction made in the winter session of 1843 for an absence of some kind. There exists a fifth bill for drawing lessons only in the autumn session of 1847:

> *Received of Dr. James Webb twenty dollars tuition of Anne and*
> *Thomas Webb the past session in Drawing.*
> *Nov. 25th 1847* R. Burwell

It is possible, however, that the Anne Webb taking drawing lessons from Signor Antonio di Martino in 1847 may not have been Henry Y. Webb's daughter.

Dr. Henry Young Webb's children were,

1. Col. Joseph Caldwell, C.S.A. Went to Texas.
2. Anne (Annie) Huske; m. Judge ____Tollman; d. 1891.
3. Ellen—left a widow.
4. James—unmarried.

Existing Webb genealogies give scanty information about Anne Huske Webb's life. She married Judge Tollman of Gadsden and had a daughter Ellen Webb Tollman, named for her mother's sister Ellen. Robert Dickins Webb in *The Webb Family* says, "She had an only daughter who is dead, but left two little boys."

The information in this sketch is from the James Webb Papers, So. Hist. Collection, UNC, Chapel Hill; William James Webb et al., *Our Webb Kin of Dixie* (Oxford, N.C., 1940); Robert Dickins Webb, MD, *The Webb Family* (Yazoo City, Miss., 1894), pp. 8–9.

## HENRIETTA WEBB
May 17, 1830–February 15, 1862
Orange County North Carolina

Henrietta Webb was one of the three Webb sisters of Oaks who attended the Burwell School. She was the eldest daughter of Alexander Smith Webb (1804–49) and Cornelia Adeline Stanford Webb (1811–91), daughter of the Hon. Richard Stanford (1767–1816). Alexander Smith Webb had moved from Harmony Hill near Mt. Tirzah in Person County in 1845 to a rocky plantation called Stony Point about a quarter mile south of Bethlehem Presbyterian Church at Oaks.

Henrietta's nine living brothers and sisters were

1. Susan A.
2. Mary Caroline, who married the Rev. Calvin N. Morrow, Presbyterian minister.
3. Addie (Adeline).
4. James.
5. Rev. Richard Stanford.
6. "Tip."
7. Samuel H.
8. The famous Sawney (William Robert).
9. John Maurice ("Old John").

Apparently Henrietta was a mentally disturbed person. Whether her alarming trouble appeared during her Burwell School years is unknown; no record mentions it. She probably did not enroll until the late 1840s. Laurence McMillin in his book, *The Schoolmaker*: "His [Sawney's] disturbed, gaunt eldest sister Henrietta had been in and out of the asylum at Raleigh." She died on February 15, 1862, at the age of thirty-two years. Her tombstone, beside her mother's, in the large cemetery at Bethlehem Presbyterian Church reads,

*Sacred to the*
*memory of*
*HENRIETTA*
*Daughter of Alexander*
*and Cornelia Webb*
*Born May 17, 1830*
*Died Feb. 15, 1862*
—
*Footstone: H. W.*

Data is from Laurence McMillin's *The Schoolmaker: Sawney Webb and the Bell Buckle Story* (Chapel Hill, 1971), p. 26.

# MARTHA (MAT) ANN WEBB
## Granville County, North Carolina

Martha (Mat) Ann Webb from Granville County was a student at the Burwell School in 1850. Her autograph, "Mat Webb," dated May 25, 1850, appears in Robina Norwood's autograph album, and her name is listed in the student roster appearing in the *Burwell School Catalogue of 1848–51.*

Martha Ann Webb married her cousin, William Peter Webb, on November 24, 1852. Their Granville County bond reads,

> *Martha Ann Webb to William P. Webb, November 24, 1852.*
> *Bond No. 6857. Bondsman: Benj. P. Thorp.*

William Peter Webb (Oct. 22, 1815–Sept. 6, 1890) was born in Lincoln County. Orphaned at an early age, he and his brothers, Hal and James, found a home with their uncle, Dr. James Webb, in Hillsborough. (The commission owns one of William Peter Webb's textbooks from these years.) He was graduated AB with high honors from University of North Carolina in 1835 and eventually became a judge of the Superior Court in Alabama. His marriage to Martha Ann Webb, who must have been his junior by perhaps sixteen years, took place when he was thirty-seven, seventeen years after his graduation.

Another William Peter Webb (b. 1875), who may have been Martha Ann's son or grandson, was a student at University of North Carolina in 1894–95, took his MD degree at South Carolina Medical College in 1897, and became a physician in Rockingham County, North Carolina

Information for this sketch is from Hicks, "History of Granville Co., N.C. Vol. I, Marriage Bonds," and the *Alumni History of the University of North Carolina* (1924 edition), p. 654.

## MARY WEBB
January 30, 1823– ?
Hillsborough, North Carolina

Mary Webb, born January 30, 1823, was the youngest daughter of Dr. James Webb and Annie Alves Huske Webb of Hillsborough. She had early attended Miss Mary Burke's little school on E. Queen Street, and in 1835 was attending the elegant Miss Maria L. Spear's classes in the Hillsborough Female Seminary (Episcopal) on E. Tryon Street. Some of her tuition receipts survive in the James Webb Papers:

> *Jan. 8th 1835      Miss Mary Webb Dr. to the Hillsboro '*
> *Female Seminary to one session's tuition in Literature*
> *$13.00*
> *Rec'd payment Jan. 9th, 1835*
> *Maria L. Spear*

> *July 7th 1836      Miss Mary Webb, dr. to the Hillsboro'*
> *Female Seminary To tuition in Literature*
> *$15.00*
> *Rec'd of Dr. Webb*
> *Maria L. Spear*

> *January 26th 1837    Miss M. Webb, dr. to the Hillsboro'*
> *Female Seminary To tuition in Literature*
> *$17.00*
> *Rec'd of Dr. Webb  Jan'y 30, 1837*
> *Maria L. Spear*

Dr. Webb, however, was a Presbyterian and encouraged Mrs. Burwell to open a new school in Hillsborough. Indeed, as a leading Presbyterian he largely underwrote the construction of the Brick House, which housed the little school when Mrs. Burwell first opened it in August 1837. Mary Webb, then aged fourteen and a half, was officially her first student. Tradition says Mrs. Burwell had two other "outside" students, little Sarah Kollock, aged eleven, and Annabella Norwood, aged six. There was, of course, her own small daughter, Mary Susan

Burwell, also aged six. Thus, Mrs. Burwell had to devise three separate courses of study.

Mary Webb remained three years (1837–41) at the Burwell School. The Webb Papers provide additional tuition receipts, but none for the first session when the Burwells were perhaps repaying Dr. Webb for the Brick House:

*Dr. Webb to M. A. Burwell Dr*
  *Jan. 15, 1838    To one session Tuition of Mary Webb*
           *$17.50*
      *1 copy Blair's Rhetoric*              *2.75*
      *1 Do Gallaudet's Nat. Theology*      *.75*
      *Recd. payment*                     *$20.50*


*Dr. Webb to M. A. Burwell Dr.*
  *Aug. 5ᵗʰ 1839    To one Session Tuition    $17.50*
        *1 Lessons in Composition           .62½*
        *"1 Scholar's Companion            .75*
                              *$18.87*

Separate tuition receipts to M. Jean Odend'hal for tutoring Mary in French at $15.00 per session in 1838 and 1839 also exist, and it is possible that M. Odend'hal was the French teacher for the first few sessions of the Burwell School.

Mary finished her course in 1841, and her daughter, Mary Alves Long, wrote this estimate of her mother's education in her book, *High Time to Tell It*:

*Mother had received the best education of her day and spoke of her teachers, Mrs. Robert Burwell and Miss Burke, daughter of Governor Burke, with the greatest respect and admiration. Besides being grounded in grammar and other branches considered essential, she had learned to paint on rice paper, to sing, and play extremely well on the piano and guitar both, by ear and by note. . . . She had a beautiful voice that charmed all her listeners when she sang "Kathleen Mavourneen," "A Wet Sheet and a Flowing Sea," "Believe Me, If All Those Endearing Young Charms," or "I Dreamt That I Dwelt in Marble Halls". . . .*

*Grammar was her specialty. She was determined we should
know grammar. . . . Mother was as sensitive to bad grammar as
she was to a false note in music.*

Mary Alves Long emphasized her mother's competence in music
and her happy youth:

*Mother had led a wonderful life in that old yellow house [on E.
Queen St.]. . . . Sometimes mother played the guitar, a beautiful
instrument which her brothers had imported from Paris for her
birthday gift. I used to marvel at its beauty and also at the contrast
between the satinwood case with its narrow band of mother-of-pearl
inlay and the plain pine of the sounding board.*

Mary Webb also had a splendid piano which accompanied her to her
new home on her marriage.

*Mary Webb Long—first student of the Burwell School.*

When Mary "graduated," at the Burwell School in 1841, Mrs.
Burwell wrote a special letter of farewell for her which was also her
diploma or "certificate" of graduation, and presented her with a brooch,

one of Mrs. Burwell's few pieces of jewelry. A letter from another one of Mary's daughters, Miss Jane Taylor Long, is included here with the "certificate."

According to Mary Alves's description, Mary Webb was "a rather small person" with curly hair, large brown eyes, arched eyebrows, a beautiful "though determined" mouth, and "a really lovely voice." On June 29, 1843, she married William John Long (1815–82), a prominent lawyer and planter of Randolph County, whose brother, Dr. Osmond F. Long, had married her older sister, Frances Helen. Mary Alves Long's *High Time to Tell It*, if not wholly a biography of Mary Webb Long and the story of her married life, comes close to it. The Longs had eight children at their Randolph County farmhouse, Peach Tree Hill:

1. Sabra Ramsey, 1844– ?
2. Annie Webb, 1846–1914.
3. Jane Taylor, 1848– ?
4. Elizabeth Strudwick, 1850– ?
5. John, 1852–54.
6. William Osmond, 1854–1928.
7. John Henry, 1856–1917.
8. Mary Alves, 1864 - ?

Two of Mary Webb's children were taught by the Burwells. Jane Taylor Long attended the Charlotte Female Institute and later became a teacher at Peace Institute [now Peace College]. Mary Alves Long spent four years at Peace where John Bott Burwell, "Mr. Johnny," was principal.

The Longs in 1882 moved from Randolph County to Minneapolis where ailing William J. Long sought to reestablish himself as a lawyer. Both Mary Webb Long and her husband are buried in a Minneapolis cemetery, as are most members of their family.

### Miss Mary Webb
*Present*

*I feel very badly at parting with you My dear Mary on many accounts. You have been my pupil for three years and have attached me very much to you by your uniform good conduct, but apart from that I feel much anxiety for you as you are now free from the restraints of school & will of course mingle more with the <u>world</u>. Beware my dear of its seducing influences, choose your associates <u>carefully</u> and your <u>intimates</u> with <u>great</u> care. Do not have too many. A few choice friends are better than a number. I remember a few lines that I learnt when a little girl. They contain good advice.*

> *Have communion with <u>few</u>,*
> *Be intimate with <u>one</u>,*
> *Deal justly by <u>all</u>,*
> *Speak evil of none.*

*But above all My Dear Mary, beware of being familiar with any one who has no regard for <u>vital religion</u>. You know not how easily one is led aside & tho' you do not profess religion yourself, you have been brought up to know your duty.*

*I send you a breast pin as a remembrance and token of my sincere regard. Wear it for my sake — it is, I think, a useful ornament. May you possess that which in the sight of God is of great price "a meek and quiet spirit."*

*Farewell (as my scholar) dear M. May the God of all grace bless you abundantly not only in this life, but in that which is to come.*

> *Very affectionately,*
> *Your friend*

> *M. A. Burwell*

*St. Louis, Mo.*
*April 11, 1927*

*My dear Mary,*
    *While overhauling a box of family letters and souvenirs I found the enclosed which I thought might interest you, your daughters, and granddaughters.*

    *I wrote you that my mother (Mary Webb) was the first pupil of your grandmother in that little school in Hillsboro which was the seed from which Peace Institute really sprang.*

    *There was no real curriculum or graduation in those early days, but this little note is a quasi-diploma. It surely expresses the ideals of the school and its founder. You will see that it was written before the days of envelopes and bears the mark of seal. I wish it was dated. I think it must have been about 1842. [Probably one year earlier, at least.]*

    *I could not help smiling at the warning she gave concerning the seductions of the world. Hillsboro was my mother's world. What could she say today as she would see the girls plunge into the maelstrom among the sweet girl graduates of today.*

*Affectionately,*
*Jane T. Long*

Mary Webb's "certificate" and the accompanying letter by Jane Taylor Long were given to the commission by Mary Lacy McAden (Mrs. R.Y. McAden), 118 E. Peace St., Raleigh, N.C. Webb genealogy is chiefly from *Our Webb Kin of Dixie,* by W. J. Webb et al. (Oxford, N.C., 1940); receipts for Mary Webb's tuition are in the James Webb Papers, So. Hist. Collection, UNC, Chapel Hill. Mary Alves Long's *High Time to Tell It* (Durham, 1950), pp, 79, 88–89, is the source of much detail.

# MARY CAROLINE WEBB
June 15, 1833–September 15, 1904
Orange County, North Carolina

Mary Caroline Webb, or Caroline as she was always called, was born June 15, 1833, at Stony Point near Oaks in southwestern Orange County, the third daughter of Alexander Smith Webb and Cornelia Adeline Stanford Webb. She was the sister of Henrietta, Susan A. (Suny), Addie, William Robert (Sawney), John Maurice ("Old John") of Bell Buckle, Tennessee, James, the Rev. Richard Stanford Webb, "Tip," and Samuel H. Webb—nine living brothers and sisters, all told.

Caroline is listed in the *Burwell School Catalogue of 1848–51,* as are her sisters Henrietta and Susan (Suny), and it may be that she enrolled slightly after Susan's departure since home circumstances at Stony Point could hardly have permitted all the sisters to have absented themselves at the same time.

When she was twenty-six years old, Caroline Webb in September 1859 married a long-time neighbor, "the boy next door," Calvin Newton Morrow, son of John and Rachel Thompson Morrow of the old Oaks community, a former Bingham School student at Oaks and a UNC graduate.

Dr. Herbert Snipes Turner writes of the Morrows' life together in his book, *Church in the Old Fields:*

> He *[Calvin Morrow]* received both the B.A. and M.A. degrees *[from UNC]* in the spring of 1859. The following September he married lovely Mary Caroline Webb, one of the most popular and charming young girls of the Oaks community. . . . The two families *[Webbs and Morrows]* were closely associated, and Calvin's sister Ellen married one of the Webb boys.
>
> In fall 1859, Morrow entered Union Theological Seminary at Hampden-Sydney. . . . He was licensed by Orange Presbytery on Oct. 22, 1860, and ordained on Apr. 12, 1862. During the war years he was an evangelist for Orange Presbytery in Randolph Co. In 1865 he returned to his home community and acted as Stated Supply for the Bethlehem Church and as a teacher in the Bingham School until he accepted the call to the Hawfields and Cross Roads Churches in 1873.

> *When he accepted the call to this field, Morrow moved to Mebane [Mebaneville] and bought a large two-story house with a spacious yard and garden lot. The family hired a Negro man, named John, who helped in the house and kept the yard and garden. John became quite famous in Mebane for the lovely flowers he grew in the Morrows' yard.*

The Rev. Morrow had long been subject to bronchitis, and failing health finally necessitated his removal to Florida in 1883. The Morrows sold their home, stored what provisions they could in their carriage, and slowly made the long trip.

On arrival in Florida, they purchased a four–acre orange grove, lived temporarily in a log cabin on their new property, and finally acquired a suitable house in the nearby town of Hawthorne. In 1893, the Rev. Morrow's health was sufficiently improved so that he could undertake occasional supply work. Caroline, however, died at age seventy-one on September 15, 1904. Her body was returned to Oaks by train and she was buried beside other members of the Webb family in the larger cemetery at Bethlehem Presbyterian Church near the shade of tree box and magnolias. Her tombstone reads,

*MARY CAROLINE*
*wife of*
*Rev. C. N. Morrow*
*and Daughter of*
*Alexander S. & Cornelia*
*Adeline Webb*

—

*Born June 15, 1833*
*Died in Hawthorne, Fla.*
*Sept. 15, 1904*

—

*"Asleep in Jesus"*

—

*Footstone: M. C. M.*

The Calvin Morrows had no children. After Caroline's death, the Rev. Morrow sold the orange grove and returned to Oaks to live with his sister, Ellen. He died a decade later on March 14, 1914. He, too, is buried in the Bethlehem Cemetery at Oaks.

Materials in this sketch are from Cemetery Records of Bethlehem Presbyterian Church; Herbert Snipes Turner, *Church in the Old Fields* (Chapel Hill, 1962), pp. 162–66; and Historic Hillsborough Commission records.

## SUSAN (SUNY) A. WEBB
November 18, 1831–March 16, 1905
Orange County, North Carolina

Susan (Suny) A. Webb, the second daughter of Alexander Smith Webb and Cornelia Adeline Stanford Webb, and the granddaughter of the Hon. Richard Stanford, was beyond question one of the most remarkable women and one of the finest teachers ever turned out by the Burwell School, rivaling Mrs. Burwell herself in physical endurance, moral courage, and simple effectiveness.

Susan enrolled at the Burwell School in July 1847, when she was fifteen and boarded at the Norwoods' Poplar Hill. Annabella Norwood reported the event on July 13, 1847, to her cousin William N. Tillinghast, "Susan Webb (I expect you saw her down at Uncle Bingham's) is going to her [Mrs. Burwell] and boards here. She is a very stout girl and quite a pleasant companion for me."

Suny returned from the Burwell School to become the dedicated teacher of her own large family of brothers and sisters at Stony Point, the family's rocky plantation a quarter mile south of Bethlehem Presbyterian Church and Bingham School at Oaks. Her frail father died in 1849 at the age of forty-seven, leaving Susan with the behest, "My daughter, teach my children"; and teach she did, in a little log building with puncheon benches that she named "Almeda Schoolhouse."

Mrs. Burwell's magnetic influence went farther than she ever knew or dreamed—two of the Webb boys, taught by Suny, became the famous teachers: Sawney (William Robert) Webb, later also a U.S. senator, and John Maurice ("Old John") Webb of the Bell Buckle School for Boys at Bell Buckle, Tennessee. Another brother was the Rev. Richard Stanford Webb, Methodist minister and C.S.A. chaplain. Susan also taught the neighbors' children at Almeda and continued to do so for forty years.

*Susan "Suny" Webb.*

An excerpt from Lawrence McMillin's book, *The Schoolmaker: Sawney Webb and the Bell Buckle Story*, gives a picture of Suny after her Burwell School days:

> *In his home Sawney found another "big personality," a girl still in her teens, the greatest teacher he said he ever knew. Susan, or "Suny," knew more than anyone else. Sawney watched her on Saturday at the dining room fireplace, baking perfect bread in "oven" pots on short legs in hot coals. . . . Cakes, biscuits, and roast ducks emerged from similar pots. . . . Suny and Black Nancy even made waffles in molds with tong-like handles, the batter ends thrust deep in ashes. . . . Suny never did wrong. She always placed her knife and fork neatly on her plate, and folded her napkin while she was still a bit hungry. She never allowed her*

*back to touch her chair. She very much resembled a good straight pen. She wrote hundreds and thousands of letters. She became the corresponding secretary of the family. She loved putting English words together. She dressed to suit herself—no trails [trains?], no silly outsized bustles, for her. She remained too busy at the vocation her father had left her to give her full heart to courting though admirers called on her from a distance. Suny never married.*

*She did teach them [her father's children], and some of their children, and neighbors' children, for forty years. She began teaching Sawney no later than the summer of 1848, and formally opened her school four months before her father died [Alexander Smith Webb died June 30, 1849]. She charged a nickel a day, a quarter per week, per child.*

*The log building daubed with mud that became "Almeda Schoolhouse" sat on the partially wooded slopes of the mountain field. The day began with a Bible passage, which her students read along with her as best they could. After a prayer, she taught.*

*"All day long in the little log cabin I sat by my little chum in a seat when our feet did not touch the floor," Sawney remembered. Even fifteen minutes was uncomfortable on backless puncheon benches, logs split or sawed in half, with the flat end to sit on. "We could not move our feet, and we were not allowed to speak a word." Her discipline was rigid. Yet she knew that a child has limits. "When she saw that her pupils were tired she would tell a story or read a beautiful poem. I never saw a little boy leave her school that did not have a love of poetry and good English. . . ."*

Susan Webb spent her entire life (she lived to be seventy-four years old) teaching in the little Almeda Schoolhouse near Stony Point. In her later years, friends recalled that Susan Webb lived in a little house nearby with a bachelor brother and raised peacocks, a yard full of them. She died on March16, 1905, and was buried between her sisters Henrietta and Mary Caroline (both Burwell School girls) near the great tree box in the larger cemetery at Bethlehem Presbyterian Church at Oaks, only a short distance from her old home and her beloved Almeda Schoolhouse.

*SUSAN A. WEBB*
*Daughter of*
*Alexander S. & Cornelia*
*Adeline Webb*
*Born Nov. 18, 1831*
*Died Mar. 16, 1905*

—

*I have so lived am*
*not afraid to die*

—

*Footstone: S.A.W.*

Information for this sketch is from W.N. Tillinghast Papers, Ms. Collection, Perkins Library, Duke Univ., and from Lawrence McMillin's book, *The Schoolmaker: Sawney Webb and the Bell Buckle Story* (Chapel Hill, 1971), pp. 15–16.

## [  ELIZABETH WHITTED
Hillsborough, North Carolina

Elizabeth Whitted was the daughter of Anna D. Faucett and Henry Whitted, a wealthy Hillsborough planter. Her mother died on August 30, 1849. Elizabeth (or Bettie) never married and became the mistress of her father's household as evidenced in the United States Census of 1860, 1870, and 1880. Her father died in 1883. No further information is known about Elizabeth. She does not have a headstone in the family cemetery (William Whitted, Jr., Family Cemetery outside of Hillsborough), but that is probably where she was buried.    ]

# DENAH McEWEN WITHERSPOON
## 1837–59
### Camden, South Carolina

Denah McEwen Witherspoon (1837–59) was the daughter of John Knox Witherspoon, Jr., and Elizabeth McEwen Witherspoon of Camden, South Carolina. Her father was the third child of the Rev. Dr. John Knox Witherspoon, organizer and first pastor of the Hillsborough Presbyterian Church, and his wife Susan Kollock Witherspoon. John Knox, Jr., was born in Hillsborough on September 25, 1816, the historic day on which the church was dedicated and the same day on which his father was to die thirty-seven years later.

John Knox Witherspoon, Jr., met Elizabeth McEwen in Camden during his father's brief pastorate (1833–37) of the beautiful Bethesda Presbyterian Church on DeKalb Street. The voluminous Witherspoon-McDowall Papers describe the Witherspoons' Camden years in detail as well as their succeeding year and a half in Columbia before their return to their farm, Tusculum, south of Hillsborough.

In Camden the Witherspoons had lived in a pleasant house (still standing) with ample grounds at York and Lyttleton streets, and it may be that the young John Knox Witherspoons continued to live there after their marriage. The younger Witherspoon spent his entire life in Camden, became an elder in his father's former church, and operated a telegraph line from Camden to Columbia.

Denah Witherspoon is known to have been a student at the Burwell School in 1851, when she was fourteen, but she probably had entered at least a year earlier. She of necessity would have been a boarder since the tragic circumstances in her ailing home at Tusculum would scarcely have permitted an additional person to join the household. Denah married James Jones of Camden as his first wife, and the couple lived in the Jones home on Lyttleton Street. She died in 1859 at the age of twenty-two.

Information in this sketch is from M.C. Engstrom's Witherspoon Family Records and from Witherspoon-McDowall Papers in the So. Hist. Collection, UNC, Chapel Hill.

# MARY NASH WITHERSPOON
July 9, 1827– ?
Hillsborough, North Carolina

It is probable that no girl who attended the Burwell School had a sadder, more tragic life than Mary Nash Witherspoon. She was the seventh and last child of the Rev. Dr. John Knox Witherspoon (Sept. 1791–Sept. 25, 1853) and Susan Davis Kollock Witherspoon (Dec. 21, 1793–Mar. 31, 1854). Although the Rev. Dr. John Knox Witherspoon had been "born with a silver spoon in his mouth," a succession of misfortunes and his natural ineptitude with money always kept his family in dire need. A few months before Mary's birth, fire destroyed the new farmhouse and school at the Witherspoon plantation south of Hillsborough, and the Rev. Witherspoon never managed to get on his feet again.

Possibly no minister of the Presbyterian church in the Southern states had anything like the prestige and authority of the Rev. John Knox Witherspoon in his early days. He had inherited the most impressive name in American Presbyterianism and was indeed a princeling of the American church. An irreconcilable difference with his Hillsborough congregation over the question of slavery led him in 1833 to sever his connection with the Hillsborough church and to accept the pastorate of Bethesda Presbyterian Church in Camden, South Carolina. Mary was only six years old at the time; she was twelve when her parents returned to Hillsborough in 1839 to try to make a living on the farm, although her father was then suffering with a fatal infection or growth in his chest.

The Witherspoon-McDowall Papers chronicle the almost heartbreaking attempts of the family to keep body and soul together. Mary Nash Witherspoon in the autumn of 1839 went to stay with the Dr. Edmund Strudwicks in Hillsborough and nominally at least attended the Burwell School. She could not pay tuition, but she taught Mrs. Burwell's younger children, a task for which she had real aptitude, thereby freeing Mrs. Burwell for other duties. She also took music lessons from Miss Caroline Heartt, which one suspects were free lessons.

Just when her severe nervous affliction began to manifest itself is uncertain—but she experienced excruciating spasms, partial paralysis, and alarming mental lapses, first at intervals, then more frequently.

There were periods of improvement—she even started a school at Tusculum, the Witherspoon farm, and in 1846 she taught school briefly at Camden. But as her parents' fortunes and health went downhill, so did Mary's. When she slipped into insanity, and the spasms and pain became unbearable, her mother scraped together enough money to take her to Philadelphia for treatment on two occasions.

Mary was in Philadelphia when her father died penniless in the Tusculum farmhouse on September 25, 1853. Her mother, worn out and exhausted, died in Camden a few months later on March 31, 1854. Two of Mary's aunts then attempted to commit her to a lunatic asylum, but they may not have been successful. On April 7, 1855, the *Sessions Book of the Hillsborough Presbyterian Church* entered the dismissal of Miss Mary Witherspoon "at her own request" to "connect herself with the Presbyterian Church in Philadelphia under the pastoral charge of the Rev. Boardman." On November 14, 1857, there is the surprising entry in the Orange County Marriage Bonds of Mary Witherspoon's marriage to William G. Bowers by M. Baldwin, Minister. Nothing further is known of Mary Nash Witherspoon Bowers.

Information is from the Witherspoon-McDowall Papers, Southern Historical Collection, UNC, Chapel Hill, and from Mary Claire Engstrom's Witherspoon Family Records, the Orange Co. Marriage Bonds (p. 138), and the *Sessions Book of the Hillsborough Presbyterian Church* (p. 48).

## MARY WORTHAM
Granville County, North Carolina

Mary Wortham was a student at the Burwell School in the spring of 1852. Her roommate, Elizabeth Coit of South Carolina, wrote to her sister on May 29, 1852,

> *Our session will soon be out, the girls have begun to go home allready [sic], five of our boarders went off this morning. Two of them were my roommates, Jennie Speed and Mary Wortham. Mary Wortham is my bedfellow.*

Both Jennie Speed and Mary Wortham were going to Granville County. Mary Wortham, like her cousin Fannie Amis, was a member of the large Webb clan of Granville. Her mother, Lucy A. Wortham, wife of Robert Wortham, had been Lucy A. Webb (b. Aug. 28, 1814), the daughter of John Webb (d. Apr. 14, 1858) and Margaret Howard Webb. The Robert Worthams had three children:

1. John; m. Miss Lorena Warren.
2. Graham.
3. Mary; m. Maurice Blackwell.

The Robert Worthams later moved to Alabama. Mary Wortham Blackwell had one daughter, named Lucy for her mother, Lucy A. Webb Wortham.

Elizabeth Coit's letter is in the Records Room, Burwell School. Genealogical data about Mary Wortham is from William James Webb et al., *Our Webb Kin of Dixie* (Oxford, N.C., 1940), p. 20.

# Abbreviations

| | |
|---|---|
| accs | accounts |
| afft. | affectionate |
| b. | born |
| c. or ca. | circa |
| cr | credit |
| C.S.A. | Confederate States of America |
| d. | died |
| dau. | daughter |
| Decr | December |
| Do. | ditto |
| Dr | director |
| dtr. | daughter |
| d.y. | died young |
| Inst. | Instant/this month |
| Kt. | Knight |
| m. | married |
| No. Ca. | North Carolina |
| QM | quarter master |
| s. | son |
| s. | student |

# Index

## A

## B

Glass, Lizzie, 31
Glenn, Stephen W., 129–30
Graham, Archibald, 183–84
Grant, Richard S., 142–43
Green, James G., 80–81
Greensboro College (formerly Greensboro Female College), 20
Greensboro Museum, 127
*Greensboro, 1808–1904* (Albright), 125, 126n, 127
*Greensboro Patriot*, 203
Grice, Sarah (Sallie), 31, 96, 151, 155
Grigory, Rodger, 35–36

# H

Hall, S., 31
Hammond, Ella, 31, 65, 96
Hampden-Sydney College, 8, 204–05, 224
"Hannah Arnett's Faith . . . A Centennial Story . . ." 100
Harris, Robert Harrison, 170–73
Harrison, Cassandra, (Mrs. Bryan S. Rhodes), 31, 42, 97
Hawks, Hannah, 31, 42, 97–98
Heartt, Dennis, 39, 93, 111, 123n, 147, 190; *Catalogue of the Caldwell Institute, 1848–49*, 36n
Heartt-Wilson Papers, 207
*Heritage County, North Carolina, The* (Bizzell, ed.), 58n
*Heritage of Harnett County, North Carolina, The*, 186
*Heritage of Johnston County, North Carolina, The*, 186
*Hermit* (Beatty), 208–209
Hermitage Plantation, 184
Hickerson, Thomas Felix: *Echoes of Happy Valley*, 113n, 161, 164n
*High Time to Tell It* (Long), 106, 129, 219–20, 223n
Hill, John H., 57–58
Hillsborough Cemetery Records, 80n, 167n
Hillsborough Female Academy, 137
Hillsborough Female Seminary, 218
Hillsborough House, 146
Hillsborough Memorial Cemetery, 79, 80, 92, 116, 132, 199, 213
Hillsborough Methodist Church, 37
Hillsborough Presbyterian Church, 8, 91, 230, 232
*Hillsborough Recorder*, 40, 55, 78, 81, 88, 89n, 90, 92, 111, 113, 114, 132, 133, 146, 159, 160n, 168, 174, 175n, 179, 185, 196, 200, 207
Hillsborough's Old Town Cemetery, 39, 43, 48, 51, 68–69, 78, 80, 99, 105–06, 108–09, 125, 159–60, 160n, 161, 164n, 166–67, 167n, 170
Hill-Webb-Matheson House, 91

Historic Hillsborough Commission, 9, 12–13, 14, 15–16, 17, 25, 60, 62, 77, 78–79, 80, 81, 87n, 119, 129, 132, 139n, 154n, 165, 187–88, 189, 213n, 225

Historic Register of Historic Places, 193

*History of Alamance County* (Stockard), 51n, 144n

"History of Granville Co., N.C., Vol. I, Marriage Bonds" (Hicks), 217n

*History of the Churches of Hillsborough, N.C.: CA 1766–1962* (Lloyd and Lloyd), 56

*History of the Presbyterian Church in New Bern, North Carolina* (Vass), 103–04, 104n

*History of the Town of Hillsborough* (Lloyd and Lloyd), 125

*History of the University of North Carolina* (Battle), 145, 146n, 148

Hogg, James, 64, 160, 162, 164, 166

Holcomb, Brent H.: *Marriages of Orange County, North Carolina, 1779–1868*, 84n, 90n

Holditch (Holdich), Henrietta H., 20, 31, 99–101, 125

Hollister, Charles Slover, 102

"Hollister Family of New England—and New Bern, The" (McCullough), 104

Hollister House, The (New Bern), 103–04

Hollister, Janet (Mrs. Thomas George Wall), 31, 42, 97, 101–04

Hollister, Mary Bryan, 102

Hollister-Swan House, 102

Holmes, Bettie A. (Mrs. John London Meares), 31, 104–05

Holt, Annie (Mrs. William H. Foust), 31, 105–06

Holt, Frances Ann (Mrs. John L. Williamson), 32, 107–08, 185

Hooker, Margaret Parthenia (Mrs. Henry Nicholas [Nate] Brown), 32, 56, 108–10

Hooper, George William Mallett, 206

Hooper, John De Bernière; Hooper Papers, 161, 164n

Horner, C(?), 32

Horner, ___, 110–11, 178

Houston J. Walker House, 168

Howerton, Emily, 32, 111, 112

Howerton House, 111–12

Howerton, Maria (Mrs. Hasell Norwood), 32, 112–13, 196

Hughes Academy, 187

Hunt, Littleton Tazewell, 113

Hunter, William F., 44, 46–47

Huske, Benjamin R., 157–60

Huske's School. *See* Mrs. Huske's School

# I

Irwin, George W., 115–16

Irwin, John, 116

# J

# K

# L

Lindsay, Annette Eliza (Mrs. Clement Gillespie Wright), 32, 125–26, 127
Lindsay, Mary Virginia, 32, 126–27
Littlejohn, Sarah Blount (Mrs. Shepard Kosciusko Kollock), 99–101, 123
*Lives of Christian Ministers* (Kernodle), 89n
Lloyd, Allen A. and Pauline O. Lloyd: *History of the Churches of Hillsborough, N.C.: CA 1766–1962*, 56n; *History of the Town of Hillsborough*, 125
Lockhart-Phillips Cemetery, 91
Long, Helen Caldwell, 32, 127
Long, Jane Taylor, 220–21, 223
Long, Margaret (Mag) Taylor (Mrs. Rufus Barringer), 32, 128–29
Long, Mary Alves: *High Time to Tell It*, 106, 129, 219–20, 221–23
Long, William John, 105–06, 221
Long, William S, 185–86
Louisburg Female Academy, 11
Lunsford, Frances Elizabeth (Mrs. Stephen W. Glenn), 32, 129–30
Lunsford, Virginia (Mrs. Thomas Halliburton Bumpass), 32, 129–30
Lynch, Elizabeth (Lizzie) Palmer (Mrs. Calvin E. Parish), 32, 130–32
Lynch House. *See* Lemuel H. Lynch House
Lynch, Mary Jane, 32

# M

Madame Chegaray's School, 41
Mangum, Addison, 196–97
Mangum Papers, 138–39
Mangum, Sallie (Sally) Alston (Mrs. Martin Washington Leach), 19, 32, 137–39
Mangum, Willie Person, 19, 137–39
Marable, B. F., 87–88
Marriage Bonds of Orange County, 90n, 143n, 168n
*Marriages of Orange County, North Carolina, 1779–1868* (Holcomb), 84n, 90n
McAuley, Caroline, 132
McCauley, Mary Caroline, 132
McCormick, John Gilchrist: "Personnel of the [N.C. State] Convention of 1861," *James Sprunt Historical Monographs*, 57n
McCullough, Rose G.: "The Hollister Family of New England—and New Bern," *Ghosts on the River: The Sailing Ships of William Hollister of New Bern*, 104n
McDiarmid, Annie, 32, 94, 133
McDiarmid, Catharine (Mrs. Henry Clay Robinson), 32, 133–34
McKay, Flora, 32, 134–35
McKay, Isabella, 32, 134–35
McKoy (McKay), Erskine, 155–56
McKeithan (McKeithen), Margaret, 32, 135
McLester, Margaret (Maggie), 32, 135–36

# N

# O

Oates, John A., 96, 153, 155; *The Story of Fayetteville and the Upper Cape Fear*, 96n, 15
Occoneechee Hotel, 161
Old Bluff Presbyterian Church, 156
Old Chapel Hill Cemetery, 143, 210
*Old Days in Chapel Hill* (Chamberlain), 142, 143
Old Poplar, 148
Old Quaker Cemetery (Mars Hill), 90
Old Town Cemetery. *See* Hillsborough's Old Town Cemetery
"Old Yaller" (Robertson home), 168
Orange County Cemetery Survey, 82n, 92n
Orange County Court House Records, 170n
Orange County Deeds Books, 175n
Orange County Marriage Bonds, 80, 143, 147, 173–74, 175n, 232n
*Orange Democrat*, 169
"Original Bloomsburg–1797, The," *Record–Advertiser*, 93, 113n
*Our Webb Kin of Dixie* (Webb), 38n, 106, 129, 215, 223n, 233n
Owen, Mary, 33
Owen, Sally Roberta, 33

# P

Palmer, Eliza, 33, 169–70, 192
Palmer, Nathaniel J., 169–70
*Papers of Willie Person Mangum* (Shanks), 139n
*Paradise Lost* (Milton), 157
Parish, Calvin E., 130–32
Parker, Jane Rebecca (Mrs. Robert Harrison Harris), 17, 33, 170–73
Parks, Maria L. (Mrs. W. B. Routon, [Wilson B. Rowton]), 33, 173–74
Parks-Hasell House (Lemuel H. Lynch House), 37, 151
Paul, John A., 89–90
Peace College (formerly Peace Institute), 221, 223
Peach Tree Hill, 221
Pearce, Annie Blount (Mrs. James M. Turrentine), 33, 174–75
Pearce, Mary Huske, 18–19, 33, 62, 69, 95–96, 124, 161, 165, 175–78, 184
Pearce, Samuel J., 122, 123, 174, 178
Pearce's New Map of the State of North Carolina, 174–75
Pearsall, Joseph Dickson, 152–53
Perkins, Henrietta Martin, 33
"Personnel of the [N. C. State] Convention of 1861," James Sprunt Historical Monographs, (McCormick), 57n
"Pianoforte," 169
*Pianoforte-Primer, The* (Burrowes), 60
Picot's, M. (Philadelphia), 75
Pleasant Henderson dwelling, 144

# T

# U

# V

Venable, Martha, 34, 204–05
*Venables of Virginia, The* (Venable), 205n
"Vine-Gatherer's Daughter, The" (Berry), 49–50
"Visit to the 'Athens' of North Carolina, A" (Bailey), 112

# W

W.N. Tillinghast Papers, 63n, 69, 72n, 83n, 96n, 113n, 121n, 125n, 143n, 146n,
    157–58, 160n, 164n, 167n, 175, 178, 183, 184n, 203n, 229n
Waddell, Charlotte (Bella) Isabella (Mrs. George William Mallett Hooper),
    34, 206
Waddell, Maria E. (Mrs. John C. Badham), 34, 207
Waitt, Carrie (Mrs. John Sanford Spurgeon), 116
Waitt Garden. *See* Carrie Waitt Spurgeon Garden
Waitt, George Nathaniel, 116
Walker, Carlton, 209–10
Walker Family Bible, 210n
Walker House. *See* Houston J. Walker House
Walker, Jane Woodhouse, 208–10
Walker, Margaret (Mag) Isabella (Mrs. Johan Hieinrich David Carl Friedrich),
    19, 34, 208–10; "Reminicences," 19, 208
Walker-Palmer House, 170, 208
Wall, Janet, 102–03
Wall, Thomas G., 97, 101–04
Walnut Hall (Willie P. Mangum home), 137–39
War Between the States: *See* Civil War
Watkins, _____, 34
Watkins, Elizabeth (Lizzie), 34, 211
Watters, Caroline (Carrie) J. (Mrs. Edmund Strudwick), 34, 211–13
Watters, Mary Elizabeth (Mrs. Thomas Davis, Jr.), 83
Webb, Alexander Smith, 215, 224, 226, 228
Webb, Anne Huske (wife of Judge Tollman), 34, 214–15
Webb, Annie Alves Huske, 128, 165–66, 218
Webb, Cornelia Adeline Stanford, 215–16, 224–25, 226
Webb, Elizabeth G., 34; *The Webb Family* (Webb), 215
Webb, Fannie Amis, 34, 38, 85
Webb, Henrietta, 34, 215–16, 226, 224
Webb, James, 91, 105, 127, 128, 165–66, 167, 214–15, 217, 218, 224
Webb, John Henry, 37–38
Webb, Martha (Mat) Ann (Mrs. William Peter Webb), 34, 217
Webb, Mary (Graduation Certificate), 222
Webb, Mary (Mrs. William J. Long), 34, 105–06, 127, 218–23
Webb, Mary Caroline (Mrs. Calvin Newton Morrow), 34, 224–25
Webb Papers. *See* James Webb Papers
Webb, Robert Dickens: *The Webb Family*, 215n

# Burwell School Historic Site

The Burwell School Historic Site of Hillsborough, North Carolina, is a historic house museum, dedicated to preserving and interpreting the day-to-day lives of its former residents. The Burwell School, one of the earliest female academies in North Carolina, operated from 1837 to 1857. During the Civil War, it served as a refuge for the wealthy Collins family. It was also the early home of Elizabeth Hobbs Keckly, an enslaved young woman, who went on to become First Lady Mary Todd Lincoln's dressmaker and confidante. Keckly also wrote *Behind the Scenes*, a memoir chronicling her years as a slave in the Burwell household and later as a free woman.

The Burwell School Historic Site offers free docent-led and self-guided tours, a variety of cultural events, and innovative and engaging heritage education programs for children and young adults.

Please visit us at 319 North Churton Street, Hillsborough, North Carolina; phone: 919.732.7451

**To order more copies of** *The Book of Burwell Students . . .*
send a check made out to Historic Hillsborough Commission:
The price per copy:        $17.95
Shipping cost per book:     $ 4.50

Mailing Address: PO Box 922, Hillsborough, NC 27278
Email: info@burwellschool.org
Website: www.burwellschool.org

---

If you are a descendant of a Burwell School student or have information about any of the young women who attended, we would love to hear from you. This book is part of an ongoing research project, and we hope to update and expand our student profiles periodically.

---